THE FUTURE
OF AN ILLUSION

D0063931

broadview editions
series editor: L.W. Conolly

THE FUTURE
OF AN ILLUSION

Sigmund Freud

edited by Todd Dufresne
and
translated by Gregory C. Richter

broadview editions

© 2012 Todd Dufresne and Gregory C. Richter

All rights reserved. The use of any part of this publication reproduced, transmitted in any form or by any means, electronic, mechanical, photocopying, recording, or otherwise, or stored in a retrieval system, without prior written consent of the publisher— or in the case of photocopying, a licence from Access Copyright (Canadian Copyright Licensing Agency), One Yonge Street, Suite 1900, Toronto, Ontario M5E 1E5—is an infringement of the copyright law.

Library and Archives Canada Cataloguing in Publication

Freud, Sigmund, 1856-1939
    The future of an illusion / Sigmund Freud ; edited by Todd Dufresne and translated by Gregory C. Richter.

(Broadview editions)
Includes Oskar Pfister's response: The illusion of a future.
Translation of: Die Zukunft einer Illusion.
Includes bibliographical references and index.
ISBN 978-1-55481-065-9

    1. Psychology and religion. 2. Psychoanalysis. 3. Religion.
I. Dufresne, Todd, 1966- II. Richter, Gregory C. III. Pfister, Oskar, 1873-1956 IV. Title. V. Series: Broadview editions

BL53.F74 2012   200.1'9   C2012-900247-X

Broadview Editions

The Broadview Editions series represents the ever-changing canon of literature in English by bringing together texts long regarded as classics with valuable lesser-known works.

Advisory editor for this volume: Martin Boyne

Broadview Press is an independent, international publishing house, incorporated in 1985.

We welcome comments and suggestions regarding any aspect of our publications— please feel free to contact us at the addresses below or at broadview@broadviewpress.com.

North America
Post Office Box 1243, Peterborough, Ontario, Canada K9J 7H5
2215 Kenmore Avenue, Buffalo, NY, USA 14207
Tel: (705) 743-8990; Fax: (705) 743-8353
email: customerservice@broadviewpress.com

UK, Europe, Central Asia, Middle East, Africa, India, and Southeast Asia
Eurospan Group, 3 Henrietta St., London WC2E 8LU, United Kingdom
Tel: 44 (0) 1767 604972; Fax: 44 (0) 1767 601640
email: eurospan@turpin-distribution.com

Australia and New Zealand
NewSouth Books
c/o TL Distribution, 15-23 Helles Ave., Moorebank, NSW, Australia 2170
Tel: (02) 8778 9999; Fax: (02) 8778 9944
email: orders@tldistribution.com.au

www.broadviewpress.com

Broadview Press acknowledges the financial support of the Government of Canada through the Canada Book Fund for our publishing activities.

This book is printed on paper containing 100% post-consumer fibre.

Typesetting and assembly: True to Type Inc., Claremont, Canada.

PRINTED IN CANADA

This book is dedicated to our children,
Chloe Dufresne & Evan Richter.

Boa sorte sempre.

Contents

Acknowledgements

My collaboration with Greg Richter began with our Broadview volume on Freud's *Beyond the Pleasure Principle* (2011), which made possible this second volume on *The Future of an Illusion*. I could not have done any of it without Greg's unfailing good sense and support. "Richter's Freud"—meticulous and fluid—deserves a wide readership. Drafts of editorial notes for this book were created by Chris Wood, a doctoral student in philosophy at the University of Guelph, who not only eased my workload, but did so with his usual style, accuracy, grace, and speed. My sincere thanks to both of them.

Once again Broadview editors did a great job. Among them I'd like to mention Tara Lowes, Marjorie Mather, Leonard Conolly, Martin Boyne, and Leslie Dema. The book has benefitted from their professionalism and skill.

Parts of this book were funded by a grant supporting the Lakehead University Research Chair in Social & Cultural Theory, which I held between 2008 and 2010; and by a Standard Research Grant from the Social Sciences and Humanities Research Council (SSHRC).

I would also like to thank friends and colleagues in Thunder Bay who have helped me in myriad ways with my work, including Clara Sacchetti, Imre Szeman, Richard Berg, Dan Hansen, Batia Stolar, Dean Jobin-Bevans, Doug Ivison, Rui Wang, Kezia Picard, and Gail Fikis. Finally, I'd like to acknowledge my colleagues at the Institute for the History and Philosophy of Science and Technology at the University of Toronto, where I was an Affiliated Scholar from 2008-2011, and where I am currently a visiting professor. Special thanks to Denis Walsh, Mark Solovey, and Joseph Berkovitz. Cheers.

The basic idea for a book of Freud/Pfister goes back to Paul Roazen, a Freud critic with whom I worked in the early days of my graduate studies. Thanks, Paul.

Todd Dufresne
Toronto

Permissions Acknowledgements

The new English translations of Freud texts by Gregory C. Richter are based on the original German texts, with the permission of Sigmund Freud Copyrights, The Marsh Agency Ltd.

Oskar Pfister. "Die Illusion einer Zukunft: eine freundliche Auseinandersetzung mit Professor Doktor Sigmund Freud." *Imago*, v. 14, 1928: pp. 149-84.

Oskar Pfister. *Zur Psychologie des philosophischen Denkens (On the Psychology of Philosophical Thought.)* Bern: Bircher, 1923.

The publisher has endeavoured to contact the rights holders of all copyrighted works and translations published in this text and would appreciate receiving any information regarding errors or omissions so that we may correct them in future reprints and editions of the work.

Introduction

Todd Dufresne

> What will they do with my theory after my death? Will it still resemble my basic thoughts?
>
> —Sigmund Freud (in Choisy 5)

The Future of an Illusion is an unusual work within Sigmund Freud's oeuvre. First of all, it seems a throwback to eighteenth-century critiques of religion, a redux of Enlightenment values in the twentieth century. To Voltaire's[1] plea for liberty and reason in the face of religious intolerance—"*écrasez l'infâme*," crush the infamy—Freud adds his own plea for "my god, Logos" in his diatribe against religious belief. To Kant's[2] description of Enlightenment as "man's emergence from his self-incurred immaturity" ("An Answer" 54), Freud adds: "People cannot remain children forever; they must ultimately go out, into 'hostile life.' One may call this 'education to reality'" (p. 108). Freud's essential contribution is to update Enlightenment critiques with diagnostic insight from psychology: religion, the therapist declares, is "the universal obsessional neurosis" (p. 103).

It's not just that Freud's pose as eighteenth-century *philosophe* is strangely anachronistic in 1927. It is rather that this pose runs against the grain of Freud's other public and private pronouncements—from the pre-psychoanalytic essays of the 1880s to his last works in 1939, and throughout his thousands of letters to friends and colleagues. For Freud scholars, therefore, the positivistic side of the *Future* is a puzzling enigma, Freud's arguments an unconvincing paean for reason by the last figure of the counter-Enlightenment.

---

1 *Nom de plume* of prolific French Enlightenment writer François-Marie Arouet (1694–1778). Arouet's works advocating civil liberty and social reform were a driving force behind the American and French Revolutions of the eighteenth century.

2 German philosopher Immanuel Kant (1724–1804), known for providing the Age of Enlightenment with its motto, "*Sapere aude!*" ("Dare to know!"), and for having reconciled the hitherto irresolvable debate between rationalism and empiricism—a contribution that Kant himself saw as nothing short of a "Copernican revolution" in the history of philosophy.

Indeed, far from being a Voltaire or Kant for the twentieth century, Freud was our greatest Romantic. Like Schopenhauer,[1] Dostoevsky,[2] and Nietzsche[3] before him, Freud embraced the irrational facts of human suffering, masochism, and overwrought conscience, reveling in the underground current of human nature that Nietzsche dubbed *das Es*, i.e., the "it" or the "id." In similar fashion, Freud's thought echoed the nineteenth-century fascination with fractured and divided consciousness, from debates about medical hypnosis and spirit possession to literary case studies such as Stevenson's *The Strange Case of Dr Jekyll and Mr Hyde* (1886)—phenomena Freud understood as uncanny harbingers of death that pointed the way toward "thought transference" and even telepathy. In other words, like other Romantics before him, Freud understood that the diabolical discourses of the unconscious challenged the philosophy of consciousness and the presumed supremacy of reason.

The late works of Freud mark a dramatic return to, and reinvestment in, this Romantic heritage. The key text in this regard is *Beyond the Pleasure Principle* of 1920, the masterwork responsible for inaugurating this phase in the history of psychoanalysis. In it Freud offers metabiological and metaphysical speculations about the death-drive and the repetition compulsion, thereby effecting the wholesale reconstruction of the theory of psychoanalysis, to wit, the "metapsychology." The result: the lifelong dualist married the traditional territory of psychoanalysis—life, sex, and love—to death, destruction, and hate. The Freud of *Beyond the Pleasure Principle* thus returned psychoanalysis to its roots as an id psychology infused with the dark overtones of nineteenth-century Romantic philosophy, literature, and biology. Even his late interest in "ego psychology" is caught in the undertow of

---

1 German philosopher and renowned pessimist Arthur Schopenhauer (1788–1860). Schopenhauer's metaphysical analysis of human desire— broadly characterized as the "will to live"—was a highly influential precursor to modern evolutionary psychology.

2 Fyodor Dostoevsky (1821–81), author of *Crime and Punishment* (1866) and *The Brothers Karamazov* (1880). Dostoevsky's novels were notable for their vivid psychological characterizations of human experience amidst the backdrop of nineteenth-century Russian society.

3 German classicist Friedrich Nietzsche (1844–1900), well known for his proclamation "God is dead!" *Contra* Schopenhauer, Nietzsche characterized all human action as the instantiation of a single drive—the "will to power."

Beyond the Pleasure Principle, often to the great annoyance and incomprehension of later ego psychologists.

Consequently, the positivistic aspects of *The Future of an Illusion* do not fit well with the historical development of psychoanalysis, most especially with its final expression in works written between 1920 and 1939. This includes Freud's other famous cultural work of this period, *Civilization and Its Discontents* (1930). For, unlike *The Future of an Illusion*, *Civilization* is an unambiguous product of Freud's darkest ruminations about *Kultur*—and precisely in terms established in *Beyond the Pleasure Principle*. Scholars therefore have three good reasons for their continued interest in the *Future*: first, as an uncompromising, old-fashioned instance of the rationalistic critique of religion, albeit updated in terms of depth psychology; second, as an aberrant example of positivism in the context of Freud's counter-Enlightenment *raison d'être*; and third, more pointedly, as an intellectual puzzle on account of its seemingly groundless status in the context of the "late Freud," a work in some ways set apart from the theories of *Beyond the Pleasure Principle* and the contemporaneous cultural observations of *Civilization and Its Discontents*.

Freud provided his own harsh assessments of *The Future of an Illusion*. In October 1927, referring to the advance proofs of his manuscript, Freud admitted to his friend and colleague, Hungarian analyst Sándor Ferenczi (1873–1933),[1] that the *Future* "already strikes me as childish, I basically think differently, consider this work analytically frail and insufficient as a confession" (Freud and Ferenczi 326). Later, when speaking to former analysand René Laforgue (1894–1962), Freud quashed his admiration for the *Future* by declaring, "This is my worst book! It isn't a book of Freud. It's the book of an old man" (in Choisy 84). In 1927, Freud was seventy years old.

No doubt it would be churlish and uncharitable to leave it at that, since Freud's self-deprecating irony is very nearly his natural fallback position—most especially in his private correspondence. And Laforgue isn't the only one to express admiration for the book. Neo-Freudian psychoanalyst Erich Fromm (1900–80)[2]

---

1 Hungarian psychoanalyst and one of Freud's closest early followers, best remembered for his late deviations from Freud.

2 German-American "Neo-Freudian" psychoanalyst most famous in the 1960s, best remembered as an early member of the Frankfurt School and for his Marxist adjustments to traditional Freudianism. On Fromm, see Daniel Burston's 1991 book (pp. 31–36, 189–206).

refers to the *Future* as "one of his most profound and brilliant books" (*Psychoanalysis* 10).Yet I think Freud's own damning remarks about the *Future* are basically correct. The book isn't very good. It's not only derivative historically and an aberration conceptually, but it is sloppily argued, repetitive, unfocused, and at times confused. To take one example, Freud spells out a thesis for the book—a rationale—only at the end of chapter nine. The thesis concerns our "education to reality," cited above, about which he adds the following: "Must I still make it clear to you that the sole purpose of this publication of mine is to show the need for progress of this sort?" (p. 108). The answer is yes: he should have said as much in chapter one—or two or three. Arguably *The Future of an Illusion* could not get published today, at least not without extensive revisions. In fact, it would probably not have been publishable in Freud's own time were it not for Freud's reputation and the fact that Freud and Freudians operated their own publication venues.[1]

This perhaps surprisingly negative verdict doesn't mean that the *Future* isn't interesting or worth close examination. On the contrary, given Freud's stature as one of the most significant thinkers of the twentieth century, everything he wrote rewards close scrutiny—perhaps most especially those works that Freud himself recognized to be insufficiently Freudian. Certainly the specter of the book's "childish insufficiency even as a confession" raises the question, Why this book at this time? And then another: Why this apparent love letter to "my god, Logos," and, by extension, to classical philosophy?

In what follows I will sketch three plausible answers to these two questions as I expand upon the general reasons, outlined above, for our continued interest in *The Future of an Illusion*. But let's first consider the Romantic philosophy that informs Freud's work.[2]

---

1   Like many of his longer works, *Die Zukunft einer Illusion* was originally published in the *Internationaler Psychoanalytischer Verlag*, for which Freud was one of a handful of directors after its inception in January 1919. According to analyst and biographer Ernest Jones, the *Verlag* [Press] appealed to Freud's "strong desire for independence," about which he adds, "The idea of being completely free of the conditions imposed upon him by publishers, which had always irked him, and of being able to publish just what books he liked and when he liked, made a forcible appeal to this side of his nature" (30).

2   For a concise, classic overview of Freud and religion, see Jones 349–74.

The Nietzschean Critique of Reason

Psychoanalysis was devised as a corrective to, and critique of, the philosophy of consciousness advanced during the Enlightenment and then entrenched in philosophy and academic psychology. Psychoanalysts claim that reason, consciousness, and ego are only one part of the story of human psychology—and not the most interesting or important part. As Freud variously analogized, the relation of ego to id is like that of rider to horse (*The Ego and the Id*, SE[1] 19: 25; *New Introductory Lectures on Psychoanalysis*, SE 22: 77); and the relation of present to past is like that of the buildings of contemporary Rome to the ancient ruins literally buried in layers deep beneath the surface (*Civilization and Its Discontents*, SE 21: 69–70). Such was, for Freud, the singular promise of his "archeology of the mind," namely, the methodical restoration of the repressed and forgotten at both individual and group levels (since for Freud the latter is determined by the former). The human condition is therefore Romantic, even if Freud reserved for his own practice the outward vestiges of a science. According to Freud's Romantic "science," only psychoanalysis can cast light onto this psychic hell; only psychoanalysis can restore a semblance of reason in a situation structured by unreason.

Above all it was Nietzsche who taught Freud the critical power of Romantic philosophy, including the critique of religion. Following Schopenhauer and Feuerbach,[2] Nietzsche argued that classical philosophy and Christian thought invented the ideals of truth and God and then mistakenly subjected the world of differences to those concepts. Such is the cornerstone of Nietzsche's indictment of the history of philosophy as nihilism, as the denial of everyday existence. Railing against this Platonism, this "history of the error"—what we nowadays call "essentialism"—the early Nietzsche writes:

> What is truth? A mobile army of metaphors, metonyms, and anthropomorphisms: in short, a sum of human relations which have been poetically and rhetorically intensified, transferred,

---

1 The abbreviation refers to the Standard Edition of Freud's works (trans. James Strachey, 1895). See References.

2 Ludwig Feuerbach (1804–72), German philosopher and anthropologist known for his scathing critiques of modern Christianity. Feuerbach's materialistic appropriation of Hegelian philosophy—dialectical materialism—would later serve as the philosophical foundation of Marxism.

and embellished, and which, after long usage, seem to a people to be fixed, canonical, and binding. Truths are illusions which we have forgotten are illusions—they are metaphors that have become worn out and have been drained of sensuous force, coins which have lost their embossing and are now considered as metal and no longer as coins. ("On Truth and Lie" 46–47)

"All that philosophers have handled for thousands of years," Nietzsche continues twenty-five years later in *Twilight of the Idols* (1888), "have been concept-mummies; nothing real has escaped their grasp alive" (197). For Nietzsche the faculty of reason is a compensation derived of human weakness vis-à-vis other animals, a means by which we preserve and enhance our lives. In this respect reason is driven by what he eventually calls the "will to power," the everyday expression of which lies in the art of simulation: "deception, flattery, lying and cheating, talking behind the back, posing, living in borrowed splendor, being masked, the guise of convention, acting a role before others and before oneself" ("On Truth and Lie" 43). If so, the history of philosophy is the history of this will to power, that is, of lies—the history of the effacement of the role that reason actually plays in the world. This is of course a wickedly perverse conclusion, where philosophers lie about reason, inflating it beyond comprehension, in order to cover up reason's affinity with lying. The abstract world of philosophy is, therefore, Nietzsche writes, "a refuted idea: let us abolish it!" (*Twilight* 201). Consequently, just as a certain kind of "fixed, canonical, and binding" truth is found dead in the late nineteenth century, so too is the Christian conception of God. This is the conclusion for which Nietzsche, self-declared "anti-Christ," is best known: "God is dead."

This, simply put, was the godless philosophy of the mid- to late nineteenth century that Freud inherited from Nietzsche and, before him, from Schopenhauer—philosophy he read and admired as a young man (see Lehrer 13–18); studied in formal classes in philosophy (including one on the existence of God) with philosopher Franz Brentano[1] during his time as a medical student at the University of Vienna; adapted to his own theories of guilt, death, and repetition; and then did his best to disown

---

1 Franz Brentano (1838–1917), German philosopher and psychologist credited with reviving the "intentional" theory of human perception. Along with Freud, Brentano's students included Christian von Ehrenfels (1859–1932; an early purveyor of Gestalt theory) and Edmund Husserl (1859–1938; the founder of the phenomenological movement).

when constructing his own creation myths of psychoanalysis (Sulloway 467–68; Roazen, "Nietzsche"). Consequently Freud's frequent attacks and rants against philosophy and philosophers must be understood as the continuation of criticisms that Nietzsche had already made—and which took decades for institutional philosophy to forgive, if partially and begrudgingly.

Arguably, then, Freud's attitude toward the illusion of religion is informed, not just by the old Enlightenment critiques of religion, but by Nietzsche's attitude, *au courant* throughout Freud's life, toward the "illusion of truth" and its expression in classical philosophy and Christianity. Yet it must be conceded: neither the Enlightenment philosophes nor the late Romantics provide an occasion for the appearance of the *Future*. They are perhaps necessary but not *sufficient* causes. That role is left, in part, to Karl Marx (1818–83). Although he is never named, which is typical of Freud's treatment of philosophers, his work and impact are repeatedly gestured toward in the opening two chapters of the *Future*. These form the first answer to the question, Why this book now?

Freud's Alternative Theory of Political Revolution

In the early years of the new century, Freud was surrounded by a disparate group of followers, none of whom was a match for his sparkling intellect and ambition. As Freud's reputation increased, most especially after psychoanalysis was utilized as a treatment for war trauma in World War I, the quality of his followers also increased. However, "Herr Professor" Freud did not always appreciate the competition, which he read as proof that the growing psychoanalytic society was just an echo of everyday society—and so subject to natural selection and parricide. What does this have to do with *The Future of an Illusion*? The best students, sometimes as talented and ambitious as Freud, were liable to disagree with aspects of Freud's thinking. Consequently the works of Freud's middle and late periods were opportunities to correct the record, but also to admonish, discipline, erase, and blacklist his wayward disciples. Hence the brooding, self-reflecting tone of *Totem and Taboo*, which was in part a response to a "parricidal" Carl Jung,[1] and *Civilization and Its Discontents*, which

---

1 Carl Gustav Jung (1875–1961), Swiss psychiatrist and founder of analytical psychology. The publication of Jung's *Psychology of the Unconscious* (1912) demarcated his theoretical divergence from Freud and, consequently, the end of their five-year friendship.

was in part a response to a "parricidal" Wilhelm Reich.[1] "The son-religion," Freud writes in *Totem*, "replaces the father-religion"—a theory Freud describes in 1913 even as he resisted its actualization in the analytic horde (p. 166).

Reich's involvement with Freud after 1920 is also related to the appearance of *The Future of an Illusion* in 1927. From the beginning Reich disliked the death-drive theory of *Beyond*, focusing instead on Freud's early view that neurosis is caused by dammed-up libido. Reich drew the obvious inference: if neurosis is caused by the inhibited discharge of sexual energy (libido), then mental health must be improved by its free release, that is, by orgasm. Freud disagreed with, but indulged, Reich's so-called *Steckenpferd*, his "hobby-horse" (I.O. Reich 13), since it was indeed based on his own work. But Freud certainly did not approve of Reich's other hobby-horse, Marxism. Consequently Reich, the first person to attempt a systematic merger of psychoanalysis and Marxism, fell out of favor during the second half of the 1920s and into the early 1930s. "While Freud developed his death-instinct theory which said 'the misery comes from inside,'" Reich would recall, "I went out where the people were. [...] *I had drawn the social consequences of the [early] libido theory. To Freud's mind, this was the worst thing I did*" (W. Reich 51; emphasis in original). By "social consequences" Reich meant his own Marxist commitments, which were reflected in his work at free clinics for workers unable to afford psychoanalysis.

Historians often insist that the *Future* reflects a trend in Freud's thinking that goes back to "Obsessive Actions and Religious Practices" (1907) and *Totem and Taboo* (1912). And this is obviously true. But the appearance of the *Future* in 1927, so different in tone from Freud's other works, is at least in part explained by Freud's pressing need to distinguish psychoanalysis from Marxism in light of the growing cachet of the communist worldview in the 1920s. In other words, it is the specter of Karl Marx that Freud attempts to exorcise in the introductory chapters of the *Future*.

---

1   Wilhelm Reich (1897–1957), Austrian-American psychiatrist and psychoanalyst. Close to the inner circle of Freudians in the 1920s, Reich was one of the first to put Freud and Marxism together. Freud rejected this idea, and by the early 1930s their relationship soured. Reich left for America in 1939, where his militant politics and work on "character analysis" gave way to increasingly eccentric work on orgone energy and therapy, UFOs, and cloud-busting.

This is an unusual claim, so let's consult a few relevant passages from the first two chapters.

Psychoanalysis is the interpretation of individual (and collective) history as filtered through the distorting conditions of the present. And so, for example, Freud utilizes a patient's "free associations" as a way to disrupt linear reason and break through to the latent (historical) meaning of dreams. In the *Future*, Freud sets his sights on a very different goal: insight into "the future," not the past. "When one has lived for a long time in a particular culture," Freud begins the book, "and has often tried to determine the nature of its origins and developmental path, one is sometimes tempted to cast one's gaze in the other direction and ask what further fate awaits this culture and what changes it is fated to undergo" (p. 73). This first sentence is highly strategic. With it, Freud establishes his singular credentials for providing a prediction about the future: as an old man at the end of his life, someone who has gained critical distance from what he calls "the naïve present"; and as the first psychoanalyst, someone intimate with the repressed past (p. 73).

Long consumed with his own legacy, Freud in the 1920s thought he was near death and thus removed from the vagaries of everyday life (see Jones 42; Dufresne, *Tales* 20, 39–41). He was diagnosed with cancer of the jaw in 1923 and, after the removal of parts of his upper palate, was given a poorly fitting and painful prosthesis. "It seemed as though my life would soon be brought to an end," Freud reflects in 1935, "but surgical skill saved me in 1923 and I was able to continue my life and my work, though no longer in freedom from pain" (SE 20: 71). The experience left Freud a changed man. As he put it to Lou Andreas-Salomé[1] in May 1925, invoking the theories of *Beyond the Pleasure Principle*, "A crust of indifference is slowly creeping up around me; a fact I state without complaining. It is a natural development, a way of beginning to grow inorganic. The 'detachment of old age,' I think it is called" (Freud and Andreas-Salomé 154). This peculiar yet typical way of positioning himself influenced the production of the *Future* and his subsequent perceptions about the book. Consider the entirety of Freud's critical remarks to Laforgue:

---

1   In addition to being one of the first female psychoanalysts, Russian-born Salomé (1861–1937) was well known for her diverse interests and, consequently, for her ongoing correspondences with many of the most prominent intellectuals of her day, including Richard Wagner, Rainer Maria Rilke, and Nietzsche.

This is my worst book! It isn't a book of Freud. It's the book of an old man. Besides, Freud is dead now, and believe me, the genuine Freud was a really great man. I am particularly sorry for you that you didn't know him better. (in Choisy 84)

Not incidentally, this "dead" Freud perfectly meets the conditions he describes in the *Future*. "[T]here is the remarkable fact," Freud writes, "that people generally experience the present naively, so to speak, without being able to appreciate its contents; they must first gain some distance from it, i.e., the present must have become the past before one can derive from it clues for making judgments about the future" (p. 73). Suitably mortified, Freud in 1927 had become a classic anti-subject, a Romantic figure of death against whom nothing critical could be said. For his pronouncements on the future were oracular, truths delivered at the end of life—if not beyond.[1]

Of course "the future" is precisely what interests Marxists, especially those late "scientific socialists" who predicted the future communist utopia out of the resolution of the contradictions of capitalism. From Freud's perspective, however, they could not possibly know a future that is determined by a repressed prehistory that is revealed only through psychoanalysis, is conditional upon the psychoanalytic resolution of individual neuroses (of the would-be historian) today, and, in any case, is limited to those who occupy a critical distance from the present.

Having met these three exclusionary conditions—publicly and obliquely in the *Future*, and privately and explicitly in his various asides—Freud begins his indirect discussion of Marxism. "Human culture," he says, has "two sides": "It includes on the one hand all the knowledge and power that people have acquired in order to master the forces of nature and gain material wealth for the satisfaction of human needs, and on the other hand it includes all the institutions necessary to regulate the relations of humans to each other, especially the distribution of the attainable material wealth. These two orientations

---

1 In *Beyond the Pleasure Principle*, Freud argues that one chooses one's own path to death once all the stages of development have been exhausted, that is, when the detour of life, ontogenetically stored, has finally been spent. In this sense one is finally free from deterministic biology; i.e., one is "beyond" it. Freud often implies that his late return to cultural questions is just such a freedom.

of culture are not independent ..." (p. 73). Freud goes on to discuss the difficulties of "communal existence," one that is fatally compromised by a dark realization central to the late Freud: individuals must choose between sadism (destroying others) and masochism (destroying oneself). "A sad disclosure indeed," Freud chortles elsewhere, "for the moralist!" (*New Introductory Lectures*, SE 22: 105; see Fromm 1973: 275). Freud therefore concludes that all aspects of culture—specifically "organizations, institutions, and laws"—must defend against this innately destructive individual. He adds:

> These [goals of culture] aim not only to effect a certain distribution of material wealth, but also to maintain that distribution. Indeed, they must protect against people's hostile impulses all those things that serve for the conquest of nature and the production of material wealth. Human creations are easy to destroy.... (p. 74)

Freud then wonders if "a reorganization of human relations"—he avoids naming it, but he means "communism"—could ever "nullify the sources of dissatisfaction with culture" that he associates with our raging drives. Although "that [reorganization] would be a golden age," Freud insists that human nature is not equal to the ideal. "On the contrary," he adds, "every culture must be based on coercion and the renunciation of drives," drives that are for Freud the *sine qua non* of human biology (p. 74; cf. "Scientific Interest in Psychoanalysis," Appendix B3, p. 167). The upshot, delivered as a "psychological fact," is that some individuals will always remain "anti-social and anti-cultural." In this respect Freud perfectly echoes Schopenhauer's sentiments from "Sufferings of the World": "If all wishes were fulfilled as soon as they arose," Schopenhauer writes, "how would men occupy their lives? What would they do with their time? If the world were a paradise of luxury and ease ... men would either die of boredom or hang themselves; or there would be wars, massacres, and murders; so that in the end mankind would inflict more suffering on itself than it has now to accept at the hands of Nature" (p. 6).[1]

---

1   For a quick but insightful comparison of Freud and Schopenhauer on religion, see Philip Rieff [Susan Sontag] 322–25.

Freud's opinion about *Massenpsychologie* owes everything to the influence of Hobbes,[1] Schopenhauer, Nietzsche, and Gustave Le Bon (1841–1931)—the French psychologist responsible for *The Psychology of Crowds* and influential for Freud's *Group Psychology and the Analysis of the Ego* (1921). Like Le Bon, but owing as much to the others, Freud agreed that the *Masse*—the mass or mob—would always need a leader, *Der Führer*. "For the masses," Freud concludes, "are indolent and stupid," uninterested in work, and insensible to reasoned argument (p. 75). *Kultur*, therefore, is what Freud means by the force that keeps our Manichean, practically unchangeable and essentially anti-social, biology in check: a thin veneer, recently acquired, that only partially covers over our innate, and therefore ancient, destructive ids. This is why Freud speaks of deterministic "fate" rather than freedom and change when he predicts "the future."

Marx would have none of this pessimism, however. Marx thought that psychology merely described epiphenomena of a more fundamental economics; that the masses had been stupefied by nurture, not nature; and that, therefore, any significant change to the economic structure would result in a change to human *Kultur*, including its mass psychology. Because his thought was dialectical rather than dualistic, Marx assumed a level of change and progress that reflected the ideals of human and social perfectibility common to the Enlightenment. And so he is a nineteenth-century optimist, which is precisely why people such as Reich—and, over two decades later, Freudo-Marxists such as Herbert Marcuse[2] and Norman O. Brown[3]—thought

---

1 English political philosopher Thomas Hobbes (1588–1679). Hobbes is best known as the author of *Leviathan* (1651)—one of the earliest and most influential formulations of modern social-contract theory. Therein he famously characterizes life in the state of nature as "solitary, poor, nasty, brutish and short."

2 Herbert Marcuse (1898–1979) was a German-Jewish philosopher, sociologist, and prominent member of the famed Frankfurt School of critical theory. His *Eros and Civilization* (1955) sought to delineate the relationship between alienated labor and the sexual drives, ultimately arguing that, in an advanced industrial society, the suppression of the latter is a product of the former, and that in a true socialist society, *Eros* would be recognized as a liberating—rather than debilitating—force.

3 American classicist Norman O. Brown (1913–2002). In *Life against Death: The Psychoanalytical Meaning of History* (1959), Brown attempts to derive a psychoanalytic account of cultural history, arguing that Freud's dual instincts (of *Eros* and *Thanatos*) are, in fact, dialectical in their relationship rather than diametrically opposed.

that a dash of Marx would repair an unduly pessimistic Freud. Obviously this Marxist perspective on psychoanalysis entails a serious critique of psychoanalytic praxis *qua* therapy. For how can a therapy so intrinsically resigned to fate and biology, so stuck in the past, so much a product of brooding late Romanticism, ever make room for change, hope, progress—for the future? How could a Freudian psychoanalysis ever claim to "cure" patients, since cure is based on the possibility of breaking with old patterns? Similarly, how could Freud's instrumental and wholly defensive conception of culture square with its constructive aspects? "I can only feel stupefaction," huffs the poet T.S. Eliot,[1] "on reading such a course of argument" (351; see also Kiell 576).

★★★

It is no accident that Freud's newfound interest in "the future" is connected to his newfound interest in the conditions of "material wealth." But just in case the reader misses his meaning about the ideal of "communal existence" and the "reorganization of human relations," Freud spells it out at the close of chapter one—albeit negatively, in relief, disowning the very territory he just covered. Freud concludes:

> I do not want to create the impression that I have wandered far off the path envisioned for my investigation. I shall therefore expressly affirm that I have no intention of assessing the great cultural experiment currently underway in the vast country between Europe and Asia. I have neither the expertise nor the ability to determine its practicability, to test the appropriateness of the methods applied, or to measure the width of the inevitable cleft between intention and execution. What is being prepared there remains incomplete and eludes the examination for which our long-consolidated culture provides the material. (p. 76)

Freud speaks of a "path," one that he has "wandered" away from, although not far; apparently the thesis or rationale for the book remains close at hand. The truth is, however, that Freud has yet to spell out a thesis for *The Future of an Illusion*—at least beyond

---

1 Thomas Stearns Eliot (1888–1965), American-British literary critic, poet, and playwright.

his opening remarks that he is interested in looking at the future of *Kultur*, that is, of culture, society, and civilization. Consequently Freud can't wander "off the path envisioned for [his] investigation" when wandering itself verily describes the process of his investigation thus far. Unless, of course, wandering *is* the path Freud doesn't so much follow as makes up as he goes along. A new reader of the *Future* could therefore be forgiven for thinking that the book has nothing to do with religion, since the opening chapters function as primers of psychoanalysis in 1927, the critical foil played by the alternative theory of communism associated with Karl Marx. Then again, the future at stake in the *Future*, as elsewhere in Freud's work, is always the future of psychoanalysis defined against its many enemies.

Chapter two is much the same: Freud returns to psychology but quickly wanders back into a discussion of economics. The key paragraph concerns what Freud calls a "crude and always unmistakable situation." Under repressive conditions the "lower classes" are unable to discharge the "excess of privation" (p. 78), *Mehr von Entbehrung*, that is its lot in life. When people suffer such over-privation they lose the capacity to identify with the aims of culture, in other words, to absorb the prohibitions of law that enforce civility. In the case of political revolution, the "excess of privation" floods the defensive barrier influenced by *Kultur* and formed by psychology, namely, the superego of each individual of the lower classes. Conscience is thus weakened to its breaking point, and the destructive energy of the *Masse* is released. The situation is analogous to the etiology of trauma that Freud describes in 1895 and again in 1920, where a "surplus of excitation," *Überschuss an Erregung*, floods or breaches the defenses of the mental apparatus (*Beyond the Pleasure Principle* 67–72; cf. *Project for a Scientific Psychology*). On this analogy, however, it is not the lower classes that are traumatized, for example, by the "energy" of culture; culture is, on the contrary, the force that dams up the energy (see p. 79) and so causes neurosis and unhappiness. The direction of energy is otherwise: it's the state apparatus that is overwhelmed and traumatized by the release of hostile energy from the now un-repressed, uncoerced *Masse*. In short, freed of the ego and superego functions of culture that Freud associates with "organizations, institutions, and laws," the lower classes revolt; the state apparatus is breached, flooded, traumatized by the frenzied and pleasurable release of tension in the *Masse*. This is the realization of

Rousseau's[1] "state of nature," which Freud mocks as untenable at the beginning of chapter three, and which necessitates "the chief task of culture": defense against nature (p. 81). As Freud says, civilization is "easy to destroy." "It is hardly necessary to say," Freud concludes, "that a culture that leaves so many of its members unsatisfied, driving them to insurrection, has no prospect of perpetuating itself. Nor does it deserve to do so" (p. 79).

And so ends the lesson. Freud may agree with some Marxist conclusions about religion, but he can't accept their reasoning. As Marx puts it in the "Introduction" to *A Contribution to the Critique of Hegel's* Philosophy of Right (1843):

> Religion ... is the opium of the people. The abolition of religion as the illusory happiness of the people is a demand for their true happiness. The call to abandon illusions about their condition is the call to abandon a [materialist, economic] condition which requires illusions. Thus the critique of religion is the critique in embryo of that vale of tears of which religion is the halo. (131)

Marx claims that revolution is based on the internal contradictions of capitalism, on economics, while Freud claims that it is really all about the psychological conflict between our ancient, innate, biologically expressed drives, and the more fragile forces of our recent, nurture-based, sociologically expressed laws. Simply put, Freud believes that Marx mistakes the mob, the *Masse*, of present-day capitalist society for "the people," the *Volk*, of a very distant, idealized utopia of the future—and on this basis has expectations for human reason that ignore our animal origins, thus inflating the actual achievements of *Kultur*. Such is the essence of Freud's psychoanalytic theory of political revolution—the masses revolt when their animal origins and needs are not adequately tended—which he proposes as an alternative theory to the kind we associate with the "cultural

---

1   Genevan political philosopher and Romantic novelist Jean-Jacques Rousseau (1712–78). *Contra* Hobbes, Rousseau maintained that a "natural" morality was innate to pre-societal humans. His principal political text *The Social Contract* (1762) opens with his famous assertion, "man was born free, and he is everywhere in chains."

experiment currently underway in the vast country between Europe and Asia." Freudo-Marxism is therefore incoherent, indeed oxymoronic.

Freud was not shy about his own political beliefs. To his friend and colleague Arnold Zweig,[1] Freud described himself as "a liberal of the old school" (Freud and Zweig 21). He certainly never warmed to Marxism or Bolshevism, claiming in 1933 that "although practical Marxism has mercilessly cleared away all idealistic systems and illusions, it has itself developed illusions which are no less questionable and unprovable than the earlier ones" (*New Introductory Lectures*, SE 22: 180). In the *Future* of 1927, Freud isn't quite ready to spell out his views, and instead he challenges Marxism and the Russian "cultural experiment" by an indirection appropriate to his procedural wandering. It is only in chapter five of *Civilization and Its Discontents*, three years later, that Freud finally discusses the principles of communism (e.g., the abolition of private property) that he alludes to and sometimes skirts in the *Future*; and here too he finally names "Russia" and "the Soviets" rather than gestures toward them in an incredibly awkward locution ("between Europe and Asia").

As for religion, the theme for which the book is primarily known, it arrives only in chapter three of the *Future*.

Dialogical Thought and the Trial of Religion

The common man cannot imagine this Providence other than in the person of an immensely exalted father.... All of this is so obviously infantile, so far from reality, that it is painful to anyone with convictions friendly toward humanity to think that the great majority of mortals will never be able to raise above this view of life. (Freud, *Civilization and Its Discontents*, Appendix B4, p. 169)

Between June and September of 1926 Freud quickly wrote and published *The Question of Lay Analysis*. In it he defends the right of "lay" or non-medical analysts to practice psychoanalytic treatment, a right challenged in the Vienna courts by an American

---

1 Freud's friend and correspondent, German anti-war activist Arnold Zweig (1887–1968).

patient who charged Freud's colleague, Theodor Reik,[1] with "quackery." Freud returned to the subject again in June 1927 in a "Postscript" to a fresh debate about lay analysis among psychoanalysts. These defenses of psychoanalysis in 1926 and 1927 help determine *The Future of an Illusion*, in particular its dialogical style and aberrant positivism.

These, too, are unusual claims, so let's compare and contrast some relevant passages from *Lay Analysis* and the *Future*.

In *Lay Analysis* Freud rationalizes the theory and practice of psychoanalysis to an "Impartial Person" of his own imagination, purportedly based on a "high official" of the Vienna courts (SE 20: 251), from whom he hopes to win "a just judgement" concerning the legitimacy (and thus the legality) of non-medical analysis in Austria (208). Consequently this latest "trial" of psychoanalysis (207) is loosely structured like a Socratic dialogue— where the give and take of question and answer propels the argument forward. As Freud puts it to the Impartial Person, "interrupt me whenever you feel inclined, if you cannot follow me or if you want further explanations" (191).

Freud introduces a similar style of presentation in the fourth chapter of the *Future*: another faux dialogue, this time with an imaginary opponent, or enemy. About these proceedings, he writes:

> An investigation that proceeds uninterrupted, like a monologue, is not completely free of danger. One may too easily yield to the temptation to push aside thoughts that seek to interrupt, and end up instead with a feeling of uncertainty, which in the end one tries to overpower through excessive assertiveness. I will therefore imagine an opponent [*einen Gegner*] who attends to my arguments with mistrust; here and there I will let him express himself. (p. 85)

While Freud very often entertains likely criticism the better to defeat it, thereby winning the reader's confidence, the personification of criticism only becomes a *method* in *The Question of Lay Analysis* and *The Future of an Illusion*. Nowhere else does Freud

---

1   Theodor Reik (1888–1969), Viennese psychoanalyst and early student of Freud. Much of Reik's work examined the role of repressed impulses in everyday behavior, including, most notably, those said to be present in the therapist–patient relationship.

structure his works in this unusual way, and it behooves us to wonder why.

One answer is that Freud, in these two works of public accounting, literally *performs* the Romantic theory of the divided self. As he characterizes the divided self in *Lay Analysis*, one carries secrets "that one would not care to admit to oneself"— closely echoing the insights of Dostoevsky's *Notes From Underground* (1864). Or as Freud clarifies, this time echoing Stevenson's *Jekyll and Hyde*: "It looks as though his own self were no longer a unity which he always thought it to be, as though there were something else as well in him that could confront that self" (SE 20: 188). That "something else" is the Impartial Person of *Lay Analysis* and the imaginary opponent of the *Future*, both of whom play the role of prosecutor, conscience, and superego to Freud's two defenses of psychoanalysis. Of course it is Freud, at this point in his life literally silenced by the painful prosthesis in his mouth (Jones 1957: 292), who plays both parts himself, who decides if and when the voice interrupts and what it has to say, and who dramatizes the proceedings—presumably staging it all for the theatrical, cathartic, and judicial benefit of his readers (Dufresne, "After *Beyond*"). This assumes, of course, that Freud is able to keep the two voices (of Freud) apart, and that the dialogical approach still follows the dictates of reason and consciousness. For just who directs whom has yet to be decided, which is probably the quintessential question of "the future," i.e., the question of who should speak for Freud when he can no longer speak for himself, and which agents should speak for psychoanalysis. To this end *Lay Analysis* is all dress rehearsal.

The theme of judicial authority arrives in chapter three of the *Future*, and not long after Freud has introduced a straightforward thesis about religion. The crux of his argument: religion is an infantile desire for Daddy's protection from a world of natural threats and, later on, from "the inadequacies and hurts of culture" (p. 83). "Thus a store of ideas is created," Freud writes, "born of the need to make human helplessness bearable, and constructed with the material of recollections of the helplessness of one's own childhood and that of the childhood of the human race" (p. 83). In short, God represents the protective force of culture writ large on the stage of the universe—a "supreme judicial authority with incomparably more might and consistency" (p. 84). The goal of religion: to allay our (reasonable) anxieties about the dangers of the external world, and to compensate us for the inadequate balm that is *Kultur*. "These [religious] ideas,"

Freud concedes, "are deemed the most precious possession of culture, as the most valuable thing it has to offer its members" (p. 85).

By contrast, religion arrives in *Lay Analysis* in chapter one, immediately following Freud's discussion of the therapeutic "magic" of words and his invocation of the divided self (SE 20: 187–88). More precisely, it arrives when the Impartial Person notices the similarity between Freud's cathartic therapy and that of the "Confession, which the Catholic Church has used from time immemorial in order to make secure its dominance over people's mind" (189). Freud rejects the claim, after which the Impartial Person raises the stakes: "as an analyst you gain a stronger influence over your patient than a Father Confessor over his penitents," and this because "the miraculous results of your treatment are the effect of hypnotic suggestion" (189). The connection between word magic, the divided self, and the problem of suggestion is not incidental. Freud studied hypnosis, translated the work of a hypnotist-therapist (Hippolyte Bernheim),[1] and in his early practice utilized hypnosis with patients; hypnosis evokes trance states that were thought to confirm the reality of divided consciousness; hypnotic trances are very often effected through the magic of words; and, finally, hypnosis is connected historically with discourses of spirit possession that go back to Mesmerism, animal magnetism, and, before that, to early Christianity (Crabtree; Dufresne, "Strange Case").

Freud, therefore, had very good reasons for contesting the criticism that psychoanalysis not only was compromised by suggestion, as many of his early critics had already claimed, but had actually perfected the therapeutic successes of the Catholic Confession. In *Lay Analysis* Freud responds as follows:

> Our Impartial Person cannot be either so ignorant or so perplexed as we thought to begin with. There are unmistakable signs that he is trying to understand psychoanalysis with the help of his previous knowledge, that he is trying to link it up with something he already knows. The difficult task now lies ahead of us of making clear to him that he will not succeed in this: that analysis is a procedure *sui generis*, something novel and special, which can only be understood with the help of

---

1 French neurologist Hippolyte Bernheim (1840–1919), known as an early advocate of clinical hypnosis.

new insights—or hypotheses, if that sounds better. (189–90; emphasis in original)

Freud saves psychoanalysis from the Impartial Person's (arguably fatal) charges by refusing the inheritance of it all and by insisting on the originality of his findings: psychoanalysis cannot be linked to the Confession, or to the suggestive authority of the priest, because it is "novel and special," "new," a "procedure *sui generis*," utterly unique. Of course the desperate lengths of this alibi— demonstrably false in every way, as even our cursory review of Romantic thought shows—is commensurate with the seriousness of the criticism. Clearly Freud has no good answer to the charges, neither here nor anywhere, but instead just a schoolyard assertion about the divine revelation that is psychoanalysis: psychoanalysis cannot be hypnosis because hypnosis is old and psychoanalysis is new. Of course the defense of psychoanalysis on this ground only strengthens its ties with religion, where the word of Freud functions like dogma for disciples.

Perhaps Freud realizes as much, because in chapter two of *Lay Analysis* he quickly invokes the scientific nature of psychoanalysis, an invocation repeated in the *Future*. Psychoanalysis is not complete or tidy, "like a philosophical system," but evolves and changes over time. He continues:

Science, as you know, is not a revelation; long after its beginnings it still lacks the attributes of definiteness, immutability and infallibility for which all human thought so deeply longs. But such as it is, it is all that we can have. If you will further bear in mind that our science is very young, scarcely as old as the century [i.e., twenty-six years old], and that it is concerned with what is perhaps the most difficult material ..., you will easily be able to adopt the correct attitude toward my exposition. But interrupt me whenever you feel inclined, if you cannot follow me or if you want further explanations. (191)

The incompleteness of psychoanalysis is itself a feature of its scientific nature, and also of its difficult subject matter and relative youth. In this context the invitation to interrupt is an invitation to "adopt the correct attitude toward my exposition," which Freud equates with the spirit of scientific inquiry, openness, and youthfulness. Freud will show us how it's done.

Freud echoes these views about science in the *Future*, but also vastly inflates his commitment by invoking empirically based reality. In fact the status of reality has already been debated with respect to the challenge of Marxism, but it is explicitly taken up again (at the beginning of chapter five) in the context of religion. Freud asks himself (not in the guise of an imaginary opponent, but as himself, without italics) how he should categorize the psychological significance of religious ideas. His answer: "After eliminating various formulations, we will stand by just one: religious ideas are teachings and pronouncements about facts and states of external (and internal) reality that convey something one has not discovered for oneself and which assert the right to be believed" (p. 88). Just as Freud reduced child's play to proto-scientific research about sexuality (e.g., Little Hans),[1] he reduces religion to a primitive form of reality testing—to a kind of botched science. As he clarifies elsewhere, the religious phase lies between the phases of primitive animism and mature science ("Scientific Interest," Appendix B3, p. 167).

Freud goes on to investigate the status of our variously acquired beliefs: arguments from authority, from tradition, and from prohibitions (p. 89). But since our religious beliefs and doctrines are "not residues of experience or the final results of thought," they are "illusions—fulfillments of the oldest, strongest and most fervent wishes of humanity" (p. 92). In short, they are like dreams, Freud's classic example of wish fulfillment; or again, as he adds in *Civilization*, they are like "mass delusions," that is, illusions shared with others (see Appendix B4, p. 169). Since religion, cut off from experience, is a form of wish fulfillment, Freud says that "we disregard its relation to reality, just as the illusion itself abjures confirmations" (p. 94). Science is another matter: "Only slowly do the riddles of the universe unveil themselves to our investigations; for many questions, science still cannot provide answers today. But scientific work [*wissenschaftliche Arbeit*] is the only path that can lead us to knowledge of reality outside ourselves" (p. 94). Or as Freud already said in *Totem and Taboo* (1913), "the scientific phase has its complete counterpart in the stage of maturity in which individuals have renounced the pleasure principle, and, adjusting themselves to reality, seek their object in the external world" (see Appendix B2, p. 162). In the

---

1 "Little Hans" refers to Freud's analysis of Herbert Graf (1903–73). In *Analysis of a Phobia in a Five-year-old Boy* (1909), Freud suggests that the young Herbert's fear of horses was caused, in large part, by his confused understanding of sexuality supplied by Herbert's father, Max (e.g., a "stork theory" to explain the arrival of Herbert's sister).

Future, wandering leads to dialoguing, and dialoguing to science—"the only path that can lead to knowledge of reality outside ourselves." Freud's constant recourse to the "reality outside ourselves," to the external world of "experience" (and by implication to empiricism), has him align psychoanalysis to this end. Anything less risks illusion. Yet this alignment results in a remarkably un-Freudian claim. Freud continues:

> Again, it is merely illusion to expect anything from intuition and introspection; these can only give us information about our own mental life—information difficult to interpret—never information about the questions that religious doctrine answers so effortlessly. It would be criminal to let one's own arbitrary opinion enter the void and, according to one's own personal estimation, to declare one aspect or another of the religious system more acceptable or less so. For such an approach, these questions are too significant—one might even say too sacred. (p. 94)

Let's unpack Freud's meaning. "Religious doctrine," based on "intuition and introspection," may tell us something about our inner lives, but nothing at all about the external world. Consequently only "arbitrary opinion" could decide which religious beliefs are right and which are wrong. The significant questions concern "knowledge of reality outside ourselves," questions that are, ironically, "too sacred" for any "religious system."

By the end of the chapter Freud will claim that "the truth value of religious doctrine is not within the plan of this investigation" (p. 95). But this is an empty gesture, similar in tone and effect to Freud's earlier disinclination to discuss the Russian experiment with communism, since he has already found the truth value of religion lacking—a finding, or verdict, that he repeats again a few pages later (p. 98). But the prosecution of religion comes at the very high price of denigrating, first, "intuition and introspection"—operations central to the foundation myth of psychoanalysis—and, second, the presumed connection between mental and physical realities, internal and external experiences, individual and collective truths, present and past events. In this sense *The Future of an Illusion* vitiates the "findings" of *The Interpretation of Dreams* of 1900, nullifying the (Romantic) basis of Freud's famous self-analysis: introspection and self-discovery as a basis for scientific insight into the object world. In this sense, just as Freud himself said, *The Future of an Illusion* really doesn't seem like a book of the genuine Freud at all, but of an imposter. If true, this is a radical conclusion, since it means that what began as a dramatization of the voice of an imaginary opponent, what began as *fiction*, quickly became reality: the Freud of the *Future* really does become divided against himself, unable to know which agency, which voice of Freud, is directing the other. "Freud" loses his way, the way of psychoanalysis.

Freud must realize that he is lost, or worse, that he has slid down a slippery slope of his own making. For at the outset of chapter seven he openly asks (of himself, without italics) what "other cultural assets" are caught in the undertow of his critique of illusion. "Once our suspicion has been stirred up," Freud continues, "we shall not shrink back from asking also whether the basis is any better for our conviction that we can learn something about external reality through the application of observations and rational thought in scientific work. Nothing should hold us back from approving the turning of our observation to our own being, from approving the application of thought to criticism of thought itself" (pp. 95-96). Nothing *should* hold us back from "such a comprehensive task" of critical self-examination, of critique in the Kantian sense, especially since Freud acknowledges the need. The problem is Freud's own inadequacies to this end: "the capabilities of the author do not extend to such a comprehensive task; of necessity, he must restrict his work to pursuing just one of these illusions—that of religion" (p. 96).

To his credit, "the author"—Freud refers to himself, "he," in the third person—doesn't "un-ask" the tough questions, doesn't erase or edit them, but leaves them for us to ponder. The upshot is that Freud and the reader both know that Freud has flirted with and then preserved an enduring suspicion: perhaps even that cultural asset called psychoanalysis is an illusion. The suspicion hangs over the *Future* and its *mise en scène*.

Later on, in chapter eight, Freud moves on to the idea that religion is not just a wish fulfillment, but contains "significant historical reminiscences" (p. 103). In effect he moves from religion's dubious "truth value" as it concerns external reality to what he calls its "historical value" (p. 104; cf. Appendix B5, p. 178). This is the positive value of religion that Freud, in retrospect, admits he has underplayed in the *Future* (see "Postscript" [to "An Autobiographical Study"], SE 20: 72): namely, the idea that our wishes, dreams, or religious beliefs are a distant echo of our archaic past, a past that he attempts to decode most fully in his final work on religion, *Moses and Monotheism* (see Jones

362–69; Zilboorg 19, 34, 44; see also Appendix B5). In this sense Freud (but which one?) is nearly back on the path of psychoanalysis. For the primary task of psychoanalysis is just this recovery of repressed historical truth, a task that goes well beyond questions of therapy and medicine. This is why Freud, not incidentally, argues in favor of the intellectual merits of lay analysis. If anything, the medical analysts, with their narrow "practical" and "professional" concerns, are actually a drag on the future progress of psychoanalysis. Invoking the "royal we," in *Lay Analysis* Freud delivers a lengthy salvo that resonates with the themes of *The Future of an Illusion* (particularly in its unusual concern with "the future"):

> We do not consider it at all desirable for psychoanalysis to be swallowed up by medicine ... It deserves a better fate and, it may be hoped, will meet one. As a 'depth-psychology', a theory of the mental unconscious, it can become indispensable to all the sciences which are concerned with the evolution of human civilization and its major institutions such as art, religion and the social order. It has already, in my opinion, afforded these sciences considerable help in solving their problems. But these are only small contributions compared with what might be achieved if historians of civilization, psychologists of religion, philologists and so on would agree themselves to handle the new instrument of research which is at their service. The use of analysis for the treatment of the neuroses is only one of its applications; the future will perhaps show that it is not the most important one. (SE 20: 248)

Freud is clearly bullish about a future that belongs to the historians, psychologists, philologists, and all the other lay analysts, but not really to medical analysts or even analytic treatment. "I have often said," Freud said privately, "that the purely medical importance of analysis is outweighed by its importance to science as a whole, and that its general influence by means of clarification and the exposure of error exceeds its therapeutic value to the individual" (Freud and Pfister 120). In his own life Freud always favored pure research, preferring the company of students, researchers, and intellectuals to patients. The advancement of "science as a whole" was his life's work. "This prospect of scientific gain," Freud repeats in the "Postscript" of 1927, "has been the proudest and happiest feature of analytic work" (SE 20: 256).

Arguably, this is the future that Freud stakes his reputation on in *Lay Analysis*—a future when psychoanalysis will function as the indispensable key to all disciplines. The alternative would be a "gloomy future," one caused by the failure of psychoanalysis to create "an abode for itself outside of medicine" (in Jones 297). And so Freud in 1926 proclaimed that lay analysts are not quacks but are legitimate practitioners of psychoanalysis; moreover, they are an essential part of Freud's vision for the future of psychoanalysis. It cannot be surprising that medical analysts were not pleased, fearful that Freud was stripping away the science from psychoanalysis. When Reik won his suit in May 1927, the *New York Times* reported: "AMERICAN LOSES SUIT AGAINST FREUD: Psychoanalysis Discoverer Says It Can Do Good Regardless of Medical Science" (in Gay 491).

Freud–Reik may have won the battle, but they lost the war with medical analysts. Nearly one year after the court win Freud remarked that he was a "Commander-in-Chief without an army" (in Jones 297). Hence *The Future of an Illusion*, which repairs the impression that Freud is insufficiently devoted to science (in *Lay Analysis*) by trumpeting the scientific nature of psychoanalysis (in the *Future*). In short, one PR campaign led to another wherein Freud pursued the un-Freudian path of positivism for the sake of the institutional present of Freudianism—where Freud "out-sciences" his colleagues on their own terms. Eliot was the first reviewer to see through the ruse, writing, "it is naturally the adepts of the parvenu sciences, in their anxiety to affirm that their science really is a science, who make the most exaggerated claims for science as a whole" (353; see also Kiell 577).

As for Freud's uncharacteristic optimism in the *Future*, it is prefigured in *Lay Analysis*, where he concludes, first, that child analysis is "an excellent method of prophylaxis" (prevention of neuroses); second, that adult analysis might work as a "corrective" to the sacrifices we face in civilization; and third, that the future might even see "a new kind of Salvation Army!" run by "social workers" that help prepare humanity for the aforementioned "corrective" (SE 20: 249–50). More often Freud was lukewarm to such schemes, but they served his (exclamatory) purposes in the two books. All of this brings us full circle to the thesis that Freud provides only belatedly in chapter nine of the *Future*: "the sole purpose of this publication of mine," he says, is to show people the need to grow up and "go out, into 'hostile life'" (p. 108). Freud calls this "education to reality," by which he means education to the external world of others, of the *Masse*, and to the

Kultur that regulates their psychology. On this score, *Lay Analysis* and the *Future* are of one mind: the future belongs to an education influenced by psychoanalysis. (I discuss this further in the next section, pp. 40-43.)

Facetious mockery greets Freud's un-Freudian optimism at the beginning of the final chapter of the *Future*. The voice of the imaginary opponent declares:

> *That really sounds marvelous! A human race that has renounced all illusions and has thereby become capable of making life on earth bearable for itself! However, I cannot share your expectations. Not because I am the stubborn reactionary you may take me for. No, because of my prudence. It seems to me that we have now switched roles: you prove to be the enthusiast, who allows himself to be carried away by illusions, and I argue for the claims of reason, the right of skepticism.* (p. 109)

The voice concludes its lengthy and overdue criticism by charging Freud with having attempted "*to replace a well-tested and affectively valuable illusion*"—religion—"*by another one, untested and indifferent*"—the science of psychoanalysis (p. 110).

Freud is receptive to the criticism since the voice of the opponent is a genuinely Freudian one. The two voices have indeed "switched roles." "Maybe the hopes I have confessed," Freud admits, "are also illusory" (p. 110). If so, then the real and "sufficient" confession missing from the *Future* is the one voiced by the imaginary opponent, Freud's ventriloquist dummy.

Freud is not quite there, not yet, and so takes pains to distance himself and his science from the conclusion that psychoanalysis is just another illusion. Freud summarizes his response as follows: "We believe it is possible for scientific work to learn something about the reality of the world; through such knowledge we will be able to increase our power, and in accord with it we will be able to arrange our life. If this belief is an illusion, then we are in the same position as you are [i.e., the imaginary opponent, defender of religion], but through its numerous and significant successes science has given us proof that it is no illusion" (p. 112). In this passage Freud takes steps to counter the (hysterical) fear that his findings are illusory by tying psychoanalysis to science, science to proof, and proof to reality. For if psychoanalysis is science, and science is reality, then, Q.E.D., psychoanalysis isn't an illusion. He continues:

Science has many open enemies and even more hidden ones among those who cannot forgive her for having weakened religious faith and for her threat to overthrow it. People reproach her for how little she has taught us and for the incomparably greater amount she has left in darkness. But in doing so, they forget how young she is, how difficult were her beginnings, and how infinitesimally short has been the period of time since the human intellect has had the strength for scientific tasks. (p. 112)

This passage, which echoes *Lay Analysis*, is crucial. In it Freud compares the "infinitesimally short" time of science in general, and of psychoanalysis in particular, with the deep time of evolution. His argument is brilliant, if diabolical: if psychoanalysis, like science, can boast only modest results, it is because its development has been "infinitesimally short"—as he points out in 1926, psychoanalysis is scarcely twenty-six years old. "Are we not wrong," Freud therefore asks, "to base our judgments on excessively brief periods of time?" (p. 113). Freud's answer, insufficiently appreciated in the secondary literature, is classically Freudian in its total pessimism: "We should take geologists as our example." This dark conclusion marks the moment, more dramatic than the faux drama of the dialogue, when the two voices of the *Future* collapse, when the tension between narrator and imaginary opponent is dropped, and when Freud regains his genuine Freudian voice. Or, if you prefer, when Freud's positivism self-deconstructs (see DiCenso 30).

Marx believed that the future had already arrived, or had very nearly arrived, with industrial capitalism, and that the *Masse* was nearly a *Volk*, a people. With his appreciation of Darwinian evolution and Lamarckian[1] inheritance, Freud knew better: humanity's relatively recent experiences of science, and for that matter of *Kultur*, could only become a thing of nature, of biological inheritance, if they were (compulsively) repeated

---

1 Charles Darwin (1809–82), celebrated English naturalist who proposed and essentially proved the theory of evolution through natural selection in his 1859 book *On the Origin of Species*. Jean-Baptiste Lamarck (1744–1829), French naturalist and early proponent of evolutionary theory. Lamarck hypothesized that organisms are continually driven toward increasing levels of complexity and that differences between organisms are determined, in part, by differences between the organisms' natural environments.

for millennia.[1] Consequently, only our very distant descendents could speak of a cultural drive, an innate drive to create and foster and protect; that is to say, only the future—"far, far ahead, but probably not infinitely far" (p. 139)—could benefit from the accumulated experiences of the life drive. Until that probable time we should certainly speak out in favor of the future of science and culture, of the battle to master the external world; but in the meantime we should not forget to attend to the psychology of everyday life in our conflictual present, since it is still governed by our animal past.

And that is how Freud, after ten chapters, suspends the tension between Enlightenment and Romanticism, between the dream of progress and the devil of regress, between life and death-drives. Simply put, life is for the future, death is for the present. *The Future of an Illusion* is therefore very much a product of *Beyond the Pleasure Principle* and the death-drive theory. Indeed, the greatest illusion generated by the *Future* is the commonplace belief that its surface rationalism is derived from Enlightenment critiques and values, whereas it is part and parcel of Freud's brooding Romanticism. In this sense, it is not quite the case, as Fromm has it, that Freud's theories are "the fruitful synthesis of rationalism and romanticism" (*Psychoanalysis* 37). Nor is it quite the case, as W.W. Meissner has it, that Freud has "second thoughts" about his scientific claims toward the end of the *Future* (101). It is rather that Freud's late Romanticism indulges but ultimately suspends, or destabilizes, the scientific rationalism that is its Other. Indeed, the importance of Enlightenment thought to the *Future*, or to Freud's thought more generally, is very nearly a red herring, one that has misled readers from the moment the *Future* was published in 1927—beginning, as we will see, with Oskar Pfister.

Pastoral Work and the Cure of Souls: Philosophy against Freud

A powerful-minded opponent of religion is certainly of more service to it than a thousand useless supporters.
—Oskar Pfister to Freud (Freud and Pfister 110)

Let's summarize the argument thus far. Freud in the 1920s worries about the future of psychoanalysis, and so he takes pains

---

1 This is precisely the biological significance of Freud's theory of the "repetition compulsion," *Wiederholungszwang*, something widely misunderstood in the secondary literature. See Sulloway; Dufresne, *Tales*.

to distinguish it from medicine, from Marxism, and finally from religion. "Science" becomes the site where the battle is waged on all three fronts, and in both *The Question of Lay Analysis* and *The Future of an Illusion* Freud flirts with a positivism that is not just old-fashioned but remarkably un-Freudian: only empirical knowledge of the external world is real, thus rendering religion an illusion. Freud escapes the implications of his positivism, however, by invoking the deep history of evolution with which he predicts the development of the future. This way he has his cake and eats it too: positivistic science remains the hope of a "geologically" distant future, even though we are governed by our animal pasts today. The master key in these respects is the death-drive theory, which reveals that supposed progress in our present lives is a kind of illusion, that biology and death will win out over culture and life for the foreseeable future. And so the future he predicts for humanity (and for psychoanalysis) in the *Future* is ultimately the same as the one he pitches in *Beyond the Pleasure Principle*. There is no contradiction between the two works.

There is, however, at least one more significant piece of the puzzle that helps account for the appearance of the *Future* in 1927, and for its unusual positivism: namely, Freud's relationship with the world's first lay analyst, Oskar Pfister (1873–1956). Let's turn to this relationship now.

It is often claimed that the formal argument between psychoanalysis and religion in the *Future* repeats the informal argument between a "godless" Freud and his devout friend, the lay analyst and Swiss pastor Oskar Pfister (Meissner 64, 73, 82; Roazen, "Introduction" 557). On this reading the "imaginary opponent" in the *Future* is a personification of Pastor Pfister, the voice of opposition delivered from within psychoanalysis itself. Freud himself certainly admits that he had Pfister in mind when composing the book. "In the next few weeks," Freud tells him, "a pamphlet of mine will be appearing which has a great deal to do with you. I had been wanting to write it for a long time, and postponed it out of regard for you, but the impulse became too strong" (Freud and Pfister 109).

By 1927 Freud had known Pfister for nearly twenty years, the two sharing a bond over psychoanalysis, friendly exchanges, and family. In 1909, Pfister began utilizing psychoanalysis with his Protestant (Lutheran) parishioners in Zurich, especially young adults, a practice he called "pedagogic psychoanalysis (paedanalysis)"—the application of analysis to education (Freud and Pfister 78; see Meissner 73–74; Irwin "Oskar Pfister"). But that is not all. In addition to his many articles and books on analysis, in late 1912 Pfister sided with Freud against that other Swiss, Carl Jung, seven years later helping to establish the Swiss Society for Psychoanalysis. Freud rewarded Pfister for his loyalty, writing a short "Introduction" to Pfister's *The Psychoanalytic Method* in February 1913; not incidentally, it is the first defense of lay analysis ever published. In a rehearsal of arguments outlined in greater depth in *The Question of Lay Analysis*, Freud's "Introduction" already entertains the optimistic idea that psychoanalysis could be a prophylactic against future neuroses. To this end Freud favorably compares psychoanalysis to education and the kind of pastoral work that Pfister was practicing with young adults (SE 12: 330). "Let us hope that the application of psychoanalysis to the service of education," Freud concludes, "will quickly fulfill the hopes which educators and doctors may rightly attach to it. A book such as this of Pfister's, which seeks to acquaint educators with analysis, will then be able to count on the gratitude of later generations" (331). Freud's hopes were borne out. In a letter to Pfister in 1926, Freud wrote, "of all the applications of psychoanalysis the only one that is really flourishing is that initiated by you in the field of education" (Freud and Pfister 106).

Pfister insisted on the relevance of psychoanalysis to "all those who come into the field of the cure of souls" (104), from alcoholics to frustrated artists, a feature he thought was missing from *Lay Analysis*. Surprisingly, Freud agreed:

> I am glad that on the whole you like my pamphlet. But do not judge it as an objective, scientific piece; it is a piece of polemics written for a special occasion. Otherwise I should certainly not have omitted the application of analysis to the cure of souls. I considered doing so, but in Catholic Austria the idea of a "churchman's" working with analysis is totally inconceivable, and I did not wish to further complicate the issue. (Freud and Pfister 105)

Freud's "Postscript" of the following year was an opportunity to correct (and to "complicate") the public record concerning "the cure of souls," and once again to register his favorable views about pastoral work. In it Freud writes:

> A professional lay analyst will have no difficulty in winning as much respect as is due to a secular pastoral worker. Indeed, the words, "secular pastoral worker," might well serve as a

general formula for describing the function which the analyst, whether he is a doctor or a layman, has to perform in his relation to the public. Our friends among the protestant clergy, and more recently among the catholic clergy as well, are often able to relieve their parishioners of the inhibitions of their daily life by confirming their faith—after having first offered them a little analytic information about the nature of their conflicts. (SE 20: 255–56)

In the *Future*, Freud admits that religion can be psychologically effective against neuroses, something he mentioned in his "Obsessive Actions and Religious Practices" of 1907 (see Appendix B1, p. 155) and in the Wolf Man case study of 1918: "it may be said that in the present case religion achieved all the aims for the sake of which it is included in the education of the individual" (SE 17: 114). To Pfister Freud conceded the "possibility of sublimation to religion" (Freud and Pfister 63). Freud is thus far from distancing analysis from the religious context altogether, especially in its connection to Pfister's Protestantism. He even embraces the words "secular pastoral worker" as central to the identity of psychoanalytic practice. Freud is careful, however, to qualify his remarks in the "Postscript"—and he throws "socialism" (still used interchangeably with "communism" in some circles) into the mix as well:

We who are analysts are set before us as our aim the most complete and profoundest possible analysis of whoever may be our patient. We do not seek to bring him relief by receiving him into the catholic, protestant, or socialist community. We seek rather to enrich him from his own internal sources, by putting at the disposal of his ego those energies which, owing to repression, are inaccessibly confined in his unconscious, as well as those which his ego is obliged to squander in the fruitless task of maintaining those repressions. Such activity as this is pastoral work in the best sense of the words. (SE 20: 255–56)

I have taken pains to expose the textual and thematic connections between *Lay Analysis* (and the "Postscript") and the *Future*. But the truth is that Freud himself revealed "the secret link" between *Lay Analysis* and the *Future* in a letter to Pfister. "In the former," he wrote in November 1928, "I wish to protect analysis from the doctors and in the latter from the priests. I should like to hand it [psychoanalysis] over to a profession which does not yet exist, a profession of *lay* curers of the souls who need not be doctors and should not be priests" (Freud and Pfister 126; emphasis in original).

In a way Freud holds out Pfister as a rough model of the future analyst, which is a remarkable tribute to the man and his commitment to the "cure of souls." Certainly he held Pfister in high esteem, almost uniquely so in the history of the movement. Their mutual respect is much in evidence in the correspondence, each man outdoing the other in praise—Pfister is praised for his integrity, enthusiasm, and optimism; Freud is praised for his genius and generosity with his work. Each seems to function as the other's ego ideal, the kind of opponent one gladly invites to family dinners.

Pfister's private criticisms of the *Future* therefore came as no surprise to Freud, who agreed with Pfister's suggestion that he formalize them in an essay for the psychoanalytic journal *Imago*—where "The Illusion of a Future" was indeed published in 1928. Naturally, though, a number of criticisms were first floated in the correspondence. For example, in a long letter of 24 November 1927, Pfister challenged Freud's recourse to "'pure' experience" as a "fiction," insisting that "there can be no such thing as a pure empiricism" (Freud and Pfister 114; cf. Appendix B6, p. 191). Pfister may also have been the first to see in Freud's *Future* an echo of Enlightenment ideals. "Your substitute for religion," Pfister told Freud, "is basically the idea of the eighteenth-century Enlightenment in proud modern guise" (Freud and Pfister 115).

As for Pfister's essay response to the *Future* (see Appendix A), it is a work balanced between *pro forma* praise and informed criticism. After an opening declaration of his affection, the essay is divided into two sections: "Freud's Criticism of Religion" and "Freud's Scientism." In the first Pfister quickly outlines Freud's charges against religion and then begins his defense. He accepts the evolutionary grounds that Freud favors, but with a twist: "just as tadpoles offer up their tails" to become frogs, so too has mature religion left behind its admittedly neurotic origins to become a culturally significant force of love, community, and ethics (p. 119). Religion is therefore a part of the "biological-ethical progress of humanity," a claim that informs Pfister's entire critique. Next he criticizes Freud's reduction of science to experience and delivers a Nietzschean-sounding charge: all concepts "were long ago invented by epistemology as rather clumsy, if indispensable, anthropomorphisms" (p. 128). Consequently, "[w]hy should religion and theology form an exception?" The problem, mentioned in the correspondence, is that even if we grant "a surplus of pure objectivity" to the "exact natural sciences, they are lacking just what empirical criticism sought so passionately and unsuccessfully: pure experience" (p. 129). Here, as elsewhere, Pfister implicitly invokes Kant's Critical Philosophy, even as he offers a back-handed compliment to American pragmatism (p. 129). The upshot: religion is neither so bad, nor science so perfect, that we should invest our "entire fortune in the single bank of science" (p. 131).

To Freud's charge that religion stupefies people, Pfister lists off the achievements of brilliant believers of the past, from Descartes[1] and Newton[2] to Goethe[3] and Schiller[4] (pp. 133-34; cf. p. 146). To Freud's hope that a secular education is a healthier choice, Pfister points to neurotic atheists and communists and declares that "history has thus far pronounced another verdict" (p. 135). Later Pfister adds, mischievously, that we should be careful assuming that non-believing intellectuals are necessarily morally superior to regular believers. "Hasn't Alexander von Öttingen[5] demonstrated that the highly educated include proportionately more criminals than do those of average intelligence? Do we not sometimes encounter an incredible meanness

---

1   French mathematician and philosopher René Descartes (1596–1650), widely regarded as the "father" of both analytic geometry and modern philosophy. In philosophy, Descartes is primarily known for his arguments for the existence of God, his theory of mind–body dualism, and the oft-repeated *cogito ergo sum*—"I think, therefore I am."

2   English physicist, theologian, astronomer, and philosopher Sir Isaac Newton (1643–1727). Newton's *Mathematical Principles of Natural Philosophy* (1687) (in which his law of universal gravitation and three laws of motion are presented) is one of the most influential texts in the history of modern science.

3   German polymath and famed author of *Faust*, Johann Wolfgang von Goethe (1749–1832).

4   Johann Christoph Friedrich von Schiller (1759–1805), German poet, playwright, and philosopher.

5   Baltic-German statistician and theologian Alexander von Öttingen (1827–1905). His *Moral Statistics* (1868) maintained that regularities in human behavior are the result of social living and that, despite the statistical predictability of certain group behaviors, individual actions remain free rather than determined.

of spirit among academics?" (p. 147). Touché. Freud felt the same way about psychoanalysts, and Pfister knew as much.

Section one ends with a persuasive critique of Freud's reduction of culture, and of religion therein, to the "police-like mission" of taming our hostile instincts. Like Eliot, Pfister reminds us of the positive and creative side of culture: mature religion elevates humanity, "calling to life a higher, inwardly richer humanity, better corresponding to the true demands of human nature and ethics" (p. 137; cf. Meissner 71–72). This recognition of progress in and through religion is for Pfister "genuine realism," against which he contrasts "bad realism"—a term he associates, implicitly, with Freud's thinking.

Pfister's discussion of Freud's "scientism" in section two is philosophically informed, fairly sophisticated, and deepens the charges leveled in section one. It is no doubt of interest to philosophers curious about psychoanalysis. According to Pfister, Freud invokes a particular notion of "science" but avoids posing the question of its epistemology. Pfister makes a virtue of Freud's avoidance of philosophy, but then he delivers a wallop:

> Freud is a positivist and for that we can thank God. Without his concentrated dedication to the empirical he would not have become the great pioneer that he is. With such a successful and pioneering genius, one can make allowances if at the moment when he attempts to smother religious illusion, he sets up science as the Messiah, without observing that this belief too is permeated with illusion. (p. 138; cf. p. 144)

The charge that Freud overvalued science is of course telegraphed in the title of his essay: the illusion of a future supposedly perfected by science (cf. Reik 123).

Pfister praises Freud's self-criticism about his faith in science but then fails to recognize it as a totally empty gesture in the *Future*. As for Freud's "dedication to the empirical," Pfister takes Freud's professed positivism at face value. How it resonates, or fails to resonate, with Freud's other works is never explored. Pfister's innocence on this score is nearly laughable, since no well-regarded scientist in the history of science has been *less* dedicated to "the empirical" than Freud; no well-regarded scientist has so brazenly over-determined his observations through pre-existing theories, as Freud did, for example, when positing the truth of childhood sexuality years in advance of the confirming "observations" of children in analysis.

On the other hand, Pfister at least spells out the latent epistemological tenets of the *Future* and so holds Freud to account.
Such clarity allows Pfister to go beyond the minimalist claim that
The Future of an Illusion echoes Enlightenment critiques of religion, to actually compare Freud with other empiricists. On this
score Pfister is useful, not least because he notes a major difference between Freud and the early empiricists. "His empiricism
differs completely from that of the English empiricists," Pfister
explains, "who seized the world of experience with the greatest
precision but simultaneously, in the realm of action, left control
to natural instinct and to the conscience—no longer to science"
(p. 139). If anything, Freud is a more radical, or more naïve,
empiricist, someone totally uninterested in the ethical accommo-
dations offered by positivists such as Mill,[1] Comte,[2] Strauss,[3]
and Dietrich.[4]

Pfister, therefore, underscores and rejects Freud's unthinking
disregard for the epistemological debates of modern philosophy.
In what may be the most important passage of "The Illusion of a
Future," the Pastor delivers a quick history lesson and an
informed warning:

> May one ignore the entire history of modern philosophy,
> which begins with Descartes and his absolute skepticism; then
> goes on to Hume, who destroys the illusion of guaranteed
> causality; to Kant, who overturns the illusion of empirical
> knowledge as a conception of the world in itself; and then to
> the most recent natural science that invokes a veritable twilight

---

1 John Stuart Mill (1806–73), British economist and social and political
  philosopher closely associated with classical liberalism and utilitarianism.
2 French philosopher Auguste Comte (1798–1857). Comte is best known
  as the founder of sociology and positivism—the view that the scientific
  method provides the best approach for explaining and understanding
  reality.
3 German theologian David Friedrich Strauss (1808–74), known for his
  historical investigation, *The Life of Jesus: Critically Examined* (1860), in
  which Christ's divine nature is denied.
4 French-German writer Paul Heinrich Dietrich (1723–89), later known
  as Baron d'Holbach. D'Holbach was known for his anti-religious works,
  most notably *The System of Nature* (1772), in which he re-formulates the
  universe within the framework of philosophical materialism. As such,
  d'Holbach denies the existence of a free will and reduces mental acts to
  the physical brain.

of false gods? Has no one yet realized what sort of scientific labyrinths one enters into when epistemological and metaphysical concepts are carelessly included under the descriptive label of natural science? [...] Natural science without metaphysics does not exist. [...] The world is accessible to us only through our mental organization and indeed not only through the gates of the senses, which of course still yield no knowledge. Our categories of thought, whether understood in Kant's way or otherwise, are always involved. Therefore, we must develop a critical theory of knowledge. (pp. 141-42)

"Thoughts without content are empty," as Kant famously argues in the *Critique of Pure Reason* (1781), and "intuitions without concepts are blind" (93). And that really is the crux of Pfister's criticism of Freud's "scientism" in the *Future*: Freud's dubious embrace of empirical science and positivism is conceptually blind, a "negative dogmatism" offered "in the muddled manner of an amateur" (p. 142; cf. Meissner 93). Or as John Irwin surmises, "The criticism here is that Freud is unconscious of his metaphysical assumptions, and that they are in any case invalid" ("Pfister and Freud" 322).

The difficult part for Freud, no doubt, is that this fair and accurate portrait of Freud in the *Future* does not do justice to the long history of Freud's freewheeling theorizing, his wild abandon with the facts of "experience," and his fundamental disregard for therapeutic efficacy and clinical observation. The truth is that Freud never lets the facts get in the way of what he calls his "Witch Metapsychology" (SE 23: 225); and he is often quite aware, as poststructuralists insist, of the analogical and metaphorical status of his ideas. So yes, Freud was a blind dogmatist—just not the kind that Pfister diagnoses in his essay on the basis of one work, *The Future of an Illusion*. And not even then. Like many others, Pfister fails entirely to account for the role of the death-drive theory in the *Future*, and fails to register the dark irony of Freud's closing remarks about the science he champions. Of course Pfister may have purposefully avoided this discourse, since even to engage with Freud's death-drive would be to validate a discourse that Pfister (implicitly but quite obviously) rejects. Perhaps that explains why Pfister often speaks of love but not of Eros, a word Freud used interchangeably with the life drive, *Lebenstrieb*.

***

Let's summarize. Pfister believes that religion is a part of culture, like art, that moves humanity forward; is the basis of ethics, justice, love, and communal feeling; and is an "objective" and realized, justified and "realistic" part of our store of knowledge today. Religion is therefore no illusion at all, but "an educator" (p. 149 the role Pfister himself, the "paedanalyst," plays in the history of psychoanalysis. As we've seen, Freud is surprisingly receptive to Pfister's work, indeed would like to "hand [psycho-analysis] over to a profession which does not yet exist, a profession of lay curers of the souls" (Freud and Pfister 126). Freud even suggests that analytic work is a kind of "secular pastoral work" (SE 20: 256). But they part company on the foundations of Freud's late work: a pessimistic theory of human nature and progress based on the death-drive theory. "In instinctual theory," Pfister told Freud, "you are a conservative while I am a progressive" (Freud and Pfister 131).

As for "illusions," Pfister convincingly turns the tables on Freud: Freud's positivistic future, stripped of ethics and philosophy, is the actual illusion. And it is an illusion on the grounds that Freud suggests: a species of wishing, where science plays the role of Messiah. Pfister thus counters Freud's Logos, the god of "intellect" derived from Greek reason, with one derived from the Christian Gospel of John, the god of "divine wisdom and love" (p. 151)—where Jesus is the incarnation of Logos. And with this last formula an insurmountable difference between the two men is revealed, since clearly the theoretician of the "son-religion" cannot accept the Pastor's preaching about Jesus Christ.

Freud's only explicit response to "The Illusion of a Future" appeared in a private letter to Pfister. This letter of 24 February 1928 is worth citing in full:

Some of your arguments seem to me to be poetical effusion, others, such as the enumeration of great minds who have believed in God, too cheap. It is unreasonable to expect science to produce a system of ethics—ethics are a kind of highway code for traffic among mankind—and the fact that in physics atoms which were yesterday assumed to be square are now assumed to be round is exploited with unjustified ten-dentiousness by all who are hungry for faith; so long as physics extends our dominion over nature, these changes ought to be a matter of complete indifference to you. And finally—let me be impolite for once—how the devil do you reconcile all that we experience and have to expect in this world with your assumption of a moral world order? I am curious about that, but you have no need to reply. (Freud and Pfister 123)

Freud, the late Romantic, rejects the ethics of Christian humanism that Pfister requires; ethics are like the rules of the road, totally conventional. One year later Freud repeats himself: "ethics are not based on an external world order but on the inescapable exigencies of human cohabitation" (Freud and Pfister 129). As for the supposed evolution of our finer feelings, Freud sees little evidence of it in the world of 1928. In this sense Freud rejects Pfister's optimism as itself illusory—a criticism of Pfister echoed by an otherwise sympathetic Irwin ("Oskar Pfister" 193–94; "Pfister and Freud" 323–24).[1]

Many of the same disagreements returned in 1930 with the publication of *Civilization and Its Discontents*. As before, Pfister rejected the narrow role that Freud assigns to culture. It would be a mistake, Pfister wrote to Freud, "to identify with civilization its existing horrors, to which its magnificent achievements stand out in contrast" (Freud and Pfister 131). Freud's frank response of 7 February 1930, which doubled as a response to utopians of all stripes, acknowledged the fundamental importance of the death-drive theory to his thinking:

> If I could, I should gladly do as others do and bestow upon mankind a rosy future, and I should find it much more beautiful and consoling if we could count on such a thing. But this seems to me to be yet another instance of illusion (wish fulfilment) in conflict with truth. The question is not what belief is more pleasing or more comfortable or advantageous to life, but of what may approximate more closely to the puzzling reality that lies outside us. The death instinct [*Trieb*, drive] is not a requirement of my heart; it seems to me to be only an inevitable assumption on both biological and psychological grounds. *The rest follows from that.* Thus to me my pessimism seems a conclusion, while the optimism of my opponents seems an *a priori* assumption. I might also say that I have concluded a marriage of reason with my gloomy theories, while others live theirs in a love-match. I hope they will gain

---

1 About Pfister's "overarching idealism," Irwin writes, "This enabled him to see Freudian eros as one step toward Christian love, and Freud's goal of therapy [as] the first step toward the soul care practiced by Jesus" ("Oskar Pfister" 193).

greater happiness from this than I. (Freud and Pfister 133; my emphasis)

Clearly Freud imagines himself to be a tough-minded realist unwilling to indulge the illusions of others, who bases his "findings" on "biology and psychology grounds." In this respect everything, as he says, follows from the death-drive. Freud's pessimism is therefore earned, while the rosy optimism of his opponents is merely asserted, a wish "in conflict with the truth."

The *Future* in Retrospect: Closing Remarks

While the late Freud begins with tentative speculation in *Beyond the Pleasure Principle*, he becomes more dogmatic over the years. As he says in *Civilization*, ten years after *Beyond*, the death-drive has "gained such a hold over me that I can no longer think in any other way" (SE 21: 119). In this respect the *Future* is indeed a peculiar text, since the evidence of Freud's "gloomy theories" is buried under the weight of his un-Freudian calls for reason and science. But the subtext of the *Future* maintains the essence of his dark views, subtly undoing all of his apparent optimism—which properly belongs to his "opponents," including medical analysts, communists, and idealistic humanists of various stripes.

This conclusion helps us understand, once again, Freud's remark that the *Future* "isn't a book of Freud," since what is genuinely Freudian is mostly absent. There is no mystery here; we know what constitutes the genuine Freud. This is the Freud who rejects simple-minded progress; rejects optimism about human nature, morality, and ethics; and rejects the "poetical effusion" that mistakes religious illusion for a "genuine realism" with dubious philosophical overtones. Or, if you prefer, this is the Freud who embraces the discourse of the unconscious, embraces the divided self, and embraces a notion of psychoanalysis that is predisposed to lay contributions, even from religious figures like Pfister. In short, this is the Freud who knows perfectly well that the positivistic empiricism of the *Future* is false—knows it even before the book is published—and amuses himself by telling a clueless admirer as much. Laforgue may not have found the genuine Freud in the *Future*, but he obviously found him in person.

Freud does not speak in one voice in the *Future*—or even two. One voice speaks for religion, one speaks against it, and one speaks for the death-drive. And sometimes the voices speak all at once. Appropriately, the voice of the death-drive is the faintest; Freud always claimed that it did its work in silence. Yet it is also the most insistent and significant voice, since it's the one that directs all the action.

So what to make of the elaborate show that Freud puts on? Simply put, *The Future of an Illusion* is a portrait of the great man's *Realpolitik* in the face of his backsliding, myopic, and sometimes dense followers—a *Masse*, like any other, that was unable to see into the distant future, mired as they were in the ugly present. The *Future* is therefore just like *Lay Analysis*, namely, "a piece of polemics written for a special occasion" (Freud and Pfister 105). To benefit his followers, Freud holds his nose and stages a positivism that is merely strategic—good enough, perhaps, to placate medical analysts still angry about his defense of that "pastoral" pursuit called lay analysis. The *Future* thereby establishes Freud's credentials as a legitimate scientist, even as he whispers the truth to those, as Nietzsche says, with ears big enough to hear: *find me elsewhere....*

That "elsewhere" is closer to philosophy than Freud could ever admit. Yet the late Romantic thought of Freud's youth gave him his lifelong convictions and even his opponents: the philosophy of consciousness and reason. Blissfully unaware of the truth of the unconscious, Enlightenment philosophy was a lingering threat to the new thinking. As such it functions as Freud's Other—which of course isn't nothing. In this respect Freud perfectly understood a Nietzschean truism that his friend, the good and faithful Pfister, delivered as a throwaway remark: a good opponent is always worth a thousand useless supporters (Freud and Pfister 110). And so the agonistic Freud sides with philosophy against philosophy, just like the other counter-Enlightenment thinkers of the late nineteenth century.

Freud was well aware that the tone of his work had undergone a "significant change" in the final phase—what in 1935 he calls a "regressive development," a subtle, ironical, and characteristic invocation of the theories of *Beyond the Pleasure Principle* (SE 20: 71–72). "My interest," Freud reflects, "after making a lifelong *détour* through the natural sciences, medicine and psychotherapy, returned to the cultural problems which had fascinated me long before, when I was a youth scarcely old enough for thinking" (72). Freud's acknowledgement of this return is as close as he comes to spelling out his debt to the thinking of late Romanticism. What he doesn't say is that this return is a public reckoning with an influence that exists from the beginning as an otherwise inexplicable metabiology and metaphysics—i.e., as the "metapsychology." As such, the late works are the official commentary on Freudianism by Freud himself, the culmination of everything that is most genuine in his thinking. Arguably it is the philosopher's task to make sure we adequately respect this return and find Freud where he belongs—not in the illusory future he sometimes imagined for psychoanalysis, nor in the stale bureaucracy that psychoanalysis became for others.

With his thoughts on the future, Freud wondered what would become of psychoanalysis after his death, asking, "Will it still resemble my basic thoughts?" (in Choisy 5). The answer is yes and no. Freudian psychoanalysis survives as an immortal contribution to the history of philosophy that Freud, like Schopenhauer and Nietzsche before him, tried his best to revalue and overcome. Freud did not embrace this future, let alone love it, but it belongs to him as the essence of his late return to "cultural problems." As for the scientific nature of psychoanalysis, the privilege of retrospection permits a harsh verdict on Freud's own terms: it belongs entirely to the history of wishful thinking, illusion, and mass delusion. Today the scientific Freud survives only as a particularly complex expression of the philosophical Freud—namely, as a fascinating attempt to translate late Romanticism into the more acceptable language of science. While the history of this error tells us a lot about psychoanalysis, it tells us nothing about the external world that intrigued Freud in *The Future of an Illusion* and elsewhere.

Psychoanalysis began with autobiography and, as Freud sometimes feared, never really got beyond it. Instead it sucked others into its reality, which is a terrifying yet magnificent realization—one might say objectively so—about the function, and perhaps even the truth value, of human *Kultur*.

Sigmund Freud: A Brief Chronology

6 May 1856   "Sigismund" Freud is born in Moravia, the present-day Czech Republic.

1856–58   Freud has a Catholic nanny for over two-and-a-half years and later claims to have distant memories of her.

1860   The Freud family relocates to Vienna, Austria.

1860–72   The Freud family observes major Jewish holidays; Freud's father Jacob reads from the Talmud; Freud is interested in the Bible, and has some formal education in Judaism at the gymnasium. As an adult, Freud remains identified with Jews but is highly secular in outlook and everyday practices.

1873   Freud enters the University of Vienna as a medical student.

1874–75   Takes extra credit in philosophy with Franz Brentano.

1875   Under the direction of Carl Claus at the Institute of Comparative Anatomy, Freud dissects the testes of four hundred eels.

1876–82   Works as researcher under Ernst Brücke at the Institute of Physiology, where he examines the nerve cells of crayfish and the nervous system of the fresh-water crab. Meets the well-known Viennese physician, Josef Breuer, at Institute.

1880   Translates John Stuart Mill for Theodor Gomperz.

1881   Having extended his studies, Freud finally graduates as Doctor of Medicine.

1882   Engaged to Martha Bernays.

1882–85   Residency at Vienna General Hospital. Freud is a reluctant physician, preferring university life as a researcher. Anti-Semitism is a factor in career choice.

1884–87   Cocaine research, including publications. Freud advocates its usage professionally and personally. A friend, encouraged by Freud to use cocaine, dies of an overdose.

1885–86   Four months of study with Jean-Martin Charcot at the Salpêtrière in Paris. Increased interest in hypnosis and hysteria.

1886	Marries Martha Bernays and establishes private practice as a neurologist, or "nerve doctor." Translates Charcot's two latest lectures into German.
1887–1902	Meets, befriends, and then corresponds with Wilhelm Fliess, a Berlin ear, nose, and throat specialist. Wild metabiological/metaphysical ideas exchanged, including Fliess' ideas of periodicity and human bisexuality. Friendship ends in 1902.
1887	Freud begins using hypnotic suggestion in clinical practice.
1887–95	Birth of six children, Anna being the youngest.
1893	Freud and Josef Breuer publish "Preliminary Communication." Theoretical claim: "hysterics suffer from reminiscences."
1895	Publishes, with Breuer, *Studies on Hysteria*. Case studies claim that hysterical suffering is cured by cathartic talk. Includes ur-case of "Anna O." Freud later invokes and/or maligns Breuer, as circumstances permit, as their views diverge over the next ten years. Breuer distances himself formally from Freud in a separate Preface to the 1908 edition of the *Studies*.
1895	Freud attempts to bridge psychology and physiology in the never completed "Project for a Scientific Psychology."
1896	First mention of the word *psychoanalysis*.
1896–97	Freud's father Jacob, a wool merchant, dies in 1896. "Seduction theory" is proposed: trauma is caused by repressed childhood sexual abuse.
1897	To Fliess, Freud privately questions the "seduction" etiology that he has already publicly championed in essays. Freud, however, keeps his change of heart from the public for another eight years.
1897–1900	Period of "self-analysis" culminates with *The Interpretation of Dreams*. Dreams are "the royal road to an understanding of the unconscious."
1901	Publishes *The Psychopathology of Everyday Life*. As in the Dream Book, Freud examines mild pathology under conditions of outward normality, e.g., "parapraxes," or faulty acts, such as slips of the tongue.
1902	Granted the title of Professor Extraordinarius at the University of Vienna. Although it is not a paid

chair position, Freud comes to be known as "the Professor."

1902–06   "Wednesday Evening Meetings" at Freud's home; gatherings of disparate people loyal to Freud's ideas. After breaks with Breuer and then Fliess, the group is used as a sounding board for Freud's ideas.

1905   Publishes *Three Essays on the Theory of Sexuality*. Psychosexual stages of development. Psychoanalysis as the investigation of sexual fantasy (not "seduction") finally gets public currency— although without declaring that a shift had indeed occurred. Also publishes *Jokes and Their Relation to the Unconscious*.

1906–15   Founding of the Vienna Psychoanalytic Society, and with it the greater institutionalization of Freud's ideas.

1907   In January, Freud publishes his first complete essay on religion, "Obsessive Actions and Religious Practices."

1908   First International Psychoanalytic Congress in Salzburg.

1909   Freud and Carl Jung invited to lecture at Clark University in Worcester, Massachusetts, and receive honorary doctorates.

1910   Freud discusses the origins of religion in his analysis of Leonardo.

1911   Nine of 35 members of the Vienna Society, led by Alfred Adler, break with Freud and found the Society for Free Psychoanalysis.

1912   Wilhelm Stekel leaves the Vienna Society. Jung "defects."

1911–15   Freud, many years after publishing "findings" of psychoanalysis, finally publishes papers on the technique of psychoanalysis.

1913   Publishes *Totem and Taboo*, at least in part in reaction to Jung's status as heir apparent. Basic claim: society begins with parricide.

1914   Freud writes "A History of the Psychoanalytic Movement," which polemicizes against Adler and Jung.

1914   Freud publishes important essay "On Narcissism."

1914   Writes his last significant case study, "From the History of an Infantile Neurosis," a.k.a. the case of the "Wolf Man," published in 1918. None of his published cases, as Freud admits at the time or as we now know, are successful cures. Failure propels his examinations, not just of unconscious fantasy, but of "resistance," "transference," and the "negative therapeutic reaction."

1915–20 Freud develops his "metapsychology," or theory of psychoanalysis, an explicit return to "energy" themes from 1893–95. Many essays are lost. One important exception is *A Phylogenetic Fantasy: Overview of the Transference Neuroses*, published in 1987.

1916–17 Publishes *Introductory Lectures on Psychoanalysis*.

1919 International Psychoanalytic Press is founded in Vienna and England.

1919 Freud writes a "Preface" to Theodor Reik's book on religion, *Probleme der Religionspsychologie*.

1920 Publishes *Beyond the Pleasure Principle*. This culmination of the metapsychology writings re-establishes a dualistic ontology and introduces the "repetition compulsion" and "death-drive" theories. Basic claim: the aim of life is nonexistence.

1921 Publishes *Group Psychology and the Analysis of the Ego*, the flipside of his discussion of the death-drive.

1923 Publishes *The Ego and the Id*. Moves from conscious/unconscious structure of mind toward id/ego/superego "topography." Origin of "ego psychology."

1923 Learns of cancer of the jaw and undergoes first operation (of 31 in total). Eventually, pain and excision hinder speech.

1924 Otto Rank, once a close friend, adherent, and collaborator, breaks with Freud.

1925 Freud publishes "An Autobiographical Study."

1926 Publishes "The Question of Lay Analysis." Major debate, legal and intellectual, about the status of non-medical analysts. Quackery charges against Theodor Reik in Austria. Freud sides with "lay" analysts like Reik, but institutional forces are against him, especially in America.

1927 Writes and publishes *The Future of an Illusion*. Basic claim: religion is an infantile attachment to

Daddy. Beginning of the so-called cultural works of Freud's late years. Pastor Oskar Pfister responds in 1928.

1930   Hungarian analyst Sandor Ferenczi, Freud's oldest close friend and collaborator, is increasingly estranged from Freud and psychoanalysis.

1930   Publishes *Civilization and Its Discontents* and draws the conclusions of the death-drive theory. Qualifies his remarks about religion. Probably his best-known work.

1930   Wins Frankfurt city's Goethe Prize for "creative impact."

1933   Hitler elected in Germany. Freud's books publicly burned in Berlin.

1933   In the *New Introductory Lectures* Freud discusses the religious *Weltanschauung*.

1934–38   Writes *Moses and Monotheism*. His thesis extends the logic of *Totem and Taboo* to the history of the Jews. Freud's claim: Moses was an Egyptian murdered by the Jews, a (phylogenetically buried) historical "fact" that helps explain repressed Jewish guilt and the origin of Judaism.

1937   Publishes "Analysis Terminable and Interminable." Freud's own skepticism about analytic practice is made explicit.

1938   Hitler invades Austria; Freud and immediate family leave for London, England. They settle in Hampstead, north of the core.

23 September 1939
     Freud, suffering badly, requests and is administered lethal doses of morphine by his friend, the analyst-physician Max Schur.

Translator's Note

Gregory C. Richter

The current volume provides a new translation of Sigmund Freud's *Die Zukunft einer Illusion* (*The Future of an Illusion*) (1927). In that volume Freud presents his ideas on the nature of religion, its origins, and its role in society and the human mind; declaring that religion is an illusion, he adduces both its positive and negative aspects, but he ultimately determines that it must be superseded in the interest of social and psychological progress. The best-known English translation is that by James Strachey, who, in his introduction, recognizes the importance of the work: "[I]t was with *The Future of an Illusion* that [Freud] entered on the series of studies which were to be his major concern for the rest of his life" (3). The next work to appear was *Civilization and Its Discontents* (1930), Freud's magnum opus on the conflict between the individual and society; there, chiefly in chapter two, he takes up again the discussion of religion begun in *The Future of an Illusion*.

Upon publication, *The Future of an Illusion* was immediately controversial. In 1928, T.S. Eliot—clearly among the detractors—characterized the work as "shrewd yet stupid" (Kiell 575): "[T]he stupidity appears not so much in historical ignorance or lack of sympathy with the religious attitude, as in verbal vagueness and inability to reason." In discussing the value of religious doctrines, Eliot identifies Freud's main thrust as follows: "The principle thesis seems to be ... [that] 'psychologically considered' they are *illusions*" (576; emphasis in original). A discussion of the word *illusion* then ensues. Eliot quotes Freud (Strachey's translation): "I must define the meaning of the word. An illusion is not the same as an error, it is indeed not necessarily an error ..." (577), but he thereupon retorts: "A vegetable marrow [i.e., a green, elongated squash] is not the same as a pumpkin, indeed is not necessarily a pumpkin: but this would not strike Aristotle as being the definition of a vegetable marrow." Eliot's assessment is as follows: "An excellent example of 'illusion' seems to be at hand: it is an illusion for Freud to think he has defined the term 'illusion'" (577). In the concluding lines of the review, he takes a final swipe at Freud: "[I]t is naturally the adepts of the parvenu sciences ... who make the most exaggerated claims for 'science' as a whole. This is a strange book" (577).

Among other contemporary reviews, in his collection Kiell includes one by Dorian Feigenbaum, first editor of *The Psychoanalytic Quarterly*. Feigenbaum, an articulate admirer of *The Future of an Illusion*, writes, "The book impresses one as a mellow product of a midsummer's rest in the country. The presentation is always lucid and elegant, and pervaded by a warm, sympathetic earnestness" (Kiell 581). He then provides a very useful six-page summary of the book, stressing Freud's classification of religious doctrines as illusions—thus falling within the realm of psychopathology. He concludes with a powerful point: "The term religious is still synonymous with ethical, and irreligious with unethical in the minds of the majority. But now it is necessary to recognize a separation between these terms. The reader who had been prone to attribute cynicism, pessimism and nonmorality to Freud's teachings will now be compelled to recognize the high ethical caliber of his views" (587).

In order here are some comments on the genesis and style of *The Future of an Illusion* as it appears in the *Standard Edition*. Strachey (3) states that his translation is based on an earlier version by William Robson-Scott. Robson-Scott, though, comments that in producing his version he received many helpful suggestions—not only from his editor, Ernest Jones,[1] but from Strachey as well (v). Thus, while these two renderings do differ considerably, they are historically intertwined, and it is difficult to be sure where one translator may have influenced the other. Yet in producing the current translation, I have often consulted Strachey's. Indeed, it would be impossible now to produce a version free of his influence. Strachey does convey the meaning of Freud's German with a high degree of accuracy, but several issues connected with his translation deserve further discussion. With reference to the entire *Standard Edition*, Ornston (222) faults him for effecting an artificial style far more elegant than Freud's. Freud, for example, makes vivid use of the historical present, while Strachey avoids the construction, often shifting to the past tense. Freud's style features numerous elliptical sentences, while Strachey generally "corrects" these, supplying missing nouns and verbs.

While acknowledging the importance of Strachey's translation as a monumental achievement, Mahony too has some harsh

---

1 Ernest Jones (1879–1958), the first English-speaking psychoanalyst and a close associate of Freud. Jones presided over both the British Psycho-Analytical Society and the International Psychoanalytic Association and wrote the "official" biography of Freud in the 1950s.

words for him. He writes that "the vitality of Freud's prose also comes from its playfulness"—that Freud "played joyfully with language"—and chastises Strachey for his efforts to eliminate that trait: "It is deeply regrettable that the playwork in Freud's writing tends to disappear under the rigid censorship of Strachey's scientific prose" (171). Observing that Freud wrote with a substantially unified vocabulary, whether discussing commonplace aspects of life or the most abstruse theories, he states, "Strachey's translation, with its unannounced policy of lexical apartheid, stressed the difference between various aspects of reality.... How different [from Freud's] were the verbal choices of Strachey, who apparently endorsed Jones's rigid platform for a psychoanalytic vocabulary in English" (172–73). In particular, he criticizes Strachey's introduction of Greek terms where Freud uses ordinary German (159). At least one such example can be found in *The Future of an Illusion*, where Freud mentions the psychological *Anlehnungstypus* (literally "leaning-on type"). As clarified by the ensuing discussion, the German term can be rendered as *dependent type*, yet Strachey (with Robson-Scott), translates German *Anlehnung* into Greek, yielding *anaclitic type*. (To his credit, Strachey also provides a normal English equivalent, *attachment*, in square brackets.) All of this can presumably be accounted for by the considerations of audience in Freud's mind versus Strachey's. While it is clear that Freud was addressing his contemporaries, Mahony stresses that Strachey "avowedly conceived of his imaginary audience as dead" (173). Indeed, in the General Preface to the *Standard Edition*, Strachey writes, "The imaginary model which I have always kept before me is of the writings of some English man of science of wide education born in the middle of the nineteenth century" (xix). "*Traduttore, traditore* (translator, traitor)," concludes Mahony (173): "This piece of traditional wisdom defines Strachey's translation." Thus, given these considerations, there is presumably a place for new translations providing an alternative to Strachey's elevated prose and attempting to suggest something of Freud's German style. In working on the current version I have continuously kept those goals in mind.

At times Strachey's translation may seem both too free and too archaic. In Strachey's version, for example, he has Freud describe religion as cherishing the belief that "Providence ... will not suffer us to become a plaything of the ... forces of nature" (19). Translating *Spielball* more literally and selecting *allow* in lieu of *suffer* (for *zulässt*), I render the passage as "Providence ... will not allow us to become the ball played with by the ... forces of nature." Other formal or archaic terms invoked by Strachey include *needs must, whilst, sleeping draught, irreligious education* (here *non-religious education*), *proof from objections* (here *safe from objections*), *a proven illusion* (here *a well-tested illusion*), and many others. Granted, Strachey's translations are now at least fifty years old; many are much older. His stylistic choices certainly met the expectations of his own day, but many often fail to meet those of twenty-first-century readers.

Sexism should also be mentioned as a pervasive issue in Strachey's translation of *Die Zukunft einer Illusion*. For Strachey, *Mensch* (*person/mankind*), *Mann* (*man*), and even the pronoun *man* (*one*) often share the English rendering *man*. In the plural, Strachey consistently translates both *Menschen* (*humans*) and *Männer* (*men*) as *men*, though *Männer* is rare in Freud's original. Strachey's renderings may strike the contemporary reader as highly sexist. His English version would suggest that Freud's writing, too, is highly sexist, but it must be kept in mind that Freud's opus is, in fact, much less sexist than Strachey's. Still, the German language itself requires some forms that may seem sexist in English. With grammatically masculine antecedents such as *Mensch*, Freud uses forms of the pronoun *er* (*he*) as required by the language; with genderless antecedents such as *jemand* (*someone*), Freud also uses forms of *er*, given the dictates of his day. In the current translation, though, I have often made other selections from the choices available in contemporary English, including plurals (e.g., *people*), or the genderless pronoun *one*. Thus, in the first paragraph of the book, Strachey has "the less *a man* knows about the past and the present, the more insecure must prove to be *his* judgement of the future" [italics mine], while I select "the less *one* knows about the past and the present, the less reliable will be *one's* judgment about the future."

I have, however, frequently borrowed serviceable English renderings of Freud's sociological and psychological terminology; e.g., with Strachey (and Robson-Scott) I translate *Versagung, Verbot,* and *Entbehrung* as *frustration, prohibition,* and *privation,* respectively. Strachey, given his preference for Greek and Latin terms, renders *das Über-Ich* as *the super-ego,* though a more literal English version would be *the over-I.* Yet Strachey's term has solidly entered the English lexicon, so no new version is called for. In other cases, though, I have felt free to make terminological changes; e.g., for Freud's outdated *Indo-Germanisch,* which Strachey renders as *Indo-Germanic,* I substitute the now standard

Indo-European. Despite the German term, Freud is clearly referring to Greek, Roman, and other European cultures. Crucially, I take issue with Strachey's rendition of the German term *Trieb*. Throughout, I translate *Trieb* as *drive* (the etymological cognate); this solution is seldom invoked by Strachey, who prefers *instinct*. Similarly, I replace Strachey's *psyche* with *mind*, and *psychic* or *psychical* with *mental*.

Translation of the German term *Kultur* is notoriously difficult. The senses of the English term *culture* do not completely overlap with those of *Kultur* in German. In both languages, the term may refer to a social system (Neolithic cultures, hunter-gatherer societies, technologically advanced societies, etc.). In other cases the English term refers to "high art"—works by great painters, composers, dramatists, and other creative artists. In contradistinction to the English term, though, *Kultur* often refers specifically to civilization. In chapter one, Freud asserts, "I refuse to distinguish between culture and civilization" (p. 63)—and this is the only instance in which the German term *Zivilisation* appears in the work. The dictum proclaims that in this work (except for speculations on the prehistoric state of affairs), Freud will be interested only in cultures that can be described as *civilizations*. That is, in using the term *Kultur*, he is generally referring to highly developed societies with well-defined social classes, permanent dwellings, and a high degree of specialization of labor; in such societies, one would expect to see military, technological, religious, scholarly, and artistic realms as specialized (though sometimes overlapping) fields. Referring to his own version, Robson-Scott comments, "The German word *Kultur* has been translated sometimes as 'culture' and sometimes as 'civilization,' denoting as it does a concept intermediate between these and at times inclusive of both" (7). Nor does Strachey select a uniform translation, employing both *civilization* (more frequently) and *culture*. Thus, he selects *white Christian civilization*, whereas *white Christian culture* might seem more appropriate. Indeed, Strachey and Robson-Scott often disagree in their selection between the two English terms. Given the difficulties, I have not presumed to interpret the term *Kultur* in each case. For a German term so central to the text, a unified translation seems desirable, and for this purpose, *culture*, rather than *civilization*, seems most appropriate: the English term will simply serve to represent the German one, with its sometimes narrower sense. In each case, given the context, readers can select an appropriate interpretation. Throughout the entire translation process, this and similar issues have constantly presented themselves. The challenges, though, have been similar to those that arose as I translated *Beyond the Pleasure Principle*. For a more complete discussion, see the Translator's Note in that volume.

A few observations on the recent rendering by J.A. Underwood and Shaun Whiteside are in order. Like Strachey, Underwood and Whiteside generally convey the basic meaning of Freud's German with accuracy. The English text, though, is rendered in a surprisingly colloquial register of British English, and there are some errors in translation. In the discussion of privations, Underwood and Whiteside have privations imposing prohibitions ("bans") rather than vice versa: "With the bans that they imposed ..." (9). (In context, the correct resolution of Freud's ambiguous relative clause would be "With the bans that imposed them.") In the discussion of the "god *Lógos*" [Reason] in the final paragraphs of the book, the translators misplace the negative phrase, making Freud proclaim: "Our god may not be *Lógos* ..." (70), whereas Freud is actually claiming *Lógos* as his god. Minor errors include the translation of *endlich* (*finally*) as *endless*— "Endless attempts have been made" (71). Sometimes Strachey's terminology is retained (*psychical* rather than *mental*), while on other occasions new terms are introduced; e.g., Strachey's *super-ego* becomes the *Above-'I.'* There are large amounts of filler: "anyhow," "isn't that the case," "as we have seen," and "I must say" often correspond to nothing in Freud. Sometimes two English versions are provided for a single German phrase; e.g., *unvergleichlich mehr* is rendered as "very much more (incomparably more)" (70). On several occasions, a question mark appears where Freud has a period, e.g., "surely that is highly unlikely?" (24). Finally, certain word choices seem questionable, e.g., *male parent* (18) for *Vater*. *Folk* is Underwood and Whiteside's preferred rendering of *man* (*one*), as in "Folk wanted to be rewarded" (22). In several cases, though, word choices are apt improvements over Strachey's; e.g., in lieu of Strachey's *petticoat government* for *Frauenherrschaft*—which I translate here as *political dominance of women*—Underwood and Whiteside select *matriarchy* (62).

Of special significance among the materials included in this volume is a new English rendition of "Die Illusion einer Zukunft" ("The Illusion of a Future") (1928), Swiss pastor Oskar Pfister's cleverly titled response to Freud's volume (see Appendix A). In his introduction to *Psychoanalysis and Faith: The Letters of Sigmund Freud and Oskar Pfister*, Heinrich Meng cites Pfister's colleague Hans Pfenninger, who commented that as "the representative of a free Christianity he [Pfister] was opposed to all dogma, but he met with understanding and love those who held fast to dogma because of inner ties" (E. Freud and Meng 9). A close friend of Freud, Pfister made occasional visits to Vienna; Meng notes that their friendship, lasting three decades, was characterized by "sharp conflicts," but also by "true tolerance and mutual understanding" (9). Anna Freud comments, "In the totally non-religious Freud household Pfister, in his clerical garb and with the manners and behaviour of a pastor, was like a visitor from another planet" (11), but she goes on to stress his warmth and enthusiasm. Pfister's apparent role in the genesis of *The Future of an Illusion* should be emphasized. Roazen writes that it was presumably Freud's friendship and correspondence with Pfister that sparked him to write *Die Zukunft einer Illusion* (Roazen 1993: 557), and Mahony states, "[It] is probably Pfister who was the imagined interlocutor in the two final chapters" (58).

It was in a letter of 24 November 1927 that Pfister first presented Freud with his criticisms of *The Future of an Illusion*. Summarizing his thoughts, he characterized the crucial difference between Freud and himself as he saw it: "I practice analysis within a plan of life which ... I regard ... not only as a powerful aid to treatment ... but [as] in accordance with the nature of mankind and the world" (E. Freud and Meng 116); this plan of life, as Pfister clarified, was one governed by religious faith. Indeed, he was bold enough to make this request: "Would you agree to my dealing with your views in *Imago*?" (116). In his response, on 26 November 1927, Freud wrote, "I attach importance to your publishing your criticism—in *Imago*, if you like" (117), and on 11 January 1928, he wrote that Pfister's article was "awaited with interest" (119). On 20 February 1928, Pfister sent Freud his manuscript for the journal, asking for comment. Four days later, Freud responded forcefully, but in a general spirit of respect: "Some of your arguments seem to me to be poetical effusion, others, such as the enumeration of great minds who have believed in God, too cheap. It is unreasonable to expect science to produce a system of ethics ..." (123). The letter continued with further observations, some surprisingly heated ("let me be impolite for once ..."), some calm and reflective. The discussion was taken up again from time to time. In a letter of 16 February 1929, for example, Freud wrote, "[I]t is immaterial whether Christ, Buddha, or Confucius is regarded as the ideal of human conduct," and he characterizes the "essence" of the religious outlook as "the pious illusion of providence and a moral world order" (129). The correspondence continued nearly until Freud's death, and often included a back and forth on Freud's latest publications, for example, the discussion of *Civilization and Its Discontents* that ensued in 1930.

Pfister's article, arguing that psychoanalysis can best alleviate human suffering when it acknowledges the role of religion in the human mind, appeared in *Imago*, Freud's psychoanalytic journal, in 1928. The English translation by Abrams and Taylor, however, omits several passages and contains serious translation and typographical errors. These include the claim that early man "suspended a live animal in boiling water" (rather than assumed a moving animal in water as the source of boiling) (565); the claim that "Joshua's son" (rather than the sun) stood still for him (566); the claim that Homer and Aristotle criticized the Bible (567); a passage in which the Baron d'Holbach (rather than early man) humanizes the forces of nature (572); and a passage in which the "skeptic" toward science (rather than its advocate) asserts its glorious future (575). Sometimes the rendering of compounds also seems problematical: e.g., *Realbasis* appears as "real realistic substantive basis" (575). Technical terms are mainly Strachey's, e.g., *instinctual renunciations* (*drive renunciations* in the current version). In my version in Appendix A, the references section has been greatly expanded and page numbers for citations have been corrected, as have biblical verse numbers; biblical quotations are from the King James Version. While many passages in the previous translation may be useful, it is hoped that the current version will provide new renderings more closely reflecting the intent of the author.

Also included in this volume, in Appendix B, are five shorter translations from works that Freud produced over a lengthy span of time, 1907 to 1939; all are thematically related to *The Future of an Illusion*. The appendix concludes with an excerpt from Pfister's 1923 volume *Zur Psychologie des philosophischen Denkens* (*On the Psychology of Philosophical Thought*).

First among the works of Freud selected for inclusion is a new translation of "Zwangshandlungen und Religionsübungen" ("Obsessive Actions and Religious Practices"; 1907), first published in *Zeitschrift für Religionspsychologie* (see Appendix B1). In the preface to his version in the *Standard Edition* (SE 9: 116), Strachey indicates that it is based on an earlier one by R.C. McWatters. Strachey goes on to stress that the article is of interest as Freud's "introductory incursion into the psychology of religion" (116) and that it ultimately led to a much richer elaboration of the same ideas in *Totem and Taboo* (1913). Strachey's translation certainly conveys Freud's basic meaning, but one is again struck by the dated nature of his translation. A few examples are *nervous affections,* corresponding here to *nervous disorders*; *morbid,* corresponding here to *pathological*; and *psychical,* corresponding here to *mental* throughout. Issues of sexism arise in connection with Freud's term *Mädchen.* Although it was normal in Freud's day to use the term with reference to a young woman, the translation *girl* in this context no longer seems acceptable in academic English; *young woman* will surely serve better. I have previously discussed at length two terms often invoked by Strachey that appear in "Obsessive Actions" as well (Richter 39–41). The first is *cathected,* a Greek-based term coined by Strachey to represent Freud's *besetzt* (*charged*). Freud's term conveys, in very ordinary German, the metaphor of electrical charge in psychological processes, while Strachey's translation reflects a register entirely different from that of the original and lends the metaphor a scientific aura Freud probably did not intend. The second term is *instinct,* Strachey's equivalent for the German *Trieb*; as in *The Future of an Illusion,* I translate the German term as *drive.* Finally, of linguistic interest in Freud's German text is the term *Proskinesis,* Freud's misspelling of the Greek borrowing *Proskynesis.* Although the Greek term itself sometimes appears in English as well, I have selected a more familiar but literal equivalent, *prostration.* Strachey, by contrast, selects *turning to the East,* thus changing the sense considerably.

In Appendix B2 are new renditions of excerpts from Freud's 1913 work *Totem und Tabu* (*Totem and Taboo*). In the third essay in that work, "Animism, Magic, and the Omnipotence of Thoughts," Freud proposes that stages in humans' view of the universe correspond to stages in individual libidinal development: religion corresponds to the stage of attachment to the parents. In the fourth essay, "The Return of Totemism in Childhood," Freud argues that religion derives from the collective need to atone for the original murder, by the sons, of the omnipotent primeval father. Here, a major issue in translation is the racism suggested in Strachey's version: where Freud has *Primitive,* translated here as *primitives,* Strachey has *primitive races*—a solution reflecting the views of his day and implying that race predicts culture. The English term *primitives* itself is of course dubious: it presumably implies a cultural hierarchy with Western European cultures at the top and others at the bottom. Despite such considerations of political correctness, though, I have retained the term, as it best reflects Freud's own mindset and is an exact reflection of Freud's original term. The remaining issues of translation are technical ones. While Strachey sometimes introduces italics to clarify Freud's intent, I have not done this in the current translation. While Strachey corrects Freud's historical present, always recasting it in the past tense, I have retained it here to enable a more vivid depiction of the stages Freud proposes as leading to the development of Christianity.

"The Interest of Psychoanalysis from the Point of View of the History of Culture" (Appendix B3) is a new rendition of a portion of Freud's 1913 essay "Das Interesse an der Psychoanalyse" ("Scientific Interest in Psychoanalysis"). In this excerpt, Freud argues that religion, along with myth and morality, arose as means by which human beings sought compensation for those wishes that went unfulfilled in the real world. Few difficulties arose in the translation process, but here the hyphenated form *psycho-analysis* might be mentioned: in this essay, and throughout the *Standard Edition*, the hyphen always appears—simply signaling Strachey's awareness that, according to the phonological rules of Classical Greek, the vowel before *analysis* should have been elided (cf. English psych-edelic, psych-iatrist). French translators have gone further, correcting Freud's German term, *Psychoanalyse*, as *psychanalyse*. In English, though, the didactic hyphen becomes tiresome; a more contemporary rendering as *psychoanalysis* now seems entirely acceptable.

From *Das Unbehagen in der Kultur* (*Civilization and Its Discontents*; 1930), Appendix B4 contains a new translation of chapter two. Here, Freud discusses the unpleasure that individuals experience from the body, the external world, and human relationships but describes numerous paths by which they may seek personal fulfillment and happiness. He concludes by arguing that religion has the disadvantage of constraining many of these paths: in the end, the happiness religion affords may be only that of "unconditional submission." In translating this chapter, I again encountered issues related to gender-biased language. For modern readers, Strachey's translation of *Menschen* as *men* in the 1961 version of *Civilization and Its Discontents* may evoke inappropriate connotations for readers unfamiliar with his style. Such connotations are absent in the German original, since *Menschen* translates more accurately as *humans* more broadly. Thus, in translating the work, English equivalents such as *individuals*, *humans*, or *people*, will presumably be more effective. In the case of Freud's *der gemeine Mann*, however, I have selected a convenient and very literal English rendering: *the common man*. Yet Freud's *der gemeine Mann* clearly refers to ordinary people of both genders in their relation to religion. Freud, too, could be sexist!

In preparing the current rendering of the chapter, I also consulted the translation of *Civilization and Its Discontents* by McLintock. That translation is more conservative than my own version—e.g., Stracheyan terms such as *morbid*, *instinctual*, and *psychical* frequently appear—but it conveys Freud's ideas with eloquence. Indeed, each of the translations provides its own take on the text. Consider just one example. In a crucial sentence clinching much of the discussion, McLintock has "[E]veryone must discover for himself how he can achieve salvation" (26). Strachey has: "[E]very man must find out for himself in what particular fashion he can be saved" (83), and the current version reads: "[E]veryone must find his own unique path to blessed happiness" (p. 177). Here, the main difficulty is presented by the German *selig werden* (*become happy/blessed*). The term certainly has strong religious overtones, but Freud is using it figuratively; I have selected a rendering that is less strongly religious than those in the other versions cited but which fits within the semantic scope of the German term.

The last Freud work excerpted in the current volume (in Appendix B5) is *Der Mann Moses und die monotheistische Religion: Drei Abhandlungen* (*Moses and Monotheism: Three Essays*). Published in 1939 after Freud's escape from Nazi-occupied Vienna, it was one of his last publications, and certainly the last one to deal in depth with religion. Included is a portion of Essay II, "If Moses was an Egyptian...." In this excerpt, Freud argues that Jewish monotheism is of Egyptian origin: he speculates that Moses was actually an Egyptian, and that the Levites, whom he claims perpetuated monotheism after Moses was killed in the desert, were originally Egyptians who had accompanied him. Included also are portions of Essay III, "Moses, his People, and Monotheism." In these passages, Freud examines the psychological history of Judaism and Christianity to argue (as in *Totem and Taboo*) that religion arose due to guilt over the dimly remembered murder of the primeval father.

The text is extremely complex syntactically, presenting immense challenges for the translator. English cannot express the complex structures of German with equal concision, but expansions and adjustments must be carefully juggled so as to avoid introducing new ambiguities not present in the original. The need to preserve Freud's distinction between instincts (basically associated with animals) and drives is a crucial issue here. Where Freud has *instinktmässig*, and only there, I have selected *instinctively*: "We find that in a number of significant relations our children ... react ... instinctively, in a manner comparable to animals, which can only be explained as phylogenetic acquisition" (p. 187). Strachey, by contrast, generally translates both *instinktmässig* and *triebhaft* as *instinctual* or *instinctually*, thus obscuring Freud's clear distinction. Another issue is the translation of figurative language. In his translation of *Moses* in the *Standard Edition*, Strachey relates how Christianity overcame all obstacles "[w]ith the strength which it derived from the source of historical truth," while I render the passage thus: "With the strength that flowed to it from the wellspring of historical truth" (p. 190). Where Freud has *zufloss*, Strachey has *derived*, corresponding here to *flowed*; the semantics of *zufloss* also suggests that *Quelle* should be less ambiguously translated as *wellspring* than as *source*, thereby preserving the metaphor of strength as flowing water.

The appendix concludes with a brief passage from Pfister's *Zur Psychologie des philosophischen Denkens* (*On the Psychology of Philosophical Thought*; 1923), to which he refers in "The Illusion of a Future." In the section "The Significance of Psychology for Understanding and the Normative Assessment of Philosophical Thought," Pfister casts doubt on the objectivity of all philosophical argumentation that goes beyond the empirical, beyond a priori certainties, or beyond the mathematical. He argues that in many cases, philosophical argumentation is merely rationalization of the system suggested by unconscious affects in the philosopher himself. The ideas with which philosophers grapple thus have the same source as those inspired by "poetic, artistic, and religious revelations." Pfister therefore concludes that "the completely conscious development of thoughts must become the ideal of all science." These proposals serve to round off the discussion, and they are conceptually linked to his concluding words in "The Illusion of a Future" as well: "*The Future of an Illusion* and 'The Illusion of a Future' unite in a strong belief whose credo is: 'The truth shall make you free!'"

THE FUTURE OF AN ILLUSION

I

When one has lived for a long time in a particular culture and has often tried to determine the nature of its origins and developmental path, one is sometimes tempted to cast one's gaze in the other direction and to ask what further fate awaits this culture and what changes it is fated to undergo. But one will soon notice that from the very start the value of such an investigation is negated by several factors. Chief among these is the fact that there are only a few people who can clearly view the hustle and bustle of human activity in all its aspects. Most people have had to limit themselves to a single realm of activity, or just a few; but the less one knows about the past and the present, the less reliable will be one's judgment about the future. There is also the fact that precisely in this judgment the individual's subjective expectations play a role difficult to assess; these turn out to depend on purely personal factors in the individual's own experience—on the more optimistic or less hopeful orientation to life that temperament, success, or failure have prescribed. Finally, there is the remarkable fact that people generally experience the present naively, so to speak, without being able to appreciate its contents; they must first gain some distance from it, i.e., the present must have become the past before one can derive from it clues for making judgments about the future.

Those who yield to the temptation to form an opinion on the likely future of our culture should recall the reservations noted above, as well as the uncertainty inherent in every prediction. As for me, then, in hasty flight from so great a task, I shall seek out the limited domain to which my attention has previously been directed, once I have determined its place in the greater scheme of things.

Human culture—all those things in which human life has risen above its animal conditioning factors and in which it differs from the life of beasts (I refuse to distinguish between culture and civilization)—obviously shows the observer two sides. It includes on the one hand all the knowledge and power that people have acquired in order to master the forces of nature and gain material wealth for the satisfaction of human needs, and on the other hand it includes all the institutions necessary to regulate the relations of humans to each other, especially the distribution of the attainable material wealth. These two orientations of culture are not independent—first, because the mutual relations of humans are profoundly affected by the degree to which the available material wealth makes possible the satisfaction of drives; second, because an individual, with respect to another person, can take on the role of a material possession in so far as that person utilizes the other one's capacity for work or chooses the other one as a sexual object; and third, because every individual is virtually an enemy of culture even though it supposedly exists in the interest of all humanity. It is remarkable that people, as little as they are able to exist in isolation, nevertheless perceive as highly oppressive the sacrifices culture expects of them in the interest of making possible a communal existence. Thus culture must be defended against the individual; its organizations, institutions, and laws all serve that goal. These aim not only to effect a certain distribution of material wealth, but also to maintain that distribution. Indeed, they must protect against people's hostile impulses all those things that serve for the conquest of nature and the production of material wealth. Human creations are easy to destroy; the science and technology that built them up can also be used for their destruction.

One thus gains the impression that culture is something that was forced on a resisting majority by a minority who knew how to gain possession of the means of power and coercion. Of course it might easily be assumed that these difficulties are not inherent in the nature of culture itself, but result from the imperfections in the cultural forms that have thus far been developed. Indeed, it is not difficult to point out these defects. While humanity has made steady progress in the conquest of nature and can expect to make still greater strides in that direction, similar progress in the regulation of human affairs cannot be clearly identified; probably in all former times, as again now, many people have wondered if the meager acquisitions of culture are really worth defending at all. One would suppose that a reorganization of human relations should be possible which, by renouncing coercion and the suppression of drives, would nullify the sources of dissatisfaction with culture so that all people, undisturbed by mutual conflict, could devote themselves to acquiring and enjoying material wealth. That would be the golden age, but the question remains whether such conditions can be realized. On the contrary, it seems that every culture must be based on coercion and the renunciation of drives. It does not even seem clear that if coercion ends, most people will be ready to take on the amount of labor necessary for the acquisition of the new material wealth needed to sustain life. I think one must accept the fact that in all people there are destructive and therefore antisocial and anti-cultural tendencies, and that in many people these are strong enough to determine their behavior in human society.

This psychological fact has decisive significance in the evaluation of human culture. At first it was believed that the essence of culture lay in the conquest of nature for the purpose of acquiring the material wealth needed to sustain life, and that the dangers threatening culture could be eliminated through a suitable distribution of that wealth among its members. But now the emphasis seems to have shifted from the material to the mental realm. The decisive issue is whether and to what degree it will be possible to reduce the burden of the sacrifices (restrictions of drives) imposed on people, and to reconcile people to those sacrifices still necessary and compensate them accordingly. It is just as impossible to forgo minority rule of the masses as to forgo coercion in the work of culture, for the masses are indolent and stupid, they have no love for the renunciation of drives, they cannot be convinced of its inevitability by any arguments, and the individuals within the masses reinforce each other in letting their unbridled passions run wild. Only through the influence of exemplary individuals whom the masses recognize as their leaders will they accept the labors and renunciations necessary for the existence of the culture. All will be well if these leaders are persons of superior insight into the requirements of life, persons who have risen to the task of mastering their own drive wishes. For them, though, the danger exists that in order not to lose their influence they may yield to the masses more than the masses yield to them; it therefore seems necessary that through access to means of power they be independent of the masses. To summarize, there are two widespread human traits responsible for the fact that cultural institutions can be maintained only through a certain amount of coercion: people show no spontaneous desire for work, and arguments are powerless against their passions.

I know what objections will be raised against my comments. It will be said that the character of the masses as it is depicted here, intended to prove the unavoidability of coercion in the work of culture, is itself only the consequence of defective cultural institutions through which people have become embittered, revengeful, and unapproachable. New generations, brought up lovingly and taught to have great respect for rational thought, who have had early experience of the benefits of culture, will consequently have a different relation to it, will feel that it is their very own possession, and will be ready, in the interest of culture and for its preservation, to make the necessary sacrifices in labor and in the satisfaction of drives. They will require no coercion, and will differ little from their leaders. If human masses of this quality have thus far existed in no culture, it is because no culture has yet discovered the institutions that will influence people in such a way, from childhood on.

Given the present state of our conquest of nature, one may doubt whether it is possible at all, or at this point, to establish such cultural institutions; one may ask where the needed quantities of superior, infallible, unselfish leaders are to be found who must act as the educators of future generations; and one may be taken aback by the immense amount of coercion that will be unavoidable until these intentions are put in place. But the magnificence of this plan and its significance for the future of human culture are undeniable. This plan is securely based on the psychological insight that humans are equipped with the most varied tendencies with respect to their drives, and that the ultimate direction of these tendencies is determined by early childhood experiences. But the limits of human educability therefore also limit the efficacy of such a cultural change. One might question whether and to what degree another cultural milieu could obliterate the two characteristics of human masses that make the governance of human affairs so very difficult. The experiment has not yet been undertaken. Probably a certain percentage of humanity—due to a pathological tendency or excessive strength of drives—will always remain asocial, but if one can manage to reduce to a minority today's anti-cultural majority, one will have achieved a great deal—perhaps all that can be achieved.

I do not want to create the impression that I have wandered far off the path envisioned for my investigation. I shall therefore expressly affirm that I have no intention of assessing the great cultural experiment currently underway in the vast country between Europe and Asia.[1] I have neither the expertise nor the ability to determine its practicability, to test the appropriateness of the methods applied, or to measure the width of the inevitable cleft between intention and execution. What is being prepared there remains incomplete and eludes the examination for which our long-consolidated culture provides the material.

---

1 The "country between Europe and Asia" is Russia, and the "experiment" is the Russian Revolution of 1917. See Introduction, pp. 23-24.

We have inadvertently shifted from economics to psychology. At first we were tempted to seek the assets of culture in the available material wealth and the institutions through which it is distributed. Given our discovery, though, that every culture is based on coercion to work and on the renunciation of drives, inevitably provoking opposition from the people these demands affect, it is now clear that material wealth itself, the means of acquiring it, and the manner of its distribution cannot be the essential or sole content of culture. Indeed, this wealth itself is threatened by the rebellious nature and destructive obsession of the members of the culture. Beside material wealth come also the means that can serve to defend culture—coercive measures as well as others intended to reconcile people to culture and to compensate them for their sacrifices. These measures can be described as the mental assets of culture.

In the interest of uniform terminology we shall designate the case in which a drive cannot be satisfied as a frustration; the regulation that establishes this frustration as a prohibition; and the state the prohibition produces as a privation. The next step is to distinguish between privations that affect everyone and those that do not, affecting only groups, classes, or even individuals. The former are the oldest: with the prohibitions that established them, culture began its separation (an unknown number of millennia ago) from prehistoric animal conditions. It is surprising to find that these privations are still in effect, and still form the nucleus of hostility to culture. The drive wishes that suffer under them are born again with every child; there is a class of individuals, the neurotics, who directly react to these frustrations by becoming asocial. These drive wishes include incest, cannibalism, and a lust for killing. It may sound strange to group these wishes, which all people seem united in condemning, together with various others, about which there is such vigorous debate in our culture as to whether they should be permitted or frustrated. Psychologically, though, we are justified in grouping them all together. Furthermore, the position of culture toward these oldest drive wishes is by no means uniform. Only cannibalism seems to be rejected by all, and (to non-psychoanalytic observation) to have been completely surmounted. Behind the prohibition on incest, we can still feel the strength of incest wishes, and under certain conditions killing is still practiced, even commanded, by our culture. Cultural developments may await us in which the satisfaction of other wishes, entirely acceptable today, will seem just as unacceptable as does cannibalism now.

In the context of these oldest renunciations of drives, we must consider a psychological factor that remains significant for all further ones as well. It is not the case that the human mind has undergone no development since prehistoric times and is, contrasting with the advances of science and technology, the same today as at the dawn of history. Here, we can mention one of these mental advances. Human development has progressed in such a way that external coercion gradually becomes internalized: a special mental agency, the human superego, includes this coercion among its commandments. Every child shows us the process of such a transformation, and acquires moral and social capacities only through that transformation. This strengthening of the superego is a highly valuable psychological cultural asset. Those persons in whom it has occurred are transformed from opponents of culture into bearers thereof. The greater their number in a cultural region, the more secure that culture is, and the sooner it can function without external means of coercion. Yet the degree of internalization is very different for the various drive prohibitions. As for the oldest cultural demands, mentioned above, internalization seems to have been significantly achieved (disregarding the unwelcome exception of the neurotics). This situation is altered when one turns to the other demands of drives. One notices with surprise and concern that most people obey the cultural prohibitions on these matters only under the pressure of external coercion—only where that coercion can be effected, and only as long as it is to be feared. This applies also for the so-called moral demands of culture, which also apply to everyone. Most of our experience of human moral inconsistency belongs here. Countless civilized persons who would shrink back from murder or incest do not deny themselves the satisfaction of their greed, of their urge to aggression, of their sexual lusts; they do not hesitate to harm others through lies, deceit, and slander if they can go unpunished; this has presumably always been the case through many cultural ages.

With the restrictions applying only to certain social classes, one encounters a crude and always unmistakable situation. It is to be expected that these lower classes will envy the favored classes their privileges and will do everything in their power to rid themselves of their own excess of privation. Where this is not possible, a permanent quantity of discontent will make itself felt within that culture, potentially leading to dangerous uprisings.

However, if a culture has not progressed beyond the point where the satisfaction of a portion of its members is based on the suppression of another portion, perhaps the majority—and this is the case in all current cultures—it is understandable that these suppressed people should develop an intense hostility toward the culture—one they make possible through their labor, but in whose material wealth they have too little benefit. Among these suppressed people, one can expect no internalization of the cultural prohibitions. Indeed, these persons are unwilling to recognize the prohibitions, and are intent on destroying the culture itself—perhaps on eliminating even the preconditions for its existence. The hostility of these classes toward culture is so clear that the more latent hostility of the more advantaged social strata has been disregarded. It is hardly necessary to say that a culture that leaves so many of its members unsatisfied, driving them to insurrection, has no prospect of perpetuating itself. Nor does it deserve to do so.

The degree of internalization of the precepts of culture—to put it popularly and unpsychologically, the moral level of the members—is not the only mental resource one must consider in assessing a culture. There are also its assets in ideals and artistic creations—that is, the satisfactions gained from both of these.

People will be all too ready to include among the mental assets of a culture its ideals—its own determinations of which achievements are the most sublime, the most worthy of aiming for. Initially it may seem that these ideals determine the achievement of the cultural region. But the actual sequence may well be that the ideals are formed on the basis of the first achievements made possible for the culture through the interaction of innate ability and external circumstances, and that these first achievements are then retained by the ideal as something to be perpetuated. The satisfaction the ideal gives the members of the culture is thus a narcissistic one, based on pride in the achievement already attained with success. To become complete, this satisfaction requires comparison with other cultures that have thrown themselves behind other achievements and have developed other ideals. Based on these differences, every culture claims the right to look down on any other. Thus cultural ideals give rise to conflict and enmity among cultural regions, as is most clearly seen among nations.

The narcissistic satisfaction derived from the cultural ideal is also among the forces successfully opposing the hostility to culture within the cultural region itself. Not only the privileged classes who enjoy the benefits of the culture, but the suppressed ones too, have a share in this satisfaction, for the right to despise outsiders compensates them for what they have suffered within their own culture. One may be a wretched plebeian, plagued by debt and military service; still, one is a Roman, with a share in the task of ruling other nations and establishing their laws. But this identification of the suppressed classes with the ruling and exploiting class is only part of a larger context: indeed, the suppressed classes can be affectively attached to the ruling class and see their ideals in their masters, despite their hostility toward them. Were it not for these basically satisfying relations, it would be impossible to understand how so many cultures have maintained themselves for so long despite the justified hostility of large masses of humanity.

A different sort of satisfaction is supplied by art to the inhabitants of a cultural region, though it generally remains out of reach to the masses, who spend their time in exhausting labor and remain uneducated. As we learned long ago, art offers substitute satisfactions for the oldest cultural renunciations, still felt most deeply, and therefore serves best of all in reconciling the individual with the sacrifices made for them. On the other hand, artistic creations heighten the sense of identification, so essential to every cultural region, by producing communally experienced, and highly valued perceptions. Yet those creations also serve narcissistic satisfaction when they depict the achievements of a particular culture, impressively reminding one of its ideals.

We have thus far made no mention of what is perhaps the most significant part of the mental inventory of a culture—its religious concepts, broadly speaking, or in other words (to be justified later) its illusions.

III

Wherein lies the special value of religious ideas?

We have discussed the hostility toward culture engendered by the pressure culture exerts and the renunciations of drives it demands. If one imagines its prohibitions lifted—thus one may now take any woman one wishes as sexual object; may without hesitation kill one's rival in love, or anyone else standing in the way; may take anything belonging to another person without asking permission—how marvelous, what a sequence of satisfactions life would be! But one soon discovers the first problem: all

Nature = natural world
Fate = individual fate in NW

others have just the same wishes I do, and will treat me no more gently than I treat them. Essentially, then, if cultural restrictions are abolished, only one person can become unlimitedly happy: a tyrant, a dictator who has seized for himself all the means of power. And even he has every reason to hope others will at least observe the one cultural commandment: "Thou shalt not kill."

But how ungrateful, indeed how short-sighted, to aim to abolish culture! Only a state of nature would remain—harder by far to bear. True, nature would demand of us no restrictions of drives: she would let us do as we pleased. But she has her own highly effective means of constraining us. She kills us—coldly, cruelly, recklessly, it seems to us—and perhaps through the very sources of our satisfaction. Precisely because of these dangers with which we are threatened by nature, we joined together and created culture, which, among other things, is intended to make possible our communal life. Indeed, the chief task of culture, its actual *raison d'être*, is to defend us against nature. ☆

Clearly, culture already does this well enough in many aspects, and will certainly do so much better in the future. But no one is fooled into thinking that nature is already conquered; few dare hope she will ever be completely subject to humankind. There are the elements, which seem to mock all human force; the earth, which quakes and is torn asunder, burying all humanity and its works; water, which floods and drowns everything in a great cataclysm, and storms, which blow away the refuse; there are diseases, only recently recognized as the attacks of other organisms; and finally there is the painful riddle of death, against which no healing herb has yet been discovered nor probably ever will be. With these forces nature rises up against us, magnificent, cruel, inexorable, again showing us our weakness and helplessness, from which we planned to extricate ourselves through the work of culture. One of the few pleasant and uplifting impressions of humanity one can have is presented when, faced with a natural disaster, humanity forgets its cultural disunity—all the internal difficulties and hostilities—and remembers the great communal ? task: preserving itself against the overwhelming power of nature.

Just as is true for humanity in general, life is hard to bear for the individual. The culture of which one is a member imposes on one a certain degree of privation, and other people, too, create a measure of suffering—despite the precepts of the culture or as a consequence of its imperfection. There are also the injuries inflicted by untamed nature—the individual calls it fate. We would expect the consequence of this situation to be a continuing state of anxious expectation and a heavy blow to innate narcissism. We already know how the individual reacts to the injuries culture and others inflict: by developing a corresponding measure of resistance to the institutions of the culture—hostility toward it. But how does one defend oneself against the overwhelming forces of nature, of fate, which threaten the individual and all others?

Culture frees one from this task; it performs this task for everyone equally. It is also noteworthy that nearly all cultures do the same in this respect. Culture never ceases to carry out its task of defending humankind against nature, but perpetrates it by other means. The task here is multifaceted. Humankind's seriously threatened self-regard requires solace; the terrors of the world and of life must be eliminated. And human curiosity—albeit driven by the strongest practical interest—wants an answer too.

With the very first step—the humanization of nature—much is already attained. Impersonal forces and fates are unapproachable, eternally unfamiliar. But if passions rage in the elements as they do in the human soul; if death itself is nothing arbitrary, but the violent act of an evil will; if nature is filled with beings like those in one's own society, then one can breathe a sigh of relief, then one feels at home in the uncanny and can mentally work through one's senseless anxiety. One may still be defenseless, but is no longer helplessly paralyzed. At least one can react. And perhaps one is not defenseless after all. Against these violent supermen outside, one can apply the same methods used within society. One can try to conjure them up, placate them, bribe them—and through such influence rob them of some of their power. Such a substitution of natural science by psychology not only produces immediate relief, but also shows the way to further mastery of the situation.

Indeed, this situation is nothing new. It has an infantile prototype—is, in fact, only the continuation of that prototype, for one has been in a similar state of helplessness once before: as a small child in relation to one's parents. There was reason to fear them, especially the father, yet one could be sure of his protection against the dangers one knew at the time. Thus it was natural to regard the two situations as similar. Here, too, as in dream life, wishing came into its own. A premonition of death may come over the sleeper, may seek to place him in the grave. But the dreamwork knows how to choose the condition under which even that feared event becomes a wish fulfillment: the dreamer sees himself in an old Etruscan tomb he had climbed down into, happy to satisfy his archaeological interests. Similarly, one does not simply turn the forces of nature into human beings to be associated with as with equals: that would do no justice to the overpowering impression they create. Rather, one gives them the character of a father—turns them into gods. Here one follows not only an infantile prototype, but, as I have sought to demonstrate, a phylogenetic one as well.

As time progresses, humankind first observes the regularity and conformity to law of natural phenomena; thus, the forces of nature lose their human traits. Yet human helplessness remains, and with it the human longing for a father. The gods, too, remain, retaining their threefold task: warding off the terrors of nature, providing reconciliation with the cruelty of fate (particularly as it appears in death), and providing compensation for the sufferings and privations imposed on humankind by cultural, communal life.

Gradually, though, there is a shift of accent in these functions. It is observed that natural forces develop on their own, based on internal necessities. Indeed, the gods are the lords of nature; they have established nature as it is, and can now leave it to its own devices. Only rarely, in so-called miracles, do they intervene, as if to provide assurance that they have given up nothing of their original sphere of power. As for the vicissitudes of fate, an uncomfortable foreboding remains that the perplexity and helplessness of the human race cannot be ameliorated. Here, above all, the gods fail; if they themselves create fate, then one must declare their determinations inscrutable. The most gifted nation of Antiquity begins to grasp that *Moira* [Fate] stands above the gods and that the gods themselves have their own fates. The more autonomous nature becomes, and the more the gods recede from it, the more earnestly all expectations concentrate on the third function assigned to them and the more morality becomes their actual domain. The task of the gods is now to provide compensation for the inadequacies and hurts of culture, to fix their attention on the sufferings people inflict on one another in their communal life, and to watch over the execution of the precepts of culture, so inadequately observed by humankind. The precepts of culture themselves are ascribed divine origin; they are raised above human society and extended to nature and the universe.

Thus a store of ideas is created, born of the need to make human helplessness bearable, and constructed with the material of recollections of the helplessness of one's own childhood and that of the childhood of the human race. It is clear that these ideas protect humankind in two directions—against the dangers of nature and fate, and against the injuries originating from within human society itself. In summary: life in this world serves a higher purpose—one difficult to guess, but certainly signifying a perfecting of human nature. The spiritual part of humankind, the soul, which through time has so slowly and reluctantly separated itself from the body, is probably seen as the object of this elevation and exaltation. Thus, whatever happens in this world results from the intentions of an intelligence superior to us, which, albeit through ways and detours difficult to follow, ultimately steers everything toward the good—that is, toward a state of affairs pleasant for us. Over each one of us watches a kindly Providence, stern only in appearance, which will not allow us to become the ball played with by the super-strong and ruthless forces of nature. Death itself is no destruction, no return to an inorganic lifeless state, but the start of a new type of existence on the path of higher development. On the other hand, the same moral laws our cultures have established also govern all that occurs in the universe, but they are safeguarded by a supreme judicial authority with incomparably more might and consistency. All good is ultimately rewarded, and all evil punished—if not in this form of life, then in the later existences commencing after death. Thus all the terrors, sufferings, and hardships of life are destined for annihilation. Life after death, which adjoins our earthly life just as the invisible portion of the spectrum adjoins the visible portion, brings all the perfection we may have missed here. And the superior wisdom that governs this progression, the perfect goodness that expresses itself therein, the justice that asserts itself therein—these are the attributes of the divine beings who also created us and the whole universe, or rather, these are the attributes of the one divine being into whom, in our culture, all the ancient gods have been subsumed. The people that first succeeded in this concentration of the divine attributes was not a little proud of this advance. It had exposed the paternal core that had always been hidden behind every divine figure. Essentially, this was a return to the historical beginnings of the idea of God. Now that God was a single individual, relations toward him could regain the intimacy and intensity of the child's relationship to the father. But having done so much for the father, one also wanted to be rewarded, or at least to be the only beloved child, the chosen people. Very much later, pious America claims to be "God's own country," and for one form in which humanity worships the deity, this is certainly correct. The religious ideas reviewed above have of course undergone a long development and have been adopted by various cultures at various phases. From these phases, I have selected just one, which more or less corresponds to the final form in our contemporary white Christian culture. One can easily see that not all the parts of this whole accord equally well with the others, that not all the urgent questions receive an answer, and that the contradiction supplied by daily experience can be dismissed only with difficulty. But such as they are, these ideas—broadly speaking, religious ones—are deemed the most precious possession of culture, as the most valuable thing it has to offer its members, far more valued than any skill in winning treasure from the earth, in providing humankind with sustenance, or in preventing disease, etc. People believe they could not bear life if they did not attribute to these ideas the value claimed for them. And now we must ask: what are these ideas in the light of psychology? What is the source of their high regard? And, to continue timidly, what is their true worth?

IV

An investigation that proceeds uninterrupted, like a monologue, is not completely free of danger. One may too easily yield to the temptation to push aside thoughts that seek to interrupt, and end up instead with a feeling of uncertainty, which in the end one tries to overpower through excessive assertiveness. I will therefore imagine an opponent who attends to my arguments with mistrust; here and there I will let him express himself.

I hear him saying: *"You have repeatedly used the formulation 'culture creates these religious ideas,' 'culture places them at the disposal of its members.' Something about this strikes me as strange. I cannot even say why, but that does not sound as obvious as saying that culture has created regulations for the distribution of the products of labor, or concerning rights over wife and child."*

Nevertheless, I think I am justified in expressing myself that way. I have attempted to show that religious ideas have proceeded from the same need as all other cultural achievements: from the need to defend oneself against the crushing, overwhelming force of nature. There was also a second motive—the urge to correct the painfully felt imperfections of culture. Furthermore, it is especially accurate to say that culture gives the individual these ideas, for one finds them already available; they are presented complete, and one would not be in a position to find them independently. It is the heritage of many generations that one is entering, and which one absorbs just like the multiplication table, geometry, etc. There is admittedly a difference here, but it lies elsewhere and cannot yet be clarified. The feeling of strangeness you mention may arise in part from the fact that we are usually presented with this store of religious ideas as a divine revelation. But that in itself is already part of the religious system, and entirely disregards the known historical development of these ideas and their differences at different times and in different cultures.

"Another point, which strikes me as more important. You would have it that the humanization of nature proceeds from the need to put an end to human perplexity and helplessness in the face of nature's dreaded forces, to enter into a relation with them, and ultimately to influence them. But such a motive seems superfluous. Clearly, primitive man has no choice, no other way of thinking. It is natural for him, as if innate, to project his existence into the universe and to regard all the processes he observes as the expressions of beings basically like himself. That is the only method of understanding at his disposal. And it is by no means an obvious outcome, but rather a remarkable coincidence, if he succeeds in satisfying one of his great needs by thus giving free rein to his natural inclinations."

I do not find that so remarkable. Do you think human thought has no practical motives—is merely the expression of a disinterested curiosity? That is highly unlikely. I believe, rather, that humankind, even when personifying the forces of nature, follows an infantile prototype. Humans learned from the persons in their earliest surroundings that the way to influence them is to establish a relationship with them; and therefore, with the same intent, they later treat everything else they encounter just as they treated those persons. Thus I am not contradicting your descriptive observation; it is really natural for humans to personify everything they want to understand so as to control it later—mental mastery as preparation for physical mastery—but I also provide a motive and a genesis for this peculiar trait of human thought.

"And now a third point. You have previously discussed the origin of religion, in your book Totem and Taboo *[1913].[1] But there things look different. Everything is the son-father relationship; God is the exalted father; longing for the father is the root of the need for religion. Since then, you seem to have discovered the factor of human weakness and helplessness, to which, it is true, the greatest role in the formation of religion is generally ascribed, and now you transfer everything that*

---

1 See Appendix B2.

was previously the father complex to helplessness. May I ask you to clarify this change?"

I shall be glad to reply; I was only waiting for the invitation. If it really *is* a change. In *Totem and Taboo* it was not the intention to explain the origin of religions, but only that of totemism. Can you, from any standpoint you know of, explain the fact that the first form in which the protecting deity revealed itself to humankind was that of an animal, that there was a prohibition on killing and eating that animal, and that even so it was the ceremonial custom to kill and eat it communally once a year? This is exactly what occurs in totemism. And it is certainly not helpful to argue whether totemism should be designated as a religion. It is intimately connected with later god-religions. The totem animals become the sacred animals of the gods; the earliest, but most profound moral restrictions—those on murder and incest—arise from totemism. Whether or not you agree with the conclusions of *Totem and Taboo*, I hope you will admit that in that volume several highly remarkable and disparate facts are brought together as a consistent whole.

Why the animal god did not suffice in the long run, and was replaced by a human one—that was hardly touched on in *Totem and Taboo*; other problems in the formation of religion are not even mentioned there. Do you feel that such a limitation is identical to a denial? My work is a good example of the strict isolation of the contribution psychoanalytic observation can make in solving the problem of religion. If I now seek to add the other, less deeply hidden part, you should not accuse me of contradiction, as you previously accused me of one-sidedness. It is, of course, my task to point out the connections between what I said earlier and what I am asserting now, between the deeper and the manifest motivation, between the father complex and human helplessness and need for protection.

These connections are not hard to find. These are the relations of the child's helplessness to the helplessness of the adult, which continues that of the child such that, as we might expect, the psychoanalytic motivation for the formation of religion is clearly the infantile contribution to its manifest motivation. Let us transport ourselves into the mental life of the young child. You probably remember the choice of object in the *dependent* type that psychoanalysis speaks of. The libido follows the paths of the narcissistic needs and clings to the objects that ensure their satisfaction. Thus the mother, who satisfies the child's hunger, becomes the first love-object and certainly the first protection against all the vague, threatening dangers of the external world as well—the first protection against anxiety, we can say.

In this function, the mother is soon replaced by the stronger father; this function remains his for the duration of childhood. But the child's relation to the father is marked by a peculiar ambivalence. The father himself is a danger, perhaps due to the child's earlier relation to the mother. Thus one fears him no less than one longs for him and admires him. The signs of this ambivalence in the relation to the father are deeply imprinted in all religions, as demonstrated in *Totem and Taboo*. As one grows up, one finds that it is one's lot to remain always a child, and that one can never manage without protection from strange, superior powers; one then lends these the features of the father figure; one creates for oneself the gods—whom one fears, whose favor one seeks to gain, and yet whom one assigns the task of protection. Thus the motive of longing for a father is identical to the need for protection from the consequences of human powerlessness. The defense against helplessness in childhood lends its characteristic features to the reaction to the helplessness the adult must acknowledge; this reaction is the formation of religion. But I do not intend to investigate further the development of the god-idea; here, we are concerned with the complete store of religious ideas as transmitted by culture to the individual.

V

And now to take up again the thread of our investigation: what, then, is the psychological significance of religious ideas and in what category shall we classify them? Initially, the question is not at all easy to answer. After eliminating various formulations, we will stand by just one: religious ideas are teachings and pronouncements about facts and states of external (or internal) reality that convey something one has not discovered for oneself and which assert the right to be believed. Since they provide information on what is most important and interesting for us in life, they are especially highly valued. Those who know nothing of them are very ignorant; those who have taken them up in their store of knowledge can consider themselves much enriched.

There are, of course, many such teachings about a diverse range of things in this world. Every class at school is full of them. Let us take the geography class. There, we hear that Konstanz lies on the Bodensee. A student song adds: "If you don't believe it, go and see." I have been there, by chance, and can confirm that this beautiful city does lie on the shore of a wide body of water known by all who live around it as the Bodensee. Indeed, I am now fully convinced of the correctness of this geographical claim. In this connection I recall another, quite peculiar experience. I was already a grown man when I first stood on the hill of the Athenian Acropolis, among the temple ruins, with my gaze on the blue sea. Into my contentment there entered a feeling of amazement that brought forth the thought: "So it's really just as we learned at school!" What a shallow and feeble belief I must have acquired in the real truth of what I heard there, if I could be so amazed that day! But I do not want to overemphasize the significance of that experience. There is another possible explanation for my amazement; it did not occur to me at the time and is thoroughly subjective, relating to the special character of the place.

Thus, all such teachings demand belief in their content, but not without justifying their claim of authority. They present themselves as the summarized result of a lengthy thought process based on observation and clearly also on inference. To anyone with the intention of going through this process independently, rather than accepting its result, they show the way. Further, the source of the knowledge proclaimed by the teaching is always added when that source is not as obvious as it is with geographical claims. For instance, the earth is spherical; as proofs of this claim one adduces Foucault's pendulum experiment, the behavior of the horizon, and the possibility of circumnavigating the earth. Since, as all involved realize, it is impracticable to send all schoolchildren on voyages around the world, one is content to let school learning be accepted on "faith and belief"; but for those who wish to convince themselves personally, we know that the path remains open.

Let us measure religious doctrines with the same ruler. If we ask the basis for their claim that they must be believed, we receive three answers, and these show a remarkably poor mutual accord. First, these doctrines deserve belief because our forefathers already believed in them; second, we have proofs that have been passed down to us from those early times; and third, it is forbidden to question their authority in the first place. Any such attempt was formerly met with the harshest punishments, and even today society regards it with disapproval, should anyone raise the question again.

This third point must provoke our strongest reservations. Indeed, such a prohibition can only have one motivation: society understands perfectly well the insecurity of the claim it makes for its religious doctrines. Otherwise it would certainly be very willing to provide the necessary data to those desiring to find conviction on their own. Thus, with a feeling of mistrust not easily assuaged, we shall proceed to an examination of the two other arguments. We ought to believe because our forefathers believed. But those ancestors of ours were far more ignorant than we, and believed in things we could not possibly accept today. The possibility arises that religious doctrines, too, could fall in that category. The proofs our ancestors have left us are set down in writings that themselves bear every characteristic of unreliability. They are full of contradictions; they are reworked and falsified, and, where they report actual confirmations, are themselves unconfirmed. It does not help much when divine revelation is claimed as the source of their wording, or indeed merely of their content, for this claim is itself among the doctrines whose reliability is being investigated. Obviously, no pronouncement can prove itself.

Thus we reach the remarkable finding that precisely those communications from our store of cultural assets that could be the most significant for us, those assigned the task of solving the riddles of the universe and of reconciling us with the sufferings of life—precisely these have the very weakest confirmation. If it could not be better proven, we would never accept such an indifferent matter as the fact that whales bear young rather than laying eggs.

This state of affairs is in itself a very remarkable psychological problem. And no one should think the preceding comments on the impossibility of verifying religious doctrines hold anything new. This impossibility has been sensed at all times—and certainly also by those ancestors who left us this legacy. Many of them probably harbored the same doubts we do, but the pressure exerted on them was so great that they dared not express them. And since then countless people have tormented themselves with just the same doubts, which they wanted to suppress because they felt obliged to believe; many shining intellects have broken down over this conflict, and many people's characters have suffered damage through the compromises in which they sought a solution.

If all the evidence presented for the credibility of religious teachings stems from the past, the next step is to look around and see whether the present, which we can better evaluate, can also provide such evidence. If in this way we could free just one element of the religious system from doubt, the whole system would gain enormously in credibility. Here the activities of the spiritists are of interest; they are convinced of the continued existence of the individual soul, and seek to prove this one point of religious doctrine beyond all doubt. Unfortunately they cannot prove that the appearances and utterances of the spirits they invoke are not merely the products of their own mental activity. They have summoned up the spirits of the greatest individuals, of the most eminent thinkers, but all the utterances and messages received from them have been so inane, so hopelessly devoid of sense, that the only credible thing one notes is the spirits' ability to adapt themselves to the circle of people conjuring them up.

One must now recall two attempts that seem like desperate efforts to evade the problem. One of these, violent in nature, is ancient; the other is subtle and modern. The first is the *credo quia absurdum* [I believe because it is absurd] of the early Church Fathers. It seeks to assert that religious doctrines are outside the realm of reason—above reason. One must sense their truth within oneself; one need not understand them. But this *credo* is of interest only as a personal confession; as a claim to authority it is not binding. Shall I be obliged to believe every absurdity? And if not, why this particular one? There is no higher court than the court of reason. If the truth of religious doctrines depends on an inner experience attesting to that truth, what shall one do with the many people who have not had that rare experience? One can require of all people that they apply the gift of reason they possess, but one cannot, on the basis of a motive existing only for a very few, set up an obligation for all. If one person, based on a state of ecstasy experienced as deeply moving, has gained an unshakable conviction in the real truth of religious doctrines, how is that significant for others?

The second attempt is that of the philosophy of "as if." This argument claims that in our mental activity there are a great number of assumptions whose baselessness and even absurdity we fully realize. These are called fictions, but given various practical reasons, it is claimed that we must act "as if" we believed in them. This is said to be the case with religious doctrines because of their incomparable importance for maintaining human society. This argument is not far removed from the *credo quia absurdum*. But I think the demand made by this "as if" could only be made by a philosopher. A person whose thinking is uninfluenced by the artifice of philosophy will never be able to accept it: for such a person, the admission of absurdity, of being contrary to reason, puts the matter to rest. Precisely in handling one's most important interests, one cannot be expected to renounce the certainties one demands for all one's normal activities. This reminds me of one of my children, who was characterized at a young age by his high regard for accordance with reality. When the children were being told a story and were listening with fixed attention, he would come up and ask: "Is that a true story?" On hearing that it was not, he would leave with an expression of disdain. It is only to be expected that people will soon treat the tales of religion in a similar way, despite any support expressed for "as if."[1]

But now they still behave in a different manner entirely; in the past, too, religious ideas, despite their obvious lack of confirmation, have had the very strongest influence on humankind. That is a new psychological problem. The question arises: Wherein lies the inner force of these doctrines and to what do they owe their effectiveness, which has no need for approval by reason?

VI

I think we have made sufficient preparation for an answer to both questions. The answer will be found if we regard the mental origin of religious ideas. These, promulgated as doctrines, are not residues of experience or final results of thought. They are illusions—fulfillments of the oldest, strongest and most fervent wishes of humanity. The secret of their strength is in the strength of those wishes. We already know that the frightening impression of helplessness in childhood awakened the need for protection—protection through love—once provided by the father; and the realization that this helplessness will continue throughout one's entire life necessitated clinging to the existence of a father, albeit now a more powerful one. Through the kind rule of divine Providence, anxiety over the dangers of life is assuaged; the introduc-

---

1 I hope I am committing no injustice in letting the philosopher of "as if" represent a view which is not unfamiliar to other thinkers: "We include in the group of fictions not only indifferent theoretical operations but also conceptions created by the noblest minds, to which the heart of the nobler part of mankind clings and which mankind will not allow to be taken away. And this we certainly do not wish to do. We will allow all that to remain as *practical fiction*, but it perishes as *theoretical truth*" (Hans Vaihinger, 1922: 68). [Freud's note; it appears in Freud's original at the end of the fourth sentence of this paragraph.]

tion of a moral world order ensures the fulfillment of the demand for justice, so often unmet in human society. The extension of earthly existence through a future life provides the framework in space and time within which these wish fulfillments are to occur. Answers to the riddles posed by human curiosity, such as those asking about the origin of the universe or the relation between body and mind, are developed corresponding to the underlying assumptions of this system. It is a great relief for the individual psyche if the childhood conflicts arising from the father complex—conflicts never fully surmounted—are taken from the psyche and given a solution acceptable to all.

In saying that all those things are illusions, I must narrow down the meaning of the word. An illusion is not identical to an error, and is not necessarily an error. Aristotle's belief that vermin spontaneously generate from filth (a belief uneducated people still retain today) was an error, as was the belief among a former generation of physicians that *tabes dorsalis* results from sexual excess. It would be wrong to call these errors illusions. On the other hand Columbus's belief that he had discovered a new sea route to India was an illusion. In this error, the part played by his wish is very clear. One may designate as an illusion the claim of certain nationalists that the Indo-European peoples constitute the only race capable of culture, or the belief, demolished only by psychoanalysis, that the child is a being without sexuality. For illusions, the characteristic aspect remains their derivation from human wishes. In this respect they resemble psychiatric delusions, but they differ from them too—even disregarding the more complex framework of delusions. In delusions, we emphasize as the essential thing their contradiction to reality. Illusions, though, need not necessarily be false, i.e., unrealizable or in contradiction to reality. For instance, a bourgeois girl may have the illusion that a prince will come to carry her off to his home as his bride. This is possible, and cases of this sort have occurred. That the Messiah will come and establish a golden age is much less likely; based on one's personal orientation, one will classify this belief as an illusion or as analogous to a delusion. In any case, examples of illusions that have turned out to be true are not easy to find, but the illusion of alchemists that metals could be transformed into gold might be such a case. The wish to have a large amount of gold, as much as possible, has been significantly dampened by our contemporary insights into the conditioning factors of wealth, but chemistry no longer regards the transformation of metals into gold as impossible. Thus we call a belief an illusion when wish fulfillment is prominent in its motivation; in doing so we disregard its relation to reality, just as the illusion itself abjures confirmations.

Having now completed this orientation, we can turn once again to religious doctrines. We can now reiterate: all of them are illusions—indemonstrable—and no one can be forced to hold them true, to believe in them. Some of them are so unlikely, so very much in contradiction with everything we have laboriously learned about the reality of the world, that one may—with appropriate consideration of the psychological differences—compare them to delusions. As to the reality value of most of them, one can make no judgment; just as they are indemonstrable, they are likewise irrefutable. We still know too little to approach them critically. Only slowly do the riddles of the universe unveil themselves to our investigations; for many questions, science still cannot provide answers today. But scientific work is the only path that can lead us to knowledge of reality outside ourselves. Again, it is merely illusion to expect anything from intuition and introspection; these can only give us information about our own mental life—information difficult to interpret—never information about the questions that religious doctrine answers so effortlessly. It would be criminal to let one's own arbitrary opinion enter the void and, according to one's own personal estimation, to declare one aspect or another of the religious system more acceptable or less so. For such an approach, these questions are too significant—one might even say too sacred.

Here, one must be prepared for an objection. *"So, if even dogged skeptics admit that the claims of religion cannot be refuted by reason, why shouldn't I believe in them, since so much speaks for them: tradition, agreement among people, and the comforting nature of their content?"* Indeed, why not? Just as no one can be forced to believe, no one can be forced to disbelieve. But we should not deceive ourselves into thinking that with such justifications we are treading on the paths of correct thought. If the term "weak excuse" was ever appropriate, it certainly is here. Ignorance is ignorance; no right to believe derives from it. In other matters, sensible persons will never behave so carelessly or be satisfied with such feeble justifications for their opinions or the side they choose. Only in the highest and most sacred matters does one permit oneself such behavior. These are really just efforts to pretend to oneself or others that one still holds firmly to religion when one has long since become free of it. When questions of religion are involved, people commit every possible sort of insincerity and intellectual sloppiness. Philosophers overextend the meaning of words until they contain hardly anything of their original sense. They designate as "God" some hazy abstraction they have created for themselves; then, before all the world, they are deists, believers in God, and they can even boast that they have perceived a higher, purer notion of God, though their God is now only an insubstantial shadow, no longer the powerful personality of religious doctrine. Critics continue to describe as "deeply religious" anyone who has admitted to a feeling of man's smallness and powerlessness within the scope of the universe. Yet it is not this feeling that constitutes the essence of religiosity. Rather, it is the next step—the reaction to this feeling, which seeks a remedy for it. The person who goes no further, who humbly accepts the minimal part humans play in the universe, is actually irreligious in the truest sense of the word.

Stating a position on the truth value of religious doctrines is not within the plan of this investigation. For us, it suffices that we have recognized them, in their psychological nature, as illusions. But we need not conceal the fact that this finding also has a powerful influence on our attitude to the question many people surely see as the most important. We know approximately at what times religious doctrines were created, and by what sorts of people. If we also discover the motives underlying this creation, our stance toward the problem of religion will undergo a marked shift. We tell ourselves that it would be very nice if there were a God—creator of the world and kindly Providence—if there were a moral world order and a life in the hereafter, but it is quite obvious that all of this is just as we would wish. And it would be even more remarkable if our poor, ignorant, unfree ancestors had succeeded in finding the solution to all these difficult riddles of the universe.

VII

Now that we have recognized religious doctrines as illusions, the next question immediately arises: is it not the case that other cultural assets we esteem, and by which we allow our life to be ruled, are of a similar nature? Is it not the case that the assumptions regulating our state institutions must be called illusions as well, and that the relations of the sexes are clouded in our culture by an erotic illusion or a series thereof? Once our suspicion has been stirred up, we shall not shrink back from asking also whether the basis is any better for our conviction that we can learn something about external reality through the application of observations and rational thought in scientific work. Nothing should hold us back from approving the turning of our observation to our own being, from approving the application of thought to criticism of thought itself. Here, numerous investigations open themselves to us whose results would certainly be decisive for constructing a "world view." We also suspect that such an effort will not be wasted and that it will at least provide partial justification for our suspicion. But the capabilities of the author do not extend to such a comprehensive task; of necessity, he must restrict his work to pursuing just one of these illusions—that of religion.

Now the loud voice of our opponent insists that we stop. We are called to account for our forbidden undertaking:

"Archaeological interests are certainly very commendable, but one does not carry out excavations if that would undermine the dwellings of the living so that they cave in and bury people in the ruins. Religious doctrines are not a topic about which one can make clever arguments, as with other topics. Our culture is founded on them; the preservation of human society is conditioned on the majority of people believing in the truth of those doctrines. If one teaches people that there is no almighty and all-just God, no divine world order, and no life in the hereafter, they will feel free of all duty to obey the regulations of culture. Without inhibition or anxiety, they will follow their asocial, egoistic drives, and seek to exert their power. Chaos, dispelled through many millennia of cultural labor, will recommence. Even if one knew and could prove that religion does not possess the truth, it would be better to keep quiet about it and to behave as demanded by the philosophy of "as if." For everyone's preservation! And disregarding the danger of the undertaking, it is just needless cruelty. Countless people find their only comfort in the doctrines of religion, and can endure life only with the help of those doctrines. This is an attempt to rob people of their support, with nothing better to give them in its stead. You have admitted that science is not accomplishing much at present, but even if it had progressed much further, science would not suffice for humankind. Humankind has other imperative needs that can never be satisfied by cold science, and it is quite peculiar—indeed, the height of inconsistency—that a psychologist who has always emphasized how secondary, in human life, intelligence is to the life of drives now seeks to rob people of a precious wish fulfillment, and wants to compensate them for it with intellectual fodder."

So many accusations at once! But I'm ready to refute them all, and indeed I shall argue that maintaining the current relation of culture to religion is a greater danger than dissolving that relation. But I hardly know where to begin my rebuttal.

Perhaps by assuring you that I myself regard my undertaking as completely harmless and free of danger. This time I'm not the one overestimating the intellect. If people are as my opponents describe them—and I do not wish to disagree with their conclusions—then there is no danger that devout believers, overwhelmed by my arguments, will let their faith be taken from them. Furthermore, I have said nothing that other, better men have not said much more completely, forcibly, and effectively before me. Their names are well known. I shall not state them; I do not want to create the impression that I wish to place myself among them. I have merely added some psychological grounding to the criticisms put forth by my great predecessors: this is the only thing new in my presentation. It can hardly be expected that precisely this addition will achieve the effect denied to earlier contributions. Of course one might now ask me why I am writing such things if I am certain of their ineffectuality. But we will return to that later.

The only person this publication may harm is myself. I shall have to listen to the unkindest accusations over my shallowness, narrow-mindedness, and lack of idealism and understanding for humankind's highest interests. On the one hand, though, such reproaches are nothing new to me; on the other hand, if one has already learned at a young age to rise above the disapproval of one's contemporaries, how could their disapproval be of concern in old age, when one is sure to be snatched away soon, beyond reach of all favor and disfavor? In former times a different situation applied: through such utterances one gained a sure abridgment of one's earthly existence and a significant acceleration of the opportunity to acquire personal experience of the life hereafter. But I repeat that those times are in the past; their author does not place himself in danger by producing such writings today. At worst, translation and distribution of his book will be forbidden in one country or another—in a country, of course, that feels certain of its own high cultural level. But if one argues at all for the renunciation of wishes and for rendering oneself to fate, one must be able to bear this detriment too.

But then the question occurred to me whether the publication of this work might not be harmful to someone after all. Indeed, not to a person, but to a cause—the cause of psychoanalysis. It cannot, of course, be denied that psychoanalysis is my creation; toward it, people have expressed their mistrust and ill will in ample measure. If I now expound such distasteful claims, people will be only too ready for the displacement from my person to psychoanalysis. "Now one can see," they will say, "where psychoanalysis leads. The mask has fallen. It leads to a denial of God and of a moral ideal, as we indeed always suspected. To keep us from discovering this, the pretense was maintained that psychoanalysis has no world view and cannot construct one."

This hue and cry will really be disagreeable to me for the sake of my many colleagues, some of whom do not share at all my attitude to religious problems. But psychoanalysis has already survived many storms; now it must be set out in this one too. Psychoanalysis is really a research method, an impartial instrument—like the infinitesimal calculus, for example. If a physicist should calculate with its help that the earth will be destroyed after a certain time, one will still hesitate to ascribe destructive tendencies to the calculus itself and to outlaw it due to this prediction. Everything I have said here against the truth value of religions stands beyond the need for a psychoanalytic account, and has been said by others long before psychoanalysis existed. If by applying the psychoanalytic method one can gain a new argument against the truth content of religion, *tant pis* [too bad] for religion. But defenders of religion will with equal right use psychoanalysis in giving due emphasis to the affective significance of religious doctrine.

And now to carry on with the defense: religion has clearly done great services for human culture. It has contributed much to the taming of asocial drives—but not enough. It has ruled human culture for many millennia; it has had time to show what it can achieve. Had it been successful in making the majority of humans happy, in comforting them, in reconciling them to life, and in making them bearers of culture, it would occur to no one to seek any change in the existing conditions. What do we see instead? That an alarmingly great number of people are dissatisfied with culture, are unhappy in it, feel it as a yoke that one must shake off; that these people either contribute their full energies to changing that culture, or take their hostility to culture so far that they are unwilling to accept any part of culture and the restriction of drives. Here we will be interrupted with the claim that this situation actually arises because religion has lost some of its influence over the masses of humanity—due, specifically, to the regrettable effect of scientific advances. We will note this concession and the explanation provided; we will use it later for our own purposes, but the objection itself has no force.

It is doubtful whether people were, at the time of the unrestricted rule of religious doctrines, generally happier than today; they were certainly not more moral. They have always known how to externalize religious precepts, thus neutralizing their intent. The priests, charged with enforcing obedience to religion, made concessions. God's kindness had to stay the hand of his justice. One sinned, one brought sacrificial offerings or did penance, and then one was free to sin anew. Russian introspection has ascended to the conclusion that sin is indispensable for enjoying all the blessings of divine grace, and thus is basically pleasing to God. It is clear that the priests could only maintain the subordination of the masses to religion by making such great concessions to the nature of human drives. The dictum still held: God alone is strong and good, man is weak and sinful. In every age, immorality has found in religion no less support than has morality. If the achievements of religion in making people happy, adapting them for culture, and morally restricting them are no better than this, we must ask whether we are not overestimating its necessity for humankind, and whether we are wise to base our cultural demands on it.

Let us consider the unmistakable current situation. We have heard it conceded that religion no longer has the same influence on people as before. (This applies here to the European Christian culture.) Not because its promises have become fewer, but because people feel they are less credible. Let us admit that the reason for this change is the strengthening of the scientific spirit in the upper strata of human society. (This may not be the only reason.) Criticism has eaten away at the evidential force of religious documents, natural science has exposed the errors contained therein, and comparative research has noticed the fatal resemblance between the religious ideas we revere and the mental products of primitive peoples and times.

The scientific spirit engenders a particular orientation to earthly affairs; before religious ones it pauses for a while, hesitates, and finally steps over the threshold here as well. This process is unstoppable; the more people gain access to the treasures of our knowledge, the more widespread will be the falling away from religious belief—at first only from its old-fashioned and offensive garb, but then from its fundamental axioms too. Only the Americans, who conducted the "monkey trial" in

Dayton,[1] have been consistent. Elsewhere the inevitable transition is achieved via half steps and insincerities.

Culture has little to fear from educated people and those who carry out mental labor. In them, the replacement of religious motives for cultured behavior by other, worldly ones would proceed quietly—and furthermore most such people are themselves bearers of culture. But this is not the case with the great mass of the uneducated and oppressed, who have every reason to be enemies of culture. As long as they do not discover that people no longer believe in God, all is well. But they will find out, inevitably, even if this work of mine is not published. And they are ready to accept the results of scientific thought, but without the change having occurred in them that scientific thought produces in people. Is there no danger, then, that the cultural hostility of these masses will cast itself upon the weak point they have recognized in the mistress they serve? If the only reason one must not kill one's neighbor is that God has forbidden it and will exact a severe punishment for it in this life or the next, and if one then learns that there is no God and that one need not fear his punishment, then one will certainly kill one's neighbor without qualms; only through earthly force will it be possible to prevent this. The alternatives: either the strictest oppression of these dangerous masses and the most careful measures to cut them off from all opportunities for intellectual awakening, or a fundamental revision in the relation between culture and religion.

VIII

One would suppose that in carrying out this latter proposal no special difficulties stand in the way. True, some things would have to be renounced, but one would perhaps gain still more, and would avoid a great danger. Yet people are afraid to carry it out, as if, in doing so, one might expose culture to an even greater danger. When St. Boniface felled the tree the Saxons worshipped

---

1 The infamous "Scopes Trial" of 1925 in which John Scopes, a high-school biology teacher, was found guilty of teaching "that man has descended from a lower order of animals"—an act declared unlawful by Tennessee's Butler Act.

as sacred,[1] the bystanders expected a fearful event as the consequence of the sacrilege. Nothing happened, and the Saxons
accepted baptism.

When culture established the commandment to not kill the
neighbor one hates, who is in the way, or whose possessions one
desires, it clearly occurred in the interest of human communal
life, which otherwise could not be implemented: the murderer
would bring upon himself the vengeance of the victim's relatives,
and the unexpressed jealousy of others, who feel an equally
strong inner inclination to such an act of violence. Thus he would
not long enjoy his revenge or his robbery; he would have every
prospect of soon being killed in his turn. Even if he could protect
himself against an individual foe through exceptional strength
and caution, he would certainly be overcome by a band of weaker
foes. Were such a band not to form, the murdering would go on
endlessly; ultimately, humanity would bring about its own extinction. There would be the same situation among individuals as still
exists in Corsica between families, but otherwise continues to
exist only between nations. Insecurity of life, a danger equal for
all, now unifies people in a society that forbids the individual to
kill and reserves for itself the right to communally kill anyone
who violates the prohibition. This, then, is justice and punishment.

This rational foundation for the prohibition on murder,
though, we do not advertise. Rather, we affirm that God has
decreed the prohibition. Thus we presume to guess his intentions;
we find that like us he has no wish for humanity to bring about its
own extinction. In doing so we clothe the cultural prohibition
with a quite special solemnity, but we thus risk making its obser-
vance dependent on belief in God. If we take back this step, if we
no longer shift our will to God and are content with the social
foundation for the prohibition, we renounce, it is true, that transfiguration thereof, but we also avoid the threat to it. We also gain
something more. Through a sort of diffusion or infection, the
character of sanctity and inviolability—of belonging to the next

---

1   Saint Boniface (680–755), possibly born Winifrith, was a Christian mis-
    sionary. He became known as the patron saint of Germany in no small
    measure for chopping down a large oak tree known as a symbol of
    pagan belief in Thor. This act in 723 is sometimes credited with the
    origin of the Christmas tree.

world, one might say—has spread from a few great prohibitions to all other cultural institutions, laws, and regulations. On these, however, the halo is often unflattering. It is not just that they cancel each other out by producing the opposite decision at different times and places; beyond that, they exhibit all the signs of human inadequacy. One easily recognizes in them what can only be the product of short-sighted anxiety or an expression of petty interests, or a conclusion based on inadequate assumptions. To an unwelcome degree, the criticism to which one must subject them diminishes people's respect for other, better justified cultural demands. Since it is a delicate task to distinguish what God himself has commanded from what derives, in reality, from the authority of an omnipotent parliament or a high court, it would be an undoubted advantage to leave God out of the game entirely and to honestly concede the purely human origin of all the institutions and precepts of culture. Along with the sanctity they lay claim to, the inflexibility and immutability of these commandments and laws would also be eliminated. People would comprehend that these laws are created not chiefly to rule them, but rather to serve their interests; they would derive a friendlier relation to them, and would aim not for their abolition, but only for their improvement. This would constitute significant progress along the road to reconciliation with the pressures of culture.

Yet our plea for a purely rational foundation for the precepts of culture, that is, for deriving them from social necessity, is suddenly interrupted here by a doubt. As our example, we have selected the origin of the prohibition on murder. Does our presentation thereof correspond to the historical truth? We fear it does not; it appears to be only a rationalistic construction. With the help of psychoanalysis we have studied precisely this piece of human cultural history; based on those efforts, we must say that the course of events was actually different. Even in contemporary people, motives based purely on reason have little effect against passionate impulses. How much less powerful they must have been with the human animal of primeval times! Perhaps his descendants would still be killing each other today without inhibition if among those acts of murder there had not been one in particular—the killing of the primal father—that evoked an irresistible affective reaction, heavy with consequence. From this reaction arose the commandment "Thou shalt not kill," which in totemism was restricted to the father-substitute, and was later extended to other individuals, but even today is not consistently observed.

Yet as demonstrated by arguments that need no repeating here, the primal father was the earliest image of God, the model on which later generations formed the figure of God. Thus the religious account is correct. God was really involved in the genesis of the prohibition; his influence, and not insight into the social need, created it. And the displacement of the human will to God is completely justified. People knew, of course, that they had violently eliminated the father, and in their reaction to that criminal act they determined henceforth to respect his will. Religious doctrine thus tells us the historical truth, albeit somewhat modified and disguised, whereas our rational account denies the historical truth.

We now notice that the store of religious ideas contains not only wish fulfillments, but also significant historical reminiscences. As for this collaboration of past and present, what an incomparable fullness of power it must give religion! But perhaps with the help of an analogy one more insight will become clear to us. It is inadvisable to transplant concepts far from the soil in which they grew, but here we must mention a correspondence. We know that a human child cannot successfully complete the process of acculturation without passing through a phase of neurosis, sometimes clearer and sometimes less so. This is because the child cannot, through rational mental work, repress a great many of the drive demands that will later be unusable, but must bring them under control through acts of repression, behind which usually lies the motive of anxiety. Most of these childhood neuroses are spontaneously surmounted as the child grows up, and this is the destiny especially of childhood obsessional neuroses. Psychoanalytic treatment can still clear up the other ones later. Quite similarly, it seems correct to assume that humanity as a whole, as it developed through the ages, finds itself in states analogous to the neuroses, and indeed for the same reasons: because in the times of its ignorance and intellectual weakness, it was only through purely affective forces that humanity achieved the drive renunciations indispensable for human coexistence. The residues of these processes, similar to repression, that occurred in primeval times still clung to culture for a long time. Thus, religion would be the universal obsessional neurosis; like that of the child, it arose from the Oedipus complex, from the relation to the father. Given this view, we would predict that the turning away from religion must occur with the fatal inexorability of a growth process, and that just now we are in the middle of that developmental phase.

Thus our behavior should emulate that of a perceptive teacher who does not resist an imminent new development, but attempts to promote it and to stem the violence of its onset. With this analogy, however, we have not exhausted the basic nature of religion. If, on the one hand, religion brings obsessional restrictions (otherwise, these can be produced only by an individual obsessional neurosis), it also contains a system of wish-illusions and a denial of reality, otherwise found in isolated form only in amentia—a state of blissful hallucinatory confusion. But these are only comparisons with which we strive to gain an understanding of the social phenomenon of religion; individual pathology gives us no fully adequate equivalent.

As has been repeatedly pointed out (by myself and in particular by Theodor Reik[1]), the analogy of religion with obsessional neurosis can be pursued to a high degree of detail, and a great many of the particulars and predetermined factors in the formation of religion can be understood in this way. And it accords well with this that the devout believer is largely protected from the danger of certain neurotic illnesses; adopting the universal neurosis obviates the need to form a personal neurosis.

Recognition of the historical value of certain religious doctrines increases our respect for them, but does not render worthless our proposal that they be withdrawn from the set of motivations for the precepts of culture. On the contrary! With the aid of these historical residues we have reached our conception of religious doctrines as something similar to neurotic relics, and we may now state that it is probably time, as in the analytic treatment of a neurotic, to replace the effects of repression with the results of rational mental work. It is foreseeable, but certainly not regrettable, that this reworking will not be limited to renouncing the solemn transfiguration of the precepts of culture, and that such a general revision of those precepts will for many people result in their abolition. The assigned task of reconciling people to culture will thus be largely achieved. In providing rational motivation for the precepts of culture, we should have no regrets

---

1 Theodor Reik (1888–1969) was a non-medical or "lay" analyst and one of Freud's students in Vienna. Armed with a PhD in psychology from the University of Vienna, Reik became known for his analyses of literature, religion, and criminology. His first book was published in 1925, the year before he was charged with quackery by a disgruntled American patient in Vienna. Freud responded to this trial with *The Question of Lay Analysis*, his first major public defense of lay analysis. See Introduction, pp. 26-38.

about renouncing the historical truth. Indeed, the truths religious doctrines contain are so distorted and systematically disguised that the mass of humanity cannot recognize them as truth. This is similar to our telling a child that babies are brought by the stork. In doing so, we are also telling the truth in symbolic disguise, for we know what the large bird signifies. But the child does not know; the child, hearing only the distorted part of what has been said, feels deceived; and we know how often the child's willfulness and mistrust of adults stem from precisely this impression. We are now convinced that it is better to refrain from such a symbolic veiling of the truth and not to deny the child knowledge of the real situation, in a manner appropriate to the child's intellectual level.

IX

"You allow yourself contradictions that are hard to reconcile. First you claim that a work like yours is completely harmless. You claim no one will let himself be robbed of his faith by such discussions. But since you actually intend to disturb that faith—as later becomes clear—we may ask: 'Why are you actually publishing it?' Yet in a different place you admit that it can be dangerous, indeed very dangerous, for someone to find out that people no longer believe in God. The person who learns this has previously been compliant, and now casts aside obedience to the precepts of culture. Indeed, your entire argument that culture is endangered by the claim that its commandments are religiously motivated rests on the assumption that a believer can be made into an unbeliever. Yet that is a complete contradiction.

"And another contradiction: you admit on the one hand that humans cannot be guided by intelligence, that they are ruled by their passions and the demands of their drives, but on the other hand you propose replacing the affective bases of their cultural obedience with rational ones. May those who can understand this do so! To me it seems that it can be only one way or the other.

"And have you learned nothing from history? Such an attempt to replace religion with reason has already been made once before, officially and on a grand scale. Surely you recall the French Revolution and Robespierre[1]—and the brevity and pathetic ineffectuality of the

---

1 Maximilien Robespierre (1758–94), the highly controversial leader of the Committee of Public Safety during the French Revolution's "Reign of Terror."

experiment. The experiment is now being repeated in Russia, but we need not be too curious as to how it will end. Don't you think we can assume that humanity cannot manage without religion?

"You have said yourself that religion is more than an obsessional neurosis. Yet you have not dealt with this other side of religion. It's enough for you to develop the analogy with neurosis: it is from a neurosis that humanity must be freed. What otherwise is lost in the process does not concern you."

The appearance of contradiction has probably arisen because I have dealt with complex issues too hastily. Some of these issues, though, can be reexamined. I still maintain that this publication of mine is, in one sense, completely harmless. No believers will be shaken in their faith by these or similar arguments. A believer has certain affectionate ties with the contents of religion. There are certainly countless other people who are not believers in that sense. They are obedient to the precepts of culture because they allow themselves to be intimidated by the threats of religion; they fear religion as long as they must consider it part of the reality that restricts them. These are the ones who break away as soon as they are permitted to abandon their belief in the reality value of religion; nor do arguments have any effect in this process. Such people stop fearing religion when they notice that others do not fear it; regarding them, I claimed that they would discover the decline of religious influence even if I did not publish this work.

But I think you yourself place greater emphasis on the other contradiction you accuse me of. People are so little open to reasonable explanations and so completely ruled by their drive wishes. Why should one desire to take from them the satisfaction of their drives and replace it with reasonable explanations? Indeed, that's how people are, but have you asked yourself whether they must be so, whether their innermost nature requires it? Can an anthropologist calculate the cranial index of a group that practices the custom of deforming their children's little heads with bandages from a very young age? Think of the disturbing contrast between the radiant intelligence of a healthy child and the intellectual weakness of the average adult. Is it so completely impossible that religious education in particular is largely to blame for this relative atrophy? I think it would be a very long time before an uninfluenced child began to harbor thoughts about God and things of the next world. Perhaps those thoughts would then follow the same paths as they did with the child's primal ancestors. But one does not wait for this development; children are introduced to religious doctrines at an age when they have neither an interest in them nor the ability to grasp their consequences. Postponing the time of sexual development and advancing that of religious influence—those are the two main points in today's pedagogical program, are they not? Then, when the child's thinking processes awaken, the doctrines of religion have already become unassailable. But do you think it is very conducive to strengthening the thought processes when such an important field is closed to them by the threat of hellfire? Once someone has reached the point of accepting uncritically all the absurdities presented by religious doctrines, and even of overlooking their mutual contradictions, the intellectual weakness of such a person should not greatly surprise us. But in controlling our libidinal nature we have no means other than our intelligence. How can we expect people dominated by prohibitions of thought to achieve the psychological ideal, the primacy of the intelligence? You know, too, that women are commonly reputed to exhibit "physiological mental deficiency"—i.e., a lesser intelligence than that of men. The fact itself is debatable and its interpretation doubtful, but an argument for the secondary nature of such an intellectual atrophy is the claim that women suffer the harshness of an early prohibition on turning their thoughts to what would have been their strongest interest— namely the problems of sexual life. In addition to the sexual inhibition of thought, so long as the religious inhibition and the derived inhibition favoring political loyalty influence a person's early years, we cannot actually tell what that person is really like.

But I will temper my zeal and admit that I, too, could be chasing an illusion. Maybe the effect of the religious prohibition of thought is not as bad as I assume; maybe it will turn out that human nature remains the same even if education is not misused for the subjugation of humanity to religion. I do not know; nor can you. Not only do the great problems of this life seem currently insoluble; many lesser questions are also difficult to decide. But grant me this: hope for the future is justified here, it may be that there is a treasure to unearth that can enrich culture, and it is worth undertaking the experiment of a non-religious form of education. If the results should be unsatisfactory, I am prepared to abandon the reform and return to my earlier, purely descriptive judgment: man is a creature of weak intelligence, dominated by his drive wishes.

On another point I completely agree with you. There is certainly no sense in trying to eliminate religion violently and at a single blow. Mainly because such an attempt would surely fail.

Believers will not let their belief be torn from them—neither by arguments nor by prohibitions. Even if this did succeed with some individuals, it would be a cruel act. Someone who has been taking sleeping pills for decades will certainly be unable to sleep if the medication is withheld. That the effect of religious consolations can be likened to that of a narcotic is nicely clarified by the process now underway in America. The intention there—obviously influenced by the political dominance of women—is to deprive people of all stimulants, intoxicants, and pleasure-inducing substances;[1] in compensation, they are being supersaturated with piety. Once again, one need not be too curious as to how this experiment will end.

Thus I disagree with you when you later argue that humanity cannot manage without the consolation of the religious illusion, that without it people could not bear life's burden and cruel reality. Indeed, not those into whom you have poured the sweet—or bitter-sweet—poison from childhood on. But the others, who were raised sensibly? Perhaps those who do not suffer from the neurosis need no intoxicant to still it. Then, it is true, they will find themselves in difficulty; they will have to admit to themselves their total helplessness, their insignificance in the inner workings of the universe; they will no longer be the center of creation, no longer the object of tender care by a kind Providence. They will be in the same position as children who have left their father's home, where they felt so warm and comfortable. But is it not true that infantilism must be surmounted? People cannot remain children forever; they must ultimately go out, into "hostile life." One may call this "education to reality." Must I still make it clear to you that the sole purpose of this publication of mine is to show the need for progress of this sort?

Do you fear that people will not pass the difficult test? Well, let's hope they do anyway. It does make a difference to know that one must depend on one's own strength. Then one learns to use it correctly. People are not completely without means of help; their science has taught them much since the time of the Deluge and will continue to increase their power. And as for the great necessities of fate, for which there is no remedy, they will simply learn to bear them with resignation. Of what use to them is the mirage of great land holdings on the moon, of whose income no one has yet seen a thing? As honest small farmers on this earth they will know how to cultivate their clod of soil so that it feeds

---

1 National Prohibition 1920–33.

them. By withdrawing their expectations from the next world and concentrating all the energies thus freed on this earthly life, they will likely manage to make life bearable for all and see to it that culture no longer oppresses anyone. Then, without regret, they will be able to say with one of our fellow unbelievers:

> Den Himmel überlassen wir
> Den Engeln und den Spatzen.[1]

X

"That really sounds marvelous! A human race that has renounced all illusions and has thereby become capable of making life on earth bearable for itself! However, I cannot share your expectations. Not because I am the stubborn reactionary you may take me for. No, because of my prudence. It seems to me that we have now switched roles: you prove to be the enthusiast, who allows himself to be carried away by illusions, and I argue for the claims of reason, the right of skepticism. What you have been explicating here seems to me to be constructed on the basis of errors which, given your example, I may be permitted to call illusions, for they reveal clearly enough the influence of your wishes. You place your hopes on a scenario in which generations uninfluenced by religious doctrines in early childhood will easily achieve the longed-for primacy of intelligence over the life of drives. Surely that is an illusion: in this decisive point, human nature is not likely to change. Unless I am mistaken—one knows so little about other cultures—there are peoples even today that do not grow up under the pressure of a religious system, but these come no closer to your ideal than do other groups. If you want to eliminate religion in our European culture, that can only be done through another system of doctrines, and from the very start, in its own defense, that system would take on all the psychological characteristics of religion, the same sanctity, inflexibility, intolerance, and the same prohibition of thought. You must have something like this to satisfy the requirements of education. In any case, you cannot do without education. The path from the infant to the civilized person is long; too many children would lose their way, failing to fulfill their life's tasks in a timely manner if left, unguided, to their own development. The doctrines applied in their education will always limit their thinking at an older age—just as you accuse religion of doing today.

---

1 "We leave heaven to the angels and the sparrows." Heine, "Deutsch-land" ("Germany"), Part 1.

Do you not see that it is the indelible inborn defect of our culture and every culture, that it compels the child, dominated by drives and weak in intellect, to make decisions which only the mature intelligence of the adult can justify? But our culture cannot do otherwise, given the compression into a few childhood years of humanity's development through the ages, and only through affective forces can children be made to deal with the task assigned them. Such, then, are the prospects for your 'primacy of the intellect.'

"Now you should not be surprised if I argue for the retention of the religious system of instruction as the basis of education and of human communal life. This is a practical problem, not a question of reality value. Since, in the interest of preserving our culture, we cannot wait to influence individuals until they have become culturally mature (and many would never achieve that anyway), and since we must impose on growing children some system of doctrines intended to function in them as basic tenets beyond criticism, the religious system seems to me the most suitable for that purpose by far. Precisely, of course, due to its wish-fulfilling and consoling power, in which you claim to have recognized the 'illusion.' In view of the difficulties involved in learning anything about reality—indeed, given doubts as to whether we can even do so— we must not overlook the fact that human needs are also part of reality, an important part indeed, and one that especially concerns us.

"I see another advantage of religious doctrine in one of its characteristics which you seem to find particularly offensive. It permits a conceptual purification and sublimation through which most aspects evincing the traces of primitive and infantile thinking can be wiped away. What then remains is a store of ideas science no longer contradicts and cannot disprove. Such restructurings of religious doctrine, which you have condemned as half-measures and compromises, make it possible to avoid the rift between the uneducated mass and the philosophical thinker; they preserve the commonality between them that is so important for the defense of culture. Accordingly, there would be no fear that the man of the people will find out that the upper strata of society 'no longer believe in God.' Now I think I have shown that your efforts are merely an attempt to replace a well-tested and affectively valuable illusion by another one, untested and indifferent."

I hope you will not think I am unreceptive to your criticism. I know how hard it is to avoid illusions; maybe the hopes I have confessed are also illusory. But I insist on one difference. My illusions—beyond the fact that there is no punishment for not sharing them—are not uncorrectable, as are those of religion; they do not possess a delusional character. If experience shows— not to me, but to others after me who think as I do—that we have erred, we will renounce our expectations. Just take my attempt for what it is. A psychologist who does not deceive himself about how hard it is to find one's way in this world is striving to assess the development of humankind in accordance with the small insights he has gained through a study of mental processes in the individual during development from child to adult. While he is thus engaged, the idea imposes itself upon him that religion is like a childhood neurosis, and he is optimistic enough to assume that humankind will overcome this neurotic phase, just as so many children outgrow their similar neurosis. These insights from individual psychology may be inadequate, their extension to the human race unjustified, the noted optimism unfounded; I admit all these uncertainties. But often it is impossible to refrain from speaking one's mind—with the excuse that one is not presenting one's thoughts as anything more than they are worth.

And there are two points I must still dwell on. First: the weakness of my position does not signify any strengthening of yours. I think you are defending a lost cause. We may repeatedly emphasize that the human intellect is powerless compared to human drives, and we may be correct in doing so. But there is something special about this weakness; the voice of the intellect is soft, but it does not rest until it is heard. In the end, after countless rejections, it does find a hearing. This is one of the few points where one may be optimistic about the future of humankind, but in itself the point is not insignificant. To it still more hopes can be connected. The primacy of the intellect certainly lies far, far ahead, but probably not infinitely far. The intellect will presumably choose the same goals whose realization you expect from your god—a realization reduced to a human scale, of course, to the extent that external reality, *Anánke* [Necessity], permits; these goals are human love and the limitation of suffering. We may therefore tell ourselves that our mutual opposition is only temporary, not irreconcilable. We hope for the same things, but you are more impatient, more ambitious, and—why should I not say it?— more self-serving than I and those who think as I do. You want a state of bliss to begin immediately after death; you demand the impossible of that blissful state, and will not give up the claims of the individual. Of those wishes, our God *Lógos* [Reason][1] will

---

1   The paired gods Lógos [Reason] and Anánke [Necessity] of the Dutch writer Multatuli (1862). [Freud's note. Multatuli was the *nom de plume* of Eduard Douwes Dekker (1820–87), a Dutch author, satirist, and philosopher best known for his anti-colonial novel *Max Havelaar* (1860).]

fulfill what nature outside us permits, but very gradually, only in the unforeseeable future, and for new human generations. He does not promise any compensation for us, who suffer greatly from life. On the way to this distant goal your religious doctrines will have to be dropped, even if the first attempts fail, even if the first substitute constructs prove unfounded. You know why: in the long run nothing can withstand reason and experience, and religion's contradiction to both is all too tangible. Even reformed religious ideas cannot escape this fate so long as they seek to salvage a portion of the consolatory content of religion. Indeed, if they restrict themselves to proclaiming a higher spiritual being whose qualities are indeterminable, whose intentions are indiscernible, they will be safe from the objections of science, but then they will also be abandoned by human interest.

And second: notice the difference between your attitude to illusion and mine. You must define the religious illusion with all your might. If it becomes discredited—and it is certainly under significant threat—then your world collapses; your only alternative is to despair of everything, of culture and the future of humankind. From such serfdom I am, we are, free. Since we are prepared to renounce a good part of our infantile wishes, we can endure it if some of our expectations prove to be illusions.

Perhaps education freed from the pressure of religious doctrines will not change human psychology to any great extent. Our god *Lógos* is perhaps not particularly almighty, and can only fulfill a small part of what his predecessors promised. If we must face up to this, we will accept it with resignation. We will not, for all that, lose our interest in the world and in life: in one area we have solid ground which you lack. We believe it is possible for scientific work to learn something about the reality of the world; through such knowledge we will be able to increase our power, and in accord with it we will be able to arrange our life. If this belief is an illusion, then we are in the same position as you are, but through its numerous and significant successes science has given us proof that it is no illusion. Science has many open enemies and even more hidden ones among those who cannot forgive her for having weakened religious faith and for her threat to overthrow it. People reproach her for how little she has taught us and for the incomparably greater amount she has left in darkness. But in doing so, they forget how young she is, how difficult were her beginnings, and how infinitesimally short has been the period of time since the human intellect has had the strength for scientific tasks. Are we not all wrong to base our judgments on excessively brief periods of time? We should take geologists as our example. People complain about the uncertainty of science—how she announces as a law today what the next generation recognizes as erroneous and replaces with a new law considered valid just as briefly. But this is unfair and in part untrue. The transformations of scientific opinion are developments, progress—not overthrow of the old order. A law initially taken as valid without limitation proves to be a special case of a more general regularity or is limited by another law, undiscovered until later; a rough approximation of the truth is replaced by a more meticulously adapted one, which in turn awaits further steps toward perfection. In various fields, science has not yet advanced beyond a phase of research in which hypotheses are tested that soon must be rejected as inadequate; in other fields, there is already an assured and nearly unchangeable core of knowledge. Finally, an attempt has been made to radically devalue scientific endeavor based on the judgment that such an endeavor, bound to the conditions of our own organization, can produce only subjective results, while the real nature of things outside us remains inaccessible to it. Here, several factors crucial for understanding scientific work are being ignored. 1) Our organization—i.e., our mental apparatus—evolved precisely in the attempt to gain knowledge of the external world, and must accordingly have realized in its structure a certain amount of expediency. 2) It is itself a component of the very world we seek to investigate, and readily allows such investigation. 3) The task of science is fully described if we limit it to showing how the world must appear to us, given the particulars of our organization. 4) The final results of science, precisely because of how they are acquired, are determined not only by our organization but by what has affected that organization. 5) The problem of the nature of the world, approached without considering our mental apparatus engaged in perception, is an empty abstraction, without practical interest.

No, our science is no illusion. But an illusion it would be to think we can get elsewhere what science cannot give us.

Appendix A: "The Illusion of a Future": Oskar Pfister's Response to Freud's The Future of an Illusion

[The Swiss Protestant minister Oskar Pfister came to psychoanalysis in 1909, utilizing Freud's technique with young parishioners in need of spiritual counseling. The "lay analyst" was also the first person to apply psychoanalysis to the field of education, which became a special interest of Freud's daughter Anna Freud. Freud was fond of Pfister, and unlike most other relationships with followers, theirs was free of suspicion or ill will. It helped that Pfister sided with Freud against his Swiss countryman Carl Jung and was instrumental in helping to found the Swiss Society for Psychoanalysis in 1919. It also helped that Pfister could be self-effacing, if not sycophantic, in the face of Herr Professor Freud. Beyond that Freud recognized and admired Pfister for his innate goodness and moral purity, and welcomed him into his home for family meals.

In addition to writing articles and books on the convergence of psychoanalysis and education, Pfister wrote about psychoanalysis and Christianity. In their correspondence Pfister doesn't hesitate to compare Freud's work to the teachings of Jesus, going so far as to claim that the first psychoanalysis was Christianity. This tone returns at times in "The Illusion of a Future" of 1928, especially at the beginning and the end. But fortunately Pfister's critique is better than that. In fact, Pfister's critical response to *The Future of an Illusion*, published in Freud's own journal *Imago*, is the first and quite possibly the best response to appear. Pfister's two basic points are as follows: Freud's recourse to empiricism in the *Future* is untenable, based as it is on total ignorance of the epistemological debates in modern philosophy; and Freud's reduction of religion to pathology ignores the evolution of religion from its neurotic origins. For Pfister, Protestantism in particular is not as infantile and pathological as Freud contends. On the contrary, Pfister sees in modern religion a bulwark against evil and injustice in his time.

Freud, a non-practicing Jew and atheist, listened to Pfister but didn't *hear* him. And for good reason. Pfister simply did not understand the Romantic roots of psychoanalysis and therefore misunderstood the epistemological and determinative significance of the death-drive theory in all of Freud's late works. In this sense, "The Illusion of a Future" may be a decent response to Freud's *Future*, but it remains incomplete and flawed. And so, although Freud and Pfister debated one another, corresponded respectfully, and enjoyed supper together, in the end it is unclear whether either man really understood the other. Of course that fundamental misrecognition may also account for their mutual interest and respect.

"The Illusion of a Future" appears in full here, translated from the German by Gregory C. Richter.]

The Illusion of a Future: A Friendly Dispute with Professor Sigmund Freud (1928)[1]

Dear Professor:

In the kindly manner to which you've made me accustomed in nineteen years of shared work, you have expressed a desire that I make public my objections to your little book, *The Future of an Illusion*; for this purpose, with the generosity inherent in your way of thinking, you have placed at my disposal one of the journals you publish. I express to you my hearty thanks for this new proof of friendship, which by no means came as a surprise. From the very beginning, before me and the world, you have made no secret of your decided lack of belief; thus, your current prophecy of a future without religion is nothing new to me. And you will smile when I see in the psychoanalytic method, which you created, a splendid means of reforming and promoting religion, as you did at the time of the famine, when we were tramping on Beethoven's paths, through snow flurries, over the hills of Vienna; as in earlier years, we were once again unable to convince each other on this point, as willingly as I have otherwise sat at your feet and have let the riches and blessings of your intellectual abundance wash over me.

For you, your book was an inner necessity, an act of honesty and confessional courage. Your titanic life's work would have been impossible without the smashing of graven images, whether they stood in universities or church halls. Everyone who has had the pleasure of close association with you knows that you yourself serve science with a reverence and fervor that elevate your workroom to a temple. Frankly, I have a definite suspicion that it is due to religious feeling within yourself that you combat religion. Schiller[2] warmly extends a brotherly hand to you. Will you reject it?

---

1 "Die Illusion einer Zukunft: eine freundliche Auseinandersetzung mit Professor Doktor Sigmund Freud," *Imago* 14 (1928): 149–84.

2 Friedrich von Schiller (1759–1805), a Kantian philosopher known for his work in ethics and aesthetics, is perhaps best remembered as a German playwright and friendly colleague of Goethe.

And, precisely from the standpoint of faith, I see no reason to join in the scolding complaints of individual zealots. Whoever has fought for the truth on such a grand scale as you have, and has argued so heroically for the salvation of love, is, whether he wants it discussed or not, by Protestant standards a true servant of God. And he who through the creation of psychoanalysis has produced the instrument by which the fetters of suffering souls are filed through and the prison gates are opened, allowing them to hasten into the sunny land of a life-giving faith, is not far from the kingdom of God. Jesus tells a finely crafted parable of two sons, one of whom obediently promises to go into his father's vineyard, yet does not keep his word; the other obstinately rejects the father's unwelcome demand, but nevertheless obeys it (Matthew 21: 28ff.). You know the kindly manner in which the founder of the Christian religion favors the latter. Will you be angry with me for seeing you, who caught such glorious rays of the eternal light and consumed yourself in the struggle for truth and human love, as figuratively closer to the throne of God, despite your supposed lack of belief, than many a churchman who mumbles prayers and performs ceremonies, but whose heart never shone with understanding and good will toward man? And since for the Gospel-oriented Christian everything depends on doing the divine will and not on saying "Lord! Lord!", do you understand how even I could envy you?

And yet, with the firmest resolve, I oppose your judgment of religion. This I do with the modesty appropriate to an inferior, but also with the joy with which one defends something holy and beloved, and with an earnest desire for truth—an approach your strict school has promoted. Yet I do this also in the hope of once again establishing a friendly attitude toward psychoanalysis, as a method and sum of empirical insights, among some who have been scared away from it by your rejection of religious faith.

Thus, I would not like to write against you, but rather for you—for whoever enters the battle for psychoanalysis fights for you. And I too fight by your side, for nothing lies closer to your heart, and to mine, than overcoming illusion through truth. Whether you with your *Future of an Illusion* or I with my "Illusion of a Future" come closer to the ideal will be decided by a higher tribunal. Neither of us wraps himself in the prophet's cloak; rather, we are satisfied with the modest role of the meteorologist—but meteorologists can also reach the wrong conclusions.

With cordial greetings,
Yours,
Oskar Pfister

I: Freud's Criticism of Religion

1) The Accusations

In his short book *The Future of an Illusion*, Freud classifies religion as an illusion, but he gives the concept of illusion a different definition than the usual one. It usually includes the feature of deception and invalidity. Yet Freud emphasizes: "An illusion is not identical to an error, and is not necessarily an error" (p. 93[1]); "Thus we call a belief an illusion when wish fulfillment is prominent in its motivation; in doing so we disregard its relation to reality, just as the illusion itself abjures confirmations" (pp. 93-94). In another context, Freud refuses to state a position in his discussion of the truth value of religious doctrines (p. 95).

One might thus assume the possibility that religion nevertheless continues to be granted validity. This is shown by Freud's example of Columbus's illusion of having found a new sea route to India (p. 93). For if the discoverer of America did not actually reach India, others did so on the route opened up by him. The Genoan also reminds one that a very large measure of excellent realistic thought can be invested in illusion. Without observing the curved surface of the sea and the spherical form of the earth deduced from it, the bold voyage to the West would not have been undertaken. I am already pointing to the intimate melding of wishful and realistic thought; I see the question arising of whether in religion, and in a very large part of science in general, there is a clean separation, or whether in both realms practical thought strives in vain, within a broad context, to expose the pure objectivity beyond wishing or in the result of wishing. But stop! I do not want to reveal anything in advance, nor in any way state a firm position on what is to follow.

The hope that Freud might have left religion an altar at whose four corners one could find a safe haven does not last long. For we soon hear that religion is comparable to a childhood neurosis and that the psychologist is so optimistic as to assume that the neurotic phase will be surmounted. It is claimed that this is actually uncertain, but hope is clearly expressed (p. 103). The neurosis religion represents is more precisely described as "the universal obsessional neurosis" and, like that of the child, is derived from the Oedipus complex—from the relation to the father (p. 103). To this Freud links the prognosis: "Given

---

1   Page references are to the present edition, replacing Pfister's original page references.

this view, we would predict that the turning away from religion must occur with the fatal inexorability of a growth process, and that just now we are in the middle of that developmental phase" (p. 103).

A later sentence forms the main thrust of the complaint: "If, on the one hand, religion brings obsessional restrictions (otherwise, these can be produced only by an individual obsessional neurosis), it also contains a system of wish-illusions and a denial of reality, otherwise found in isolated form only in amentia—a state of blissful hallucinatory confusion" (p. 104).

Finally, religion is esteemed as a defender of culture (p. 99), yet rejected as inadequate in this regard since people do not achieve through it the desired degree of happiness and moral limitation.

Let us examine these accusations more closely.

2) Religion as a Neurotic Obsession

We begin with an investigation of the neurotic obsessional character that religion is claimed to have. Without question, Freud is completely correct in that many expressions of religious life are burdened with such a character; through this discovery, he has performed an immeasurably great service for the psychology of religion. These obsessions are unmistakable in many primitive religions, which still know nothing of the formation of an actual ecclesiastical structure as found in all orthodoxies. We know too that this flaw was laid in the cradle of religions as a result of drive repressions, which, as a necessary demand, developed from the biological-ethical progress of humanity. It is now the disagreeable fate of our species that the simple and practical is usually found only via the detour of the monstrously bizarre. The history of languages and of moral attitudes shows this as clearly as does the development of religions.

But even if this burden of neurotic obsession in the first stage of religions can hardly be denied, the question arises whether it belongs to their essence. Couldn't this collective neurotic trait very well fall aside without harm, even to the advantage of the whole, just as tadpoles offer up their tails so as to hop about the world that much more comfortably as frogs?

Drive renunciations precede religion. But is that not the case for all of culture? Whoever spends all his energies on the most fundamental things does not retain the energy needed for cultural achievements. If we imagine such a purely drive-governed existence, which, furthermore, is almost always denied to human nature though the wise frugality of nature, and often through the Ash Wednesday protest[1] too, then we will not doubt for a moment that it corresponds to the essence of most animals, but not to human nature. The concept of nature is conceived in a one-sided and completely inadequate way if one takes it to be "naturalistic." Nothing justifies the assertion that animalistic vegetating better corresponds to the essence of a human being than growth and activity in accord with culture. It is of course the natural world surrounding us that makes a necessity of intellectual advancement. Culture is always the product of two natures—of exterior nature and that within human beings. Culture is itself only developed human nature, just as the deprivations and renunciations that call it forth represent effects of nature. Whoever frees the concept of nature from its erroneous constriction will see in cultural development the same mutual harmony of the individual and the rest of the world that epistemology shows us in the process of cognition.

I am not in agreement with Freud's earlier assertion that the development of religions is grounded on renouncing the activity of egoistic drives, while neurosis requires the repression of exclusively sexual functions (Freud 1924[2]). The history of the Oedipal orientation, in particular, shows that sexuality forms an integral component of the ego drives, and vice versa. Throughout, the extraction of individual drives can be undertaken only as an abstraction; as soon as one thinks of drives as truly separate (disregarding their most primitive impulses), one becomes embroiled in error after error. This "organic point of view," as I call the correct mode of observation, is indispensable for understanding the genesis of religion. Here, I do not believe there remains a difference between Freud and myself today. Since he now claims the negative attachment to the father as the main determinant of religion, he also allows the libidinal forces to express themselves advantageously. I believe that one must seek the drive-denials leading to religion on a very broad scope, just as, on the other hand, the paths taken in the development of religion demonstrate extremely great variation. The totem cult is grounded on completely different complexes of determinants from those that underlie, for example, the social-ethical monotheism of the classical prophets of Israel; Akhenaton's[3] aesthetic and pacifist Aton-religion was grounded on com-

---

1 This term refers to public protests against social practices that run counter to Christianity, for example abortion.
2 I.e., "Obsessive Actions and Religious Practices."
3 Amenhotep IV, Pharaoh of the eighteenth dynasty of Egypt (ca. 1350 BCE). Akhenaton revolutionized religious practice in ancient Egypt by proclaiming Aton—the disk of the sun—as the only god worthy of worship.

pletely different complexes from those underlying the piety of Spanish conquistadors. But drive-denials calling forth more or less comprehensive and deep repressions must of course play a role in the development of every religion.

But must obsessional constructions really always inhere in religion? I believe that, on the contrary, the highest constructions of religions actually abolish obsession. Think of genuine Christianity! Contrasting with obsessionally neurotic nomism, which overburdens people with its literalness and uncomfortable ceremoniousness, Jesus established his "commandment" of love. "Ye have heard that it was said of them of old time.... But I say unto you ..." (Matthew 5: 21–22). There we have the powerful act of the Redeemer. And it occurs not through any new claim on one's attachments, but through the authority of that freedom won through triumphant love and knowledge of the truth. In accord with good psychoanalytical standards, Jesus overcame the collective neurosis of his people by introducing love—morally complete love, in fact—into the center of life. In his idea of the father, completely cleansed of the slag of Oedipal attachment, we see how the heteronomy and all the pain of bondage are completely conquered. What is expected of humankind is nothing but what corresponds to his being and true destiny, furthers the common good and—making room for the biological point of view—produces maximal health for the individual and the community. It is a serious misunderstanding of Jesus' commandment, "Thou shalt love the Lord thy God with all thy heart.... Thou shalt love thy neighbour as thyself" (Matthew 22: 37ff.), to understand it as being in the spirit of Mosaic law. The imperative form is retained, but who could fail to notice the delicate irony with which the content, the loving—an achievement that can only be accomplished voluntarily—cancels out the legalistic character?

The fine acuity with which Jesus practiced psychoanalysis 1900 years before Freud (one must not use the expression too strictly, of course) I have shown elsewhere (1927: 20–24).[1] I reiterate that Jesus

---

1 Pfister is referring to his work *Psychoanalytic Ministry: Introduction to Psychoanalysis for Pastors and Laymen*:

> To what extent can this [analytical] pastoral work, whether practiced by physicians or laymen, refer to the work of Jesus? This pastoral work is free of the restrictions [...] in which the pastoral work of the church became enmeshed. It deals with all types of psychological distress, and also with appropriate cases of sickness; Jesus, too, cared for the sick as a savior. [...] Jesus did not refer to any religious duty, but helped out of compassion, for God's love was strong in him. [...] But the similarities go much further. This is shown, for example by the detailed depiction of an instance *(continued)*

does not merely cure the lame man's symptom through suggestion, but enters into the underlying moral-religious conflict; he settles it, and thus overcomes the lameness from within. His belief in demons may alienate us as metaphysics, but as neurology we accept it. The historical-psychological direction in which Jesus tests Biblicist coercive authority finds the complete approval of the analyst (e.g., Matthew 19: 8, where Jesus claims the Mosaic commandment of the bill of divorce was issued due to human hardheartedness). His handling of transference, taken as love but further directed to absolute, ideal achievements so that no new attachment ensues, deserves the admiration of all pupils of Freud. So too does the dissolution—achieved through dedication to the absolute father, who is love—of the obsession-producing fixation on the parents.

Not that one should put Jesus forward as the first psychoanalyst in Freud's sense, as some mischievous young greenhorns would perhaps like to do! But in its basic traits his ministry of redemption points so decisively in the direction of analysis that Christians should be ashamed to have left to a non-Christian the utilization of these shining footprints. The reason is doubtless that the obsessional neurotic clumsiness threatening religion and all other constructions of the human spirit buried this wonderful trail too, as in the materialism of earlier psychiatry.

We could still investigate further Jesus' elimination of obsession and the weakening of its determinants; we could demonstrate how his father-idea, in comparison with Oedipal hatred, is free from all symptoms of reaction. God should not be appeased with sacrifices, but should be loved in one's brother. We could recall that brotherly love in the deepest and broadest sense constitutes the distinguishing feature and guiding star of Christian doctrine. We could recall that the goal and highest good of all striving and longing lie not in personal satisfaction, but in the kingdom of God, i.e., in the dominion of love, truth,

---

of the healing of the sick given to us in the Gospels: the healing of a lame man (Matthew 9: 2). 'And, behold, they brought to him a man sick of the palsy, lying on a bed, and Jesus seeing their faith said unto the sick of the palsy: Son, be of good cheer; thy sins be forgiven thee.' Thus, Jesus does not deal with the disease symptom first ... *but penetrates to the actual seat of the problem, to its cause—the moral-religious conflict. His pastoral care is primarily based on causation. Thus Jesus reflects the basic principle of psychoanalysis.* The healing is effected from within. The innermost distress is much more important than the symptom, which from the biological point of view is merely a sort of release valve protecting one from even more serious harm. (20; italics in original)

and justice in the individual and in the universal community, etc. But that would lead us too far afield.

And can't something quite similar be said of the religion of Akhenaton and, in a certain sense, even of Buddha? Doesn't a powerful principle of redemption lie at the foundation of Protestantism, with its freedom of belief and of conscience, but also with its commandment of love—indeed not only in the sense of liberation from religious obsession, but also as a general healing of obsessions?

It is a great pity that Freud disregards precisely the highest expressions of religion. In terms of historical development, it is not the case that religion creates obsessions and holds a person fast in neurosis. Rather, pre-religious life creates neurotic obsessions, which then lead to corresponding religious ideas and rites. The magic preceding religion is not yet religion. But then, precisely within the greatest development of religion—the Judeo-Christian—there appears time and time again a religious inspiration (revelation) kindled by a higher, ethical, and therefore also socio-biological insight. This inspiration seeks to eliminate obsession and provides liberation from it until— under conditions no one understands better than the analyst—again and again, through the need of the time, new bonds are forged that a later religious conception is called upon to break. Unmistakably, to this religious struggle for redemption there corresponds a humanizing process. Thus, in succession come pre-Israelite animism and naturism, Mosaicism, Baalism, classical propheticism, post-exilic nomism (culminating in Pharisaism), the birth of Christianity, Catholicism, the Reformation, early Protestant orthodoxy, Pietism, and Enlightenment, as well as the current derivatives of the various Christian systems producing and combating obsession.[1] However, it is worth noting that obsession-free individualism, specifically at the present time, is strongly represented within Protestantism; through its social pathos on the one hand, and its strictly critical-scholarly work on the other, it has gained no small reputation among the other academic fields.

---

1   Animism is the belief that the soul or spirit extends to physical matter. Naturism espouses harmony with nature, sometimes expressed as nudism. Mosaicism refers to the culture and religion of Jews. Baalism is based on the fertility gods of ancient Semites. Classical propheticism likely refers to the time of the great Hebrew prophets such as Isaiah, Jeremiah, and Ezekiel. In Jewish history, "post-exilic" refers to the time after the Babylonian Captivity (after 539 BCE), while "nomism" refers to the strict adherence to law in matters of religion. Pharisaism was associated with an ancient Jewish sect that advocated strict adherence to law and believed in a coming Messiah. Within seventeenth- and eighteenth-century Protestantism, Pietism sought to reform the more formal or dogmatic aspects of the German Lutheran church.

Nor should one forget that religion absolutely cannot develop while isolated within itself! If the Christians in particular periods were competitors in cruelty with the wildest barbarians, this did not occur due to a consistent realization of their religious principle, but through neurotic illnesses that distorted and devastated the Christian religion, just as research and artistic creation were exposed to and succumbed to the most abominable malformations.

Thus I absolutely deny that religion as such is characterized by a neurotic obsessional character.

3) Religion as a Wishful Construct

Freud correctly denies having originated the idea that all religions represent only wishful constructs (97). With insuperable consistency, Feuerbach, almost ninety years ago, expounded his thesis of theology as disguised anthropology and of religion as a dream (43). But in many points, with his microscope of the mind, Freud extraordinarily refined and strengthened these hypotheses. Here one must not be deceived. Just the explanation of latent wishes and their reworking for the purpose of making them conscious, and the revelation of the Oedipal situation and of repressed sadism and masochism, make it completely impossible to deny that wishes arise in the development of religion. But can all of religious thinking be explained in this way? And is this mistaken reversal of wishes unique to religion? In religion and science, and even, finally, in art and morality, won't the repression of wishful thinking through real thinking and the mobilization of real thinking through wishful thinking create the ideal toward which intellectual development strives—gasping for breath, hoping, and painfully disappointed time and time again?

Before turning to Freud's investigation, let us seek out a common starting point. I will never forget that sunny Sunday morning in the spring of 1909 at the Belvedere Park in Vienna, when Professor Freud pointed out to me, in his kindly, fatherly manner, the dangers presented by the research he was conducting. Even at that time I already declared that I was prepared to give up my beloved function as pastor if the truth required it. To proclaim a belief that reason contradicts, or to set up one's mind as a residence of unbelief and one's heart as a seat of belief—these seemed to me to be jugglers' tricks I absolutely wanted to avoid. I do not know what I ought to change in this attitude. One does not risk one's soul for illusions.

I can come a good way toward accommodation with Freud. (With his psychological critique of religious doctrines Feuerbach also found support among theologians [Pfleiderer 449].) I always knew that ideas of God and the beyond are often painted with colors from a palette of wishes. When, in a hallucinatory vision of God, I first encountered the features of my father, of various pastors, etc. (1913:[1] 222ff.), and behind them the directorship of hatred, the clarity with which the connection could be shown was quite interesting, but I felt nothing extremely new and unexpected. I have long known that the wishes of their originators are just as strongly mirrored in the Eskimo afterlife, plentiful in whales, or in the green hunting grounds of the Indians, inviting them to take scalps, or in the Germanic Valhalla, blessed with mead and graced with tournaments, as in the prayer-hall heaven of the Pietist, or in the next world of Goethe[2] with its decisive moral struggle.

Nemesis would have it that the deniers of God I have analyzed were also led extraordinarily often by wishful thinking. Which analyst hasn't often found atheists whose unbelief wasn't a disguised elimination of the father? Yet I would consider it incorrect to squeeze all rejection of religion into a wish schema.

And let us look more closely at the wishes leading to religion. It must be admitted that initially they are chiefly of an egoistical nature. Could it be any different with science? Among primitives, could one expect a disinterested thirst for knowledge? As early as the so-called child of nature, we see how moral need stirs in cult and belief, e.g., the need to atone for a committed wrong (e.g., death wishes against the father). With moral development, religious development matures as well. Selfish wishes recede more and more, even if there are continuous relapses into egoistical thinking, which show that the wild and primitive can be eradicated only with difficulty.

The classical prophets of ancient Israel renounce a personal existence after death, given the extent to which their literary creativity and their striving were absorbed in the people.

In the Gospel, we see a mighty combat against drive wishes, which becomes stronger and stronger the more the development of Jesus proceeds in a steady battle with tradition. We see the idea of reward, the idea of race, and the sensually colored conception of the afterlife all repressed; indeed, in the interpretation of psychoanalysis, the idea of reward is repressed far more skillfully and wisely than in the rigor-

---

1 I.e., *The Psychoanalytic Method*.
2 Johann Wolfgang von Goethe (1749–1832), German man of letters, artist, scientist, polymath, is best remembered for his tragic play *Faust*. Widely influential, he was one of the most significant figures of early-nineteenth-century Western thought.

ous philosophy of the categorical imperative,[1] which, without understanding, pours love away. What Jesus demands in the name of his religion is, to a great extent, directly opposed to egoism; yet Jesus, with great wisdom, by no means bans self-love, nor promotes masochism as it was practiced by the ascetics. The gentleness and humility, the self-denial, the rejection of the accumulation of wealth, the sacrifice of his own life for the highest moral values, in short, the entire manner of life demanded of his apostles by the one who was crucified at Golgotha, is diametrically opposed to the cravings of original human nature. Yet it corresponds to a higher view of human nature, which certainly could not proceed from the lowly demands of drives, but only from an ideal realism which was struggled for in the face of bitter privations and which sprang forth from a magnificent, intuitive anthropology and cosmology. In the Lord's Prayer everything egoistical disappears. The request for daily bread, this minimum of subsistence, is no longer egoistical; universal ethical ideals reign, and chief among these is bowing down before divine will ("Thy will be done"). This is not the Buddhist absence of desire, nor is it pathogenetic introversion.

The claim that, according to Christian understanding, everything denied the Christian in earthly life will be provided in the next world is false. According to Islam, renunciation of the activation of sexuality can be made up for in the next world—but not according to Christianity. Jesus stresses explicitly that sensual expectations for the life after death are to be ruled out (Matthew 22: 30). His highest ideal, the kingdom of God, has the earth as its setting and has as its content ideal ethical and religious values having nothing to do with drive wishes.

"However," the opponent may object, "doesn't religion then derive at least from wishes of a higher order?" I would reply that one must be clear about the difference between wish and postulate. In hallucinations or other phenomena that Freud has made understandable for us, the wish seeks gratification, without any concern for the actual circumstances. Similarly, we are also aware of many religious phenomena that make this illusory leap from desiring to assuming that something exists. Yet no one will claim that every wish finds gratification only in such an illegitimate way. One can aim for gratification of one's wishes in a manner very much centered on reality.

---

1   Immanuel Kant introduced the "categorical imperative," an ethical maxim, in *Groundwork of the Metaphysics of Morals* (1785): "act only in accordance with that maxim through which you can at the same time will that it become a universal law" (4: 421). (Cited in *Practical Philosophy*, ed. Mary J. Gregor [Cambridge: Cambridge University Press, 1996].)

Jesus felt within himself love-imperatives that contradicted sacred tradition. We can still observe precisely the stage at which he believed he could bring the claims of his inner demands into harmony with those of "Mosaic" commandment (Matthew 5: 17–22). But, as we have already learned (verses 27ff., 33ff., 38ff.), this view did not make headway on all fronts. Things had to come to an open break. The inner commandment had to supplant the outer one. But then this inner moral necessity itself had to come from God. And since it sought love, God had to appear as loving, and no longer as the strict, jealous god of the Old Testament. Thus, as noted above, the coercive character of the fear-instilling Torah collapsed as well.

If we want to translate this process—which played out intuitively and in an inspired manner within the soul of Jesus—into ponderous acts of cognition, we then enter the path of the postulate. The postulate does not say: "I want such and such. Therefore, it is real." Rather it concludes: "Such and such exists. What do I have to think of as real so that this definitely existing thing becomes comprehensible, was able to become real, and can be real?" The postulate proceeds from something with being—something recognized or assumed as sure—and deduces something else with being, and resulting from the former as a logical necessity.

Natural science with its hypotheses, which, with adequate corroboration, are developed into theories, in a certain sense proceeds on a similar path. But this involves existent things, from which one progresses to other existent things. In the postulate, though, a valuation or imperative forms the starting point. Kant,[1] for example, views the categorical "You should" as the Archimedes[2] point and postulates a lawgiver from it. I myself began with another ethical certainty that impressed itself upon me specifically through psychoanalytical and sociological observation: from the commandment to love one's neighbor, oneself, and the absolute ideal. In this norm, which results from the unique character of man, given that an obligation lies in that char-

---

1 Immanuel Kant (1724–1804) was a German philosopher from Königsberg (present-day Kaliningrad, Russia), credited with synthesizing the traditions of rationalism and empiricism; he is sometimes considered the greatest philosopher ever. In addition to key works on metaphysics, ethics, and aesthetics, Kant wrote widely on everything from religion and anthropology to law and history.

2 Third-century BCE Greek mathematician Archimedes is reported to have said that he could move the earth if only he had a place to stand and a long lever. Hence "Archimedes point": an imaginary or hypothetical vantage outside the object of study, a point of complete objectivity.

acter's being, I found the place from which I was obliged to deduce an absolute as the origin of being, of obligation, and of all values. This philosophical operation is basically nothing other than Jesus' empirical-intuitive certainty of God. Clearly, many wishes dictated by individual tastes and even many "needs" have to be sacrificed to the harsh knowledge of reality. And if the existential basis of the commandment of love in the highest sense is itself claimed to be intellectual and loving, is this then really contrary to thought?

Further, the question is raised: in science too, isn't the symbolic fantasy a charade-like, disguised bearer of valid knowledge? Doesn't scientific thinking also work with the heralds of anthropomorphism, which say much while also concealing much?

I shall begin with the last-noted problem. I still remember my happy amazement in reading Robitsek's important study of the scientific achievements of the chemist August Kekulé von Stradonitz[1] in the first volume of *Imago* (Robitsek). The article relates how the theory of molecular structure and of the structure of benzene arose from visual fantasies of dancing pairs and of snakes; but the dreams had to be tested by alert understanding.

One should beware of immediately seeing as the products of wishes all primitive conceptions that seem fantastic to us reality-based thinkers of the twentieth century. If the wild man assumes a living animal in boiling water, which wish is supposedly guiding him? Wasn't the obvious thing to explain boiling, which he did not understand, as analogous to the movement of water caused by a hidden animal, which he did understand?

And when human-like forces and beings are projected into natural phenomena and processes, is this an act of religion exclusively, or do we not find this process, which rests on analogical conclusions, even in the proudest halls of the natural sciences, and even in those of philosophy, more strictly disciplined still? We speak of "strength," "cause," "effect," "law," and a hundred other concepts that were long ago invented by epistemology as rather clumsy, if indispensable, anthropomorphisms. Isn't the concept of "censorship" of the same type?

The history of the sciences is that of a continuous struggle with anthropomorphisms and other impermissible projections of known facts onto unknown ones. Why should religion and theology form an exception?

But the question now is whether theology, which concerned itself with religion, has remained stuck with one foot in the stage of wishes.

---

1 Friedrich August Kekulé von Stradonitz (1829–96), founder of the theory of chemical structure.

If this is the case, then I seriously fear (or should I hope?) that it shares this fate, lamentable for a science, with the other sciences, not excluding the natural sciences and history. For philosophy, I can assert this very definitely (1923[1]), and even if a surplus of pure objectivity can be granted the strictly exact natural sciences, they are lacking just what empirical criticism sought so passionately and unsuccessfully: pure experience, from which the additional contributions of human subjectivity have been eradicated. For this reason, natural scientific observation ends with the bitter insight that one can recognize only a small bit of the surface—a small bit that can be acknowledged only as a shimmering appearance. Colors evaporate into "oscillations of the ether," and one adds with resignation that the ether is a very dubious auxiliary concept; tones turn out to be oscillations of the air, whose union as melody or symphony has no place in scientific journals and in the world of the natural sciences. The atom, which for several thousand years of experimentation and thought was recognized as an absolutely simple and unchangeable little clump of reality, and had been elevated to a position as bearer of a world view supposedly proven by the natural sciences, is smashed to smithereens one morning, like a piece of coal, and even transforms itself into another element. Natural law reveals itself to modern scientific criticism as the product of the wish that a process always occur in the same way under the same conditions. Imagine the embarrassment of mechanical engineers and bridge builders if this were not the case! If the revolutionary views of the most recent and critical natural sciences have yielded anything certain, it is the insight that in that area we are still stuck up to our necks in wishes; pragmatism, however much one may look down one's nose at it, at least has the good attribute of unveiling the interest of the practical American in an expansive use and enjoyment of reality, i.e., it unveils the wishful thinking behind knowledge.

Theology has amply shown that it is, in no small degree, ready and able to give up wishful thinking; I believe, though, that I shall be able to demonstrate this more effectively at the end of our friendly dispute. But along with theology, religion also underwent sacrifices that were highly penetrating, and of the most painful sort for wishing.

Further, one must not overlook the fact that religion, from the beginning, has been abundantly able to incorporate knowledge of nature and of values. Those who have ridiculed the sun that stood still for Joshua should have noted that the concept of a firmly established and closed natural order did not yet exist in those times, but first entered science more than two and a half millennia later, until once

---

1 I.e., *On the Psychology of Philosophical Thought.*

again losing no small portion of its credibility just recently. Christendom long opposed Copernicus[1] and the theory of evolution—far too long—but it finally came to an accommodation with them. One shouldn't take it amiss that is doesn't participate in all the scientific fads of the day. Numerous excellent scientists, up to the present, have found no difficulty in harmonizing religion and science, whereas the half-educated are actually more likely than great researchers of Freud's rank to proclaim the incompatibility of the two areas at the beer table.

In that, nothing is proven concerning the truth or untruth of religion.

But what is the situation with the contradictions in religious thought? I have already spoken of the honest effort of modern theology to overcome them. Whether it has succeeded is difficult to decide. I believe that I have attained a religiosity that has mastered the contradictions, even if, as in every other area of human thought, unsolved riddles have remained at every step. But now I turn to the other side of the question and ask: isn't empirical science bursting with contradictions as thick as your fist? I shall not even point to conceptual cripples like the ether, which supposedly is matter without consisting of atoms, and which the most respectable scientists nevertheless greeted, with a most subservient bow, as lord and master. Perhaps it is significant, though, that very important scientists and psychologists, e.g., Johann Herbart[2] and Wilhelm Wundt,[3] assign philosophy no other task than eliminating the contradictions in empirical concepts and harmonizing those purified empirical concepts with each other. Indeed, one should also proceed more cautiously with the religion of the uneducated and that of theologians.

Since Freud did not intend to address the individual contradictions, and limited himself to declaring most religious doctrines unprovable and irrefutable (p. 94), I cannot enter the defense of reli-

---

1   Nicolaus Copernicus (1473–1543) was a Renaissance polymath and astronomer whose heliocentric cosmology displaced earth as the center of the universe, thereby ushering in the scientific revolution. His thesis was published in *De revolutionibus orbitum coelestium* (*On the Revolutions of the Celestial Spheres*) in 1543, just before his death, and was rejected by Christendom only in the early 1600s. The book was officially prohibited until 1835.

2   German psychologist and philosopher Johann Friedrich Herbart (1776–1841). Herbart's philosophical position is vested in clarifying our conceptions via formal logic before any other substantive claims can be made.

3   German physician, physiologist, and philosopher Wilhelm Maximillian Wundt (1832–1920). Wundt founded the first psychology laboratory and is typically regarded as the father of experimental psychology.

gious thinking about reality in particular cases. When one recalls how modestly contemporary science has learned to think about the realm of the truly provable, it must be admitted that in the problem we are discussing the greatest caution is urgently indicated, lest one demand of other academic disciplines what one has not achieved in one's own, nor reproach other disciplines for errors one commits oneself. With what exemplary restraint Freud speaks of the degree to which his proposals have been proven! We must also very carefully avoid taking agreement among scholars for thorough investigation and validity of a doctrine. Very often, agreement is only the result of fatigue, and the gravedigger's feet may already stand at the door.

Given this situation, which makes our truly scientific assets appear somewhat doubtful compared to the liabilities, we must, now especially, guard against the danger of scientific dishonesty. Wishful thinking and the allowance of contradictions would not produce a more favorable balance of assets, but could easily endanger one's credit even more. But there is no obvious reason to invest one's entire fortune in the single bank of science and to declare all other cultural goods superfluous. We shall return to this later.

When Freud accuses religion of hallucinatory confusion, he is undoubtedly correct for some, indeed many of its forms. But does this apply to all forms of piety? I cannot concur. Again the great master seems to focus his attention on quite specific forms and to speak in overly general terms. I almost believe that he has seldom been a guest at Protestant services and that he has seldom honored critical theology with a visit. We analysts particularly, who are for the first time seriously and exhaustively addressing the psychology of genius, actually know very well that behind hallucinatory confusion there may lie something very great and deep. When Paul testifies that his sermon about the cross was only foolishness to the heathens (1 Corinthians 1: 23), that is no counterargument for him. To me, a creative Dionysian spirit of fire, or an Apollonian one,[1] pouring out its offerings not as well-aged wine but as fermenting new wine, is far more valuable than a sober scholar who consumes his life's energies in sterile conceptual juggling and pedantic precision. The degree of rationality is not necessarily the measure of value. Stormy youth, with all its follies and foolishness, is nevertheless no small distance ahead of prudent age. One cannot wait to eat and drink until physiologists have completed their analyses of foods and elaborated their nutritional theories to

---

1 In Greek mythology, Dionysus and Apollo are binary pairs that signify playful exuberance and reason, femininity and masculinity. Dionysus is the god of wine, Apollo the god of the Sun. Both are sons of Zeus.

general satisfaction. Radium baths did good service for several centuries before the discovery of radium, and with it, the cause of the therapeutic successes. Is it inconceivable that, in the intellectual realm, knowledge of causes limps, laboriously panting, behind the possession of valuable goods? Frankly, it seems to me that in contemporary Protestantism, with its exceedingly strict, sharp criticism, we have retained too little, rather than too much, of Platonic frenzy and Pauline scandal. But as for myself, I cannot do otherwise than perpetrate the reality principle with inexorable exactitude, though constantly concerned that I may be losing precious goods through the mesh of scientific concept-formation.

And it must not be forgotten that one can reject scientific hypotheses; in practical questions on whose answers the improvement of life depends, one must take a position even where stringent proofs are lacking. How else could one start a family, select a profession, etc.? Thus, in religion too there lies a trust, but woe to him who marries only according to wishes, or chooses a profession and adopts a religious faith without a scrupulously precise consideration of reality!

4) Religion as Hostile to Thought

The claim that religion in itself is hostile to thought is one I cannot agree with. Freud wrote: "If we ask the basis for their claim that they must be believed, we receive three answers, and these show a remarkably poor mutual accord. First, these doctrines deserve belief because our forefathers already believed in them; second, we have proofs that have been passed down to us from those early times; and third, it is forbidden to question their authority in the first place" (p. 89). Granted, such cases of dreadful argumentation have appeared here and there. But what educated Christian would be satisfied with such an answer today? Certainly not we Protestants. We criticize the Bible and dogmas as radically as we do Homer or Aristotle. As for the Catholics, they at least introduce their dogmatics with an apologetics intended to satisfy the demands of reason. As a philosopher, one may challenge whether thought requires this apologetics; as a pupil of Freud, one may diagnose it as rationalization; as a Protestant, one may reject at least a portion as *lettre de cachet*.[1] Yet a work of thought still remains that commands respect.

---

1 A letter containing a royal pronouncement not subject to appeal.

For our religion, we Protestants know far too well how indebted we are to thought; we will never deny thought its full scope. Even if Luther[1] did not grant reason its deserved rights, he was still a theologian and scientific thinker; otherwise, he would never have become a reformer. Zwingli[2] passed through the humanistic school, which gave his theology and piety not only their leniency, but also their clarity. Even the darkly brooding Calvin,[3] Geneva's ghastly grand inquisitor, made his juridical thinking accessible to his fortress-like theology. The religion of the reformers was also the product of their scientifically schooled professorial thinking. Modern theology, which has made considerable accomplishments in radical denial and continues to do so, is aware of serving religion most excellently precisely through its strict realistic thinking.

In my circle, I have never heard of the prohibition on thinking deeply about religious matters. On the contrary, we Protestant pastors require that our pupils engage in free critical thinking. Among liberal pastors this is taken for granted, but I know of it among many conservative ones as well. We calm frightened persons who have fallen into a crisis of belief with the assurance that God loves the sincere doubter and that a faith strengthened through thought is much more valuable than one simply taken up and learned through instruction. We also require and nurture independent thinking in the religion of adults.

Freud claims that thought is weakened by religion. Granted, he immediately adds that the effect of the religious prohibition on thought may perhaps not be as bad as he assumes (p. 107). Nevertheless, he insists that it would be beneficial to attempt to establish a system of education free from the sweet poison of religion (p. 107). Historically, it should be noted, there has unquestionably been a long series of the deepest and freest spirits who have enormously enriched the intellectual life of humanity, and who simultaneously agreed with religion and science; I cannot believe Freud assumes they would have created even greater things, had they never heard anything about religion. Physicians such as Hermann Lotze [1817–81], Wilhelm Wundt [1832–1920], Theodor Kocher [1841–1917]; physicists such as René

---

1 Martin Luther (1483–1546), German theologian and church reformer responsible for starting the Protestant Reformation when he nailed *Ninety-Five Theses* to the door of the church in Wittenberg in 1517.

2 Huldrych Zwingli (1484–1531), leader of the 1520s Protestant Reformation in Switzerland.

3 French theologian John Calvin (1509–64) and founder of Calvinism—a Protestant theological system grounded in the "five points" of total depravity, unconditional election, limited atonement, irresistible grace, and perseverance of the saints.

Descartes [1596–1650], Isaac Newton [1643–1727], Michael Faraday [1791–1867], Robert Mayer [1814–78]; chemists such as Justus Liebig [1803–73]; biologists such as Oswald Heer [1809–83], Charles Darwin [1809–82], Louis Pasteur [1822–95], Karl von Bär [1792–1876]; mathematicians such as Gottfried Wilhelm Leibnitz [1646–1716], Blaise Pascal [1623–62], Karl Gauss [1777–1855]; geographers such as Carl Ritter [1779–1859]; historians such as Johannes von Müller [1752–1809], Thomas Carlyle [1795–1881], Reinhold Niebuhr [1892–1971], Leopold von Ranke [1795–1886]; statesmen such as Abraham Lincoln [1809–65], William Gladstone [1809–98], Otto von Bismarck [1815–98]; philosophers such as Immanuel Kant [1724–1804], Johann Fichte [1762–1814], Friedrich Schelling [1775–1854], Georg Wilhelm Friedrich Hegel [1770–1831], Johann Herbart [1776–1841], John Ruskin [1819–1900], Rudolf Eucken [1846–1926], Henri Bergson [1859–1941]; writers such as Johann Wolfgang von Goethe [1749–1832], Friedrich Schiller [1759–1805], Friedrich Rückert [1788–1866], Albrecht Bitzius [1797–1854], Gottfried Keller [1819–90], Karl Ferdinand Meyer [1851–1922], Emanuel Geibel [1815–84]—from a long series of brilliant names I hastily select just a few—surely exhibit no defects in intelligence, although they believed in God, and I really do not know what might justify the assumption that their minds would have soared up to even greater achievements, had they never encountered religion. Some of those named above were surely far above the average believer in the intensity of their religious feeling, but given their great intellectual achievements, one would have to assume the contrary, were the danger of stupidity so closely linked to religion.

We can already note as well that even in the very recent past important scientists, specifically through thought, arrived at the certainty or at least probability that there is a constructive will in the universe (Albert Einstein,[1] Erich Becher,[2] Hans Driesch[3]). But we shall not base the evidence for the truth of religion on these authorities either.

In an earlier passage, Freud emphasized that children's intellectual curiosity would be damaged if one answered their questions about the

---

1 In 1929, Einstein confessed to believing in "Spinoza's God"—a God roughly equivalent to nature itself.

2 German philosopher and psychologist Erich Becher (1882–1929). Becher, a monist, saw reality as being wholly psychic and believed in a supra-individual mind distributed across all living organisms.

3 German biologist Hans Adolf Eduard Driesch (1867–1941), whose philosophy of entelechy maintained that a mind-like "life force" was responsible for embryonic development.

origin of objects in nature with a summary reference to God. I agree with him, but would like to ask if the result will be different if one said: "Nature created them"; I stress the fact that in religious instruction it is always pointed out how God is at work in natural processes and in human activity.

I myself remember how my own thinking has been generously enriched by religion. Innumerable intellectual problems were stimulated that simply must be worked out: in living one's life one must not stick one's head in the sand like an ostrich. Splendid historical figures were presented to me; my sense for greatness and moral necessity developed. I would experience it as an irreparably great loss if religious memories were wrested from my life. And the fact that the Bible was presented to me as the infallible word of God sharpened my thinking. I can still remember how as a twelve-year-old, after reading the story of the flood, I ran to the zoological museum in order to compare the measurements of the ark with those of the glass cases as the basis of a childish theory of evolution; simultaneously, I adopted a skeptical attitude toward the Bible, which later developed into free criticism.

As for Freud's suggested experiment of instruction without religion, it has certainly been conducted very often, and has been ongoing on a massive scale in communist circles for many years. In undertaking analyses, I have often come into contact with people raised without religion, but I really cannot reliably state that I discovered in them any extra intelligence, or a correspondingly more advantageous development of the intellectual capacities—as little as I have, among philosophers, recognized the deniers of God as the superior ones, e.g., a Karl Vogt [1817–95] or Jacob Moleschott [1822–93] (with some reservations, one might count Ernst Häckel [1834–1919] among this group as well). In any case, history has thus far pronounced another verdict.

5) Religion as Defender of Culture

It remains for us to examine religion as a defender of culture. In this sense, Freud assigns religion a police-like mission. "Religion has clearly done great services for human culture. It has contributed much to the taming of asocial drives—but not enough. It has ruled human culture for many millennia; it has had time to show what it can achieve. Had it been successful in making the majority of humans happy, in comforting them, in reconciling them to life, and in making them bearers of culture, it would occur to no one to seek any change in the existing conditions. What do we see instead? That an alarmingly great number of people are dissatisfied with culture, are unhappy in it, feel it as a yoke that one must shake off; that these people either contribute their full energies to changing that culture, or take their hostility to culture so far that they are unwilling to accept any part of culture and the restriction of drives" (p. 98).

I can agree completely with Freud that religion sometimes has not performed with high marks in its cultural-police function. But I must add: it strikes me as fortunate that that is the case, for religion has more important things to do than protecting that mixture of the noble and the abhorrent that is designated as culture today.

Under culture Freud understands "all those things in which human life has risen above its animal conditioning factors and in which it differs from the life of beasts" (p. 73). Freud refuses to differentiate between culture and civilization. "It includes on the one hand all the knowledge and power that people have acquired in order to master the forces of nature and gain material wealth for the satisfaction of human needs, and on the other hand it includes all the institutions necessary to regulate the relations of humans to each other, especially the distribution of the attainable material wealth" (p. 73).

In my opinion, I must confess, there is very much that is disgraceful and harmful in what raises humanity above the beasts. Knowledge and ability, material wealth for the satisfaction of human needs, the institutions for the regulation of social relations and the distribution of wealth—everything strikes me as so thoroughly permeated with cruelty, injustice, and poisonous germs that religion really has no cause to exert itself for the preservation of the existing order. War, the spirit of Mammon,[1] the pursuit of pleasure, the misery of the masses, exploitation, oppression, and innumerable other harmful things show the need to distinguish between what is good and worthy of protection and what is evil and must be fought against. It even seems to me that in the face of our culture, which has become superficial and has atrophied in its inner values—especially emotional ones—Christianity, taken seriously, must strive for very deep and revolutionary changes. The study of psychoanalysis has strengthened me in this view. Religion should become for us not a police force conserving the existing order, but a leader and a guiding light leading from our culture, one of pretense, toward a true culture.

It would also seem to me unworthy of religion to assign it, with Freud, the task of producing consolation for the drive renunciations required by culture and of providing, as it were, muzzles or handcuffs for the asocial masses (pp. 74-75). The taming of animal

---

1 In biblical literature, "Mammon" refers to the personification of wealth and greed.

instincts (to the extent that they detract from human well-being and dignity) may be only the reverse side to the solution of a positive task: religion should free the highest intellectual and emotional forces; promote the greatest achievements in art and science; fill the lives of all persons, even the poorest, with a maximum of truth, beauty, and love; help to deal with life's real needs; and pave the way for new, more substantive and truer forms of social life, thus calling to life a higher, inwardly richer humanity, better corresponding to the true demands of human nature and ethics than does our much-praised un-culture, which Nietzsche already called a thin apple peel over a flaming chaos. One totally misjudges the essence of Christianity if one thinks it offers us heaven as a substitute for the world, abandoned as it is to its misery. "Thy kingdom come!" proclaims the Lord's Prayer, and imposes the obligation of contributing all our strengths for this earthly kingdom of God, just as the commandments of the Gospel are very much oriented to this world. "Leave there thy gift before the altar, and go thy way; first be reconciled to thy brother, and then come and offer thy gift," demands the Sermon on the Mount (Matthew 5: 24). It is not the fault of Jesus that Christianity has so often misunderstood this. Freud has given us the possibility of understanding why the intentions of the founder of the Christian religion, through an obsessional neurotic development, have often been distorted to a caricature.

There is no more genuine realism than Christianity. But one must not forget that reality comprises not only the tangible, that which can be perceived by our sense of smell and by other little windows of the soul, but also what is hidden behind those windows, at the base of the soul and behind the sources of sensory stimulation. What is required is a somewhat more deeply penetrating examination of the essence, a more deeply penetrating philosophy of value, in order to realize that the neglect of these higher realities lying beyond the tangible and solid only leads to a bad realism. We shall thus delay this problem for a moment.

II: Freud's Scientism

1) The Belief in a Science that Brings Humanity Happiness

Freud contrasts religious belief with belief in the power of science (he means empirical science only) to bring humanity happiness. In science, illusion has yielded to truth. Here, the question "What is science?" apparently causes him less concern than the parallel consideration "What is truth?" caused Pilate.[1] Freud is a positivist and for that we can thank God. Without his concentrated dedication to the empirical he would not have become the great pioneer that he is. With such a successful and pioneering genius, one can make allowances if at the moment when he attempts to smother religious illusion, he sets up science as the Messiah, without observing that this belief too is permeated with illusion.

Let us allow the master to speak first. Freud is far too careful in his thinking to commit himself to the vulgar, uncritical belief in the omnipotence of the natural sciences. He does not shrink back from the question as to whether "our conviction that we can learn something about external reality through the application of observations and rational thought in scientific work" has a sufficient basis (p. 96). He continues in truly philosophical style: "Nothing should hold us back from approving the turning of our observation to our own being, from approving the application of thought to criticism of thought itself. Here, numerous investigations open themselves to us whose results would certainly be decisive for constructing a 'world view'. We also suspect that such an effort will not be wasted and that it will at least provide partial justification for our suspicion" (p. 96). "But the capabilities of the author do not extend to such a comprehensive task; of necessity, he must restrict his work to pursuing just one of these illusions—that of religion" (p. 96).

Later, however, empirical science is approached with an optimism ascending to bold perspectives for the future. After the abandonment of religion, humanity will expand its power with the help of science and learn to bear the great necessities of fate with resignation (pp. 108, 112). Granted, Freud immediately admits that this hope too may be an illusory one (p. 110). But what does he mean? Should we perhaps simply exchange the religious illusion for the scientific one? Would the difference be that the one is sure, while the other, perhaps, deceives us? Would we, then, still remain in a condition of uncertainty, and would the last word belong to skepticism, which at least has no doubts about one thing: that doubt has its fully logical justification?

Yet Freud shows that it is not only religion that has the capacity to console. Chivalrously, he takes up the cudgels for the intellect: "The voice of the intellect is soft, but it does not rest until it is heard. In the end, after countless rejections, it does find a hearing. This is one of the

---

1 In the Gospel of John (18: 37), Jesus proclaims, "the reason I was born and came into this world is to testify to the truth. Everyone on the side of truth listens to me"—to which Pontius Pilate famously retorts, "What is truth?" (18: 38).

few points where one may be optimistic about the future of humankind, but in itself the point is not insignificant. To it still more hopes can be connected. The primacy of the intellect certainly lies far, far ahead, but probably not infinitely far. The intellect will presumably choose the same goals whose realization you expect from your god— a realization reduced to a human scale, of course, to the extent that external reality, *Anánke* [Necessity], permits; these goals are human love and the limitation of suffering. We may therefore tell ourselves that our mutual opposition is only temporary, not irreconcilable. We hope for the same things, but you are more impatient, more ambitious, and—why should I not say it?—more self-serving than I and those who think as I do. You want a state of bliss to begin immediately after death" (p. 111). "We believe it is possible for scientific work to learn something about the reality of the world; through such knowledge we will be able to increase our power, and in accord with it we will be able to arrange our life. If this belief is an illusion, then we are in the same position as you are, but through its numerous and significant successes science has given us proof that it is no illusion" (p. 112). "No, our science is no illusion. But an illusion it would be to think we can get elsewhere what science cannot give us" (p. 113).

With this marvelously logical statement Freud concludes his prophecy of the downfall of religion and the glorious autocracy of science. The god Logos casts the god of religion from his throne and rules in the realm of necessity, but as for the sense of this necessity we thus far know absolutely nothing.

2) Historical Examination

I shall make only brief note of the fact that this scientific ideal too, as Freud is certainly well aware, looks back on a venerable past. But the creator of psychoanalysis has perhaps effected a certain intensification of emphasis, to the extent that in his positivism he has isolated the concept of science more strictly from philosophy than has previously been the custom. His empiricism differs completely from that of the English empiricists, who seized the world of experience with the greatest precision but simultaneously, in the realm of action, left control to natural instinct and to the conscience—no longer to science—or even, like John Stuart Mill,[1] who was raised in a completely non-religious manner, still sought in the end to borrow from religion (Pfleiderer 606). *The Future of an Illusion* also diverges totally from the positivism,

---

1   John Stuart Mill (1806–73), British philosopher and economist.

for example, of Auguste Comte,[1] who shatters first the mythological, then the metaphysical level of thought, to sing the praises of the individual sciences, the only sources of salvation, but then, after all, wants to explain the world on the basis of human moral feeling and constructs a highly romantic and fantastic religion of humanity—truly amusing evidence that he cannot manage with his scientism, which squarely rests on a broad foundation. Also David Friedrich Strauss,[2] who with his mechanical materialism seems to approach Freud quite closely—only in the assumption of a "rational and kindly universe" does he make a philosophical detour in which the opponent of religious illusion could by no means accompany him—demands an ethics which in no way finds total sufficiency in scientific production. Of the philosophers known to me, the one who most closely approaches Freud is Paul Heinrich Dietrich, Baron d'Holbach, who already derived the development of the idea of God from the wish to make the forces of nature accessible, through humanization, to influence through prayer and sacrifice; who challenged the usefulness of religion, and therefore wanted to eliminate it, and proposed lasting happiness as the object of human striving (Falckenberg 208ff.). Freud clearly towers over that eighteenth-century materialist as an empiricist, and refuses to give in to that writer's banal metaphysics.

3) Freud's Optimism about Science

We now stand before the task of examining Freud's optimism about science. First, we must focus clearly on what he understands science to be and how far his optimism goes.

On the first point, we are given no more detailed information. Previously, the attitude of the greatest of the modern pioneers in the field of mental life was decidedly negative toward philosophy. Now, though, I discover to my satisfaction that Freud fundamentally grants justification to epistemology to the extent that it seeks to answer the question of whether we can gain knowledge of external reality. Indeed, as we have heard, Freud modestly abstains from the task; yet he still explains that science should limit itself to a presentation of the world

---

1 Auguste Comte (1798–1857), French philosopher responsible for the doctrine of positivism, and for helping establish the field of sociology.
2 David Friedrich Strauss (1808–74), German theologian and writer.

as it must appear to us, given the particulars of our organization (p. 113) and that "The problem of the nature of the world, approached without considering our mental apparatus engaged in perception, is an empty abstraction" (p. 113).

There, in fact, it seems that Freud is providing epistemological results without any preceding epistemology. He takes it for granted that we are dealing only with the world of appearances. But is it not the case that the essence of science everywhere consists in dissolving this world of appearances and confronting it with abstractions capable, for the first time, of giving us an understanding of that world of the senses? Optics, as noted above, dissolves colors into oscillations of colorless "bodies," which are again deprived by physics and chemistry of their "materiality" and are analyzed into energies, electrons, and other non-material, abstract constructs. Nowhere do we see or smell causality; we interpret it into appearances.

It should be clearly understood that the "mental apparatus engaged in perception," which Freud claims all investigation of the nature of the world must consider, is by no means a clear construct safeguarded from deception. Can I measure temperatures with the thermometer without being sure of the reliability of the instrument? May one ignore the entire history of modern philosophy, which begins with Descartes and his absolute skepticism; then goes on to Hume,[1] who destroys the illusion of guaranteed causality; to Kant, who overturns the illusion of empirical knowledge as a conception of the world in itself; and then to the most recent natural science that invokes a veritable twilight of false gods? Has no one yet realized what sort of scientific labyrinths one enters into when epistemological and metaphysical concepts are carelessly included under the deceptive label of natural science? Has it been forgotten how natural science deceived us with its concept of laws of nature, of the atom, of the ether, of Laplace's[2] world formula, etc.?

---

1 Scottish philosopher, economist, and historian David Hume (1711–76). In his *Treatise of Human Nature* (1739), Hume maintains that we have no direct (perceptual) access to a "necessary connection" between a cause and its effect. Our understanding of causality is thus rather an understanding of contiguity and succession, enforced by our habitual association of conjoined events.

2 French astronomer and mathematician Pierre-Simon Laplace (1749–1827). Building upon the prior efforts of Swedish scientist Emanuel Swedenborg (1688–1772), Laplace helped develop the nebular hypothesis for explaining the formation of solar systems.

Natural science without metaphysics does not exist, has never existed, and will never exist. I myself went through the school of empirical criticism and, for a few semesters, sought "pure experience" in the sense of a knowledge of reality that would be totally free of all subjective ingredients. A vain endeavor! The world is accessible to us only through our mental organization and indeed not only through the gates of the senses, which of course still yield no knowledge. Our categories of thought, whether understood in Kant's way or otherwise, are always involved. Therefore, we must develop a critical theory of knowledge. Further, we require concepts such as cause and effect, although, as for their origins, they were invented as anthropomorphisms; we require atoms and molecules, etc. Whoever avoids abstractions must leave science alone. Even measuring and weighing involves abstractions: numerical concepts of course, like all concepts, are abstract. Philosophy, which begins immediately where experience leaves off, extends into the empirical sciences, and whoever does not seriously grapple with philosophical problems will be working in the muddled manner of an amateur.

Furthermore, how can one deal with the religious problem while disregarding basic epistemological questions? Is it not simply a negative dogmatism to declare, grasping a dictum out of thin air, that a world-will and a world-meaning do not exist?

If one believes that philosophy is an eccentricity of minds far from life and reality, it should be pointed out that the history of philosophy nevertheless exhibits a whole series of brilliant names—those of men who have made immense achievements in physics, mathematics, astronomy, etc. If today even a scientist with the reputation of a Hans Driesch, who gained fame through twenty years of work in natural science, goes over to philosophy, and if psychiatrists are choosing that same path, this should show that philosophy deals not with worthless and capricious whims, but with a reality whose existence cannot simply be brushed aside. In my opinion, this world of intellectual order, which can be deduced from the world of appearances, stands more solidly before us than the undeniably deceptive world of the senses. One can make things easy for oneself and adopt agnosticism. But neither is this declaration of intellectual bankruptcy made easy for one.

Thus, through Freud's non-technical concept of science, I do not know how far knowledge reaches, what degree of reliability it can acquire, and what opportunities are granted it. How should I know, then, whether or not there is a consciously functioning primary cause and an ordering, and thus thinking, world-will? How can I know if the extension of power through knowledge signifies an increase in happiness for humanity?

We can now approach Freud's prognosis for science. One cannot say that he gives us a rosy-fingered dawn. Freud is a much too serious and honest man to make promises he is not convinced he can keep. With the help of science, man will extend his power—how far, we are not told—and learn to bear the great necessities of fate with resignation. This is everything, absolutely everything. But here, hasn't Freud already said too much? Is it not possible that culture will soon collapse? Hasn't the demise of the Western world been prophesied by a man whose great knowledge is universally recognized? Is it unthinkable that culture guided only by science will succumb to wild passions after the World War has revealed to us the barbarism lurking in the depths of the peoples of the world? Is it not the case that Eduard von Hartmann[1] and many others assure us that the growth of science will only increase our misery? Has it been so surely decided that progress in the sciences has thus far increased the total sum of human joy in life and, if this has thus far been the case, is it certain that it will always be so? Is it certain that we feel happier than one hundred years ago? Is this at least the case with scholars? Do workers, thanks to the blessings of science, feel more satisfied than a few generations ago? Or the craftsmen? Or the farmers? What will become of the most wonderful achievements of technology if they are forced into the service of the human hunger for money, of human cruelty, of the inhuman craving for pleasure?

Freud's prognosis for science rests on a mere analogical conclusion which I do not consider certain. His reasoning is: since scientific progress has thus far brought advantages to humanity, this will also be so in the future. Or better expressed, in the background lies a hidden belief in science, whose basis Nietzsche spied with his eagle eye and which he characterized in the words: "One will have understood ... that there is still a metaphysical belief on which our belief in science rests—and that we perceptive ones of today, we godless ones and anti-metaphysicians, also still take our fire from the flame kindled by a belief thousands of years old, that Christian belief that was also Plato's belief, the belief that God is the truth, that the truth is divine. ... But what is to be done if this in fact becomes more and more unbelievable ...?" (Nietzsche: [*The Joyful Wisdom*,] Book V, Section 344).

Do we know through the pronouncement of an oracle that knowledge will contribute to an increase in human happiness, even if evil

---

1 Pessimistic German philosopher Karl Robert Eduard von Hartmann
   (1842–1906). In *Philosophy of the Unconscious* (1869), Hartmann argues that
   happiness is unattainable.

passions are dominant? Byron[1] laments that: "The tree of Knowledge is not that of Life!" [*Manfred*, I, 1]. Can exact knowledge contradict him? And if we glow with a Faustian[2] passion for knowledge, can natural science and medicine (philosophy and theology are excluded) satisfy us today or will the heart of a contemporary Faust nearly be consumed?

Freud predicts that humankind will learn to bear the great necessities of fate with resignation. Indeed, many have always been able to do so without science, and if I bow before the greatness of mind of the non-religious individual who finds this submission within himself, who will tell me that and why submission specifically has to be the last word? Some people have blown out their brains in desperation, though standing on the proud parapets of science. Others have become obsessed with a wild hatred of life and have tried to anesthetize themselves through excesses; others have turned within, with or without a kindly invitation, toward mysticism hostile to the world, etc.

Could it not be that behind Freud's belief in the ultimate victory of the intellect there lies a hidden wish, and that his prophecy of the end of an illusion includes the parade of a new, specifically scientific illusion? That the parade, for Freud, will not proceed with sprightly music and with flags waving, but only in a very muted way and with hesitant steps, reflects his modesty. But I cannot join in, simply because the reality principle admonishes me and stands in my way.

4) Freud's Belief in the Sufficiency of Science

"An illusion it would be to think we can get elsewhere what science cannot give us" (p. 113). These words form the culmination of Freud's creed. The context shows that what he has in mind is knowledge of the world. The arrangement of the whole book, however, betrays that here, as earlier (p. 109), he is also thinking of the complete replacement of what religion offered its adherents.

As joyfully and enthusiastically as I follow Freud on the wonderful paths of his empirical science, here it is impossible for me to keep pace with him. Here Freud's brilliant intellect loses its way in an intellectuality that, intoxicated by its successes, forgets its limits.

---

1 George Gordon Byron, or Lord Byron (1788–1824), celebrated English Romantic poet.
2 From the European legend of Faust, a man who sells his soul for knowledge. A "Faustian passion" is an insatiable and possibly diabolical one.

We human beings are not only thinking devices; we are living, feeling beings with wants and desires. We need goods and values, we must have something that satisfies our emotion, that inspires our wants and desires. Thought too must offer us values, logical ones—but others too. Do we not often deal in analysis with people who think clearly, but in their thinking are nearly starved and desperate? Do we not bear within ourselves a conscience that judges or rewards us? Hasn't the power of the feeling of guilt been demonstrated specifically through psychoanalysis? Doesn't Freud show more clearly than anyone else in the world the decisive importance of valuation, and of the feelings, affects, and drives?

As is well known, the intellect does not know how to perform valuations. The sharpest rational mind cannot indicate whether a symphony by Gustav Mahler[1] or a painting by Ferdinand Hodler[2] is beautiful. The cleverest person can, without internal contradiction, approve of a mean betrayal and treat with scorn a hero's death in the service of truth. A heartless scoundrel may possess a clear-sighted intelligence, and a person of low intelligence may become outraged at deceit. Science lacks the ability to assess aesthetic and ethical quantities. Indeed, one feels one is hearing echoes of Aristotle's definition of the brain as a cooling apparatus when thought is characterized or praised—not only by Spinoza[3]—as a function that dampens the emotions.

It is clear that somewhere in his scientific life-structure Freud had to make a place for the emotional values of which his own life evinces such a wonderful richness. But I do not find that place in his concept of science.

Nor do I see where he allows the temple of art to stand. Could it really be that art is only a sign of being unanalyzed, of weakness? Could science compensate for the loss of Ludwig van Beethoven's[4] symphonies or Max Reger's[5] sonatas? And the glorious works of Egyptian, Hellenic, and Christian art—are we to sacrifice them for scientific doctrines and inventions? The glorious cathedrals which con-

---

1   Austrian late-Romantic composer Gustav Mahler (1860–1911).
2   Swiss painter Ferdinand Hodler (1853–1918).
3   Dutch rationalist philosopher Baruch de Spinoza (1632–77). In his *magnum opus, Ethics* (1677), Spinoza maintained that it is only through recognizing the cause of our "passions" that we may find relief from their bondage.
4   Ludwig van Beethoven (1770–1827), acclaimed German composer and pianist.
5   Johann Baptist Joseph Maximilian Reger (1873–1916), German composer, conductor, pianist, and teacher.

stitute the pride and delight of the human race; the paintings, inspired by Christian feeling, of a Fra Angelico [1395–1455], Leonardo da Vinci [1452–1519], Albrecht Dürer [1471–1528], Hans Holbein [1497–1543], up to Eduard Gebhardt [1838–1925], Hans Thoma [1839–1924], Wilhelm Steinhausen [1846–1924]; the *Pietà* of Michelangelo [1475–1564], the *Thief* or the *Prodigal Son* of a Constantin Meunier [1831–1905], etc.—all of this should disappear? The source of Christian poetic art, as it sends out its silver waves in Lessing's [1729–81] *Nathan the Wise*, Goethe's [1749–1832] *Faust*, Dostoevsky's [1821–81] *Idiot,* Tolstoy's [1828–1910] *Resurrection*, etc. would have to dry up; instead of green pastures, there would remain only the heath of theory on which the ghosts of error flutter about threateningly? For the benefit of the skeptic, not even able to sigh with [Goethe's] Faust—"Oh, happy those who can still hope to emerge from this sea of error!"—one would stubbornly hold aloft the glorious future of science in coming millennia?

For me, art is still the herald, blessed with prophetic vision, of profound secrets—the revealer of precious treasures that escape and will continue to escape the scholar's spectacles; a wondrous source of nourishment for hungry souls; a message of peace from the realm of ideals which no thinker's fist can ever tear down because they belong to true reality more securely than do tangible things and other illusions of the senses. To work this out intellectually would require that I present long discussions in which the intellect would have only the role of a commentator serving and honoring creative genius. Oh, how I would dread a scholars' state emptied of art!

And even less can inventive science replace for us the realm of moral values and forces. Science must incorporate itself into the moral setting of goals if it is not to sink to the level of a dubious undertaking. Who would deny that for Freud science is part of an ethical plan and helps to carry it out? But if I have observed correctly, no place in his little book is accorded to this all-encompassing observation. We no longer stand on the Socratic foundation of the teaching that knowledge itself is already power. The alcoholic who knows he will be destroyed by his vice does not therefore have the strength to break with it. Nor, as we know today, does analytic insight into the dynamics of the unconscious and into its deepest roots in itself help to free one from its domination; Freud teaches us that the tightly packed drives should also be released through transference.

Has it really been determined that with increasing scientific activity the attitudes of human beings will also be purified? Hasn't Alexander von Öttingen[1] [*Morality in Its Significance for a Christian Social Ethics*] demonstrated that the highly educated include proportionally more criminals than do those of average intelligence? Do we not sometimes encounter an incredible meanness of spirit among academics? When public elementary education was established nearly a century ago, a rapid decline in criminality was expected. And what do we see today?

Where do we find the certainty that in the future the growth in science and technology will miraculously produce a rise in moral forces? In combating alcoholism, I have experienced clearly enough how little can be achieved with scientific arguments. And even if repressions were overcome, it would not be possible to obtain with the guide-rope of science that morality that gives life dignity and true inner health.

Here I have stated why I do not believe in the replacement of religion through science. Religion is the sun that has pushed forth the most glorious blossoming of art and the richest harvest of moral feeling. All truly great and powerful art is prayer and offering before the throne of God. God, for the philosopher of religion the real foundation of ideals, is for the pious man the ideal foundation of his real activity; the Pentecostal Spirit descending to the earth in tongues of fire; the Revelator, whose "Let there be light!" also illumines the darkness of human spirits with blinding clarity. Whoever could destroy religion would saw through the taproot of great art, which reveals the deepest meaning and the highest forces of life.

And in just the same way we see in religion a supporting pillar of morality. We do not overlook the fact that devout belief took up moral insight within itself and continues to do so, as is taught, for example, by the history of Christianity. Nor do we forget that only as religion were the boldest and most glorious ethical advances able to begin. For the great advances in ethics, not scientists but the founders of religion are to be thanked. Kant too, who with his elimination of love signifies a disturbing relapse with respect to the ethics of Jesus, is basically just the learned spokesman of Protestantism that has turned aside and become puritanical.

It has not even been established that ethics itself is undergoing a linear development. I cannot agree with Freud's assertion that what is

---

1   Alexander von Öttingen (1827–1905), German Lutheran minister and statistician. Öttingen came from a family of academics, including two brothers who were professors.

moral is always obvious. Indeed, as is well known, one cannot merely depend on the conscience, and in the science of morals the most diverse doctrines gesture excitedly in mutual opposition. Simple utilitarian morality[1] seems an abomination to the Kantian; eudaemonism,[2] with its shimmering uncertainties, irritates the Nietzschean, who wants and canonizes the will to power as the standard of good and evil, etc. In individual ethical problems we see a chaos of contradictory opinions, e.g., on the moral evaluation of war, the excessive accumulation of capital, free love, abortion, etc. Positivistic thinking, and science as Freud seems to conceive it, certainly cannot bring us much further, though as I have argued elsewhere it can give us highly valuable building blocks for ethics, which will always remain a philosophical discipline; crucially, beside providing these resources for sociology, it can provide them for Freud's psychoanalysis. I recently heard the Viennese jurist Hans Kelsen [1881–1973] expatiate, in a public discussion, on how positivism is not even able to create legislation (Kelsen himself is a positivist); how could it then call an ethical system into being?

Empirical science thus fails us in constructing ethical concepts. And more importantly: the bringing about of moral life has never been accomplished through dry theories and clever concepts. It would be pedantic dogmatism of the worst kind not to recognize this. Religion, with its in part awe-inspiring and in part charming symbols; with its poetic glory and its emotionally moving interpretations of reality; with its fascinating personalities who attract us through deeds and sufferings that win our hearts, who through their faults and weaknesses in part warn us, yet in part restore courage to the fallen individual to strive for his ideals with new strength; religion with its immense metaphysical background and future perspectives; with its divine sanctioning of the moral commandment and with its message of salvation—a message anticipating some of the most significant accomplishments of psychoanalysis; with its demands that overcome all the resistance of the empirical world through the certainty of a higher duty and alliance—in short, this whole ideal world (which is certain that it is only the expression of a higher, highest reality and which can incorporate all the gifts of science with ease, adding to them a unique abun-

---

1 Utilitarianism is most associated with Jeremy Bentham (1748–1832) and John Stuart Mill (1806–73). The doctrine claims that ethical action can be guided by its consequences, so that one aims to maximize good results over bad.

2 *Eudaimonia* is Greek for "complete, perfect happiness." Aristotle thought that such happiness was the highest good and turned his ethics and politics into a practical exploration of its meaning and realization.

dance of other treasures, life-goods, and life-strengths) is an educator, whom science with its theories would certainly be unable to replace. But, if the belief were untrue, we would have to combat it despite its achievements. It is better to go to hell with the truth than to go to heaven at the price of lies!

Freud, given his tolerant attitude, praised religion as a safeguard against neurosis (p. 104). In a previous publication he indicated that since the weakening of religions, the neuroses have increased extraordinarily (1925[1]). Has chivalry perhaps allowed Freud to go too far? I also see in the crowds of those with concentrated devotion a horde of hysterics and obsessional neurotics; disregarding the fact that all orthodoxies are to be viewed as collective obsessional neuroses, we find among very devout Christians a great number of psychoneurotics. Indeed, the extent to which piety has repressive effects depends very much on how it is structured. But one cannot fail to recognize that the free air of the true Gospel provides indispensible protection against the danger of neurosis.

But in saying this, the breadth of religion has not been stated exhaustively in any sense. Religion cannot be dissolved into morality, defense against neurosis, and enthusiasm for art. So much else still belongs there. Religion is concerned with the question of the meaning and value of life; with the unifying drive of reason toward a universal world view that encompasses being and obligation; with the longing for home and peace; with the drive toward *unio mystica*[2] with the absolute; with the spiritual fetters of guilt and with freedom's thirst for grace; with the need for a love that is removed from the intolerable insecurity of earthly affairs; with countless other concerns, which, unsettled, choke the soul and fill it with anxiety, but through religious compensation lift up human life to radiant mountain peaks with indescribably delightful views into the distance, strengthen the heart, and through the imposition of very heavy moral obligations in the spirit of love, enhance the value of existence. The non-religious person cannot share in this feeling, just as little as the unmusical person can sense the content of a composition by Brahms.[3] Indeed, religion is far less aristocratic than art and higher science. It is itself a stream in which lambs swim and elephants can drown. Here, though, the New Testament citation applies: "For all men have not faith" (2 Thessalonians 3: 2).

---

1 I.e., "The Future Prospects of Psycho-Analytic Therapy."
2 Latin: mystical union.
3 Johannes Brahms (1833–97), highly popular German composer often referred to—alongside Johann Sebastian Bach (1685–1750) and Ludwig van Beethoven—as one of the "Three Bs" of classical music.

But under belief we understand not only a conception, but rather the emotionally moving experience of a person's entire inner being.

How poor science seems to us in comparison with this abundance, of which we have only been able to suggest a small portion, given the lack of space for further discussion and because the inexpressible cannot at all be conveyed in words! It does not surprise me at all that some of the most important researchers have seen their activities as service to God, and that some of the greatest artists and poets have humbly laid their laurel wreaths before His altar.

Conclusion

How should we imagine the future of the illusion Freud objects to? I agree that it must fall and disappear if it is only an illusion. But Freud, of course, did not want to pose the question of truth at all; he expressly emphasizes that illusions can be true (p. 93).

I am therefore of the opinion that realistic thinking must advance absolutely as far as permitted by the nature of reality. How this could occur, I have sketched in the brief comments of my treatise "Weltanschauung und Psychoanalyse" [Worldview and Psychoanalysis] (in 1920: 289ff., 364ff.[1]). I suggested how a metaphysics could result from empirical science as a necessary logical completion, but also—and this is even more important for religion—how, arising from moral destiny, conclusions about the meaning and will of the world are possible and in fact necessary.

A clarified religion can result only from the harmonious integration of belief and knowledge and from the exhaustive mingling of wishful and realistic thinking, provided the content of the real thinking does not undergo any falsification of facts or relations through the wishful thinking.

But in this synthesis, doesn't the actual content of religion run into danger? Freud suspects this (p. 95), but I cannot share his assumption. I feel that the substance of Christianity is in no way attacked if we deny miracles in the sense of God's intervention in the course of nature; in any case, it is a fact the millions of Christians have done so for centuries and yet saw in their religion their most sacred object. The god of philosophically processed modern theology, who is free from crude anthropomorphisms, the world-will aiming for the realization of love in the highest moral sense, is loftier than the God who strolls in the evening coolness and personally closes the door of the ark, and

---

1 I.e., *Some Applications of Psycho-Analysis*.

loftier also than the God who uses the earth as his footstool; the allegorical language of piety must entail no relapse into inferior wishful thinking. Moral precepts—which we no longer simply allow sacred texts to dictate to us, but, as autonomous children of God, derive from the essence of humankind and the human community, reverently examining the ethical knowledge of early times and reserving the right to object or reject—are no less sacred to us than the statutes of any religious documents. The Bible has become not smaller for us, but more glorious, now that we no longer suspect it of being a paper pope and an infallible oracle, or the legal basis for the trials of heretics, but on the strength of evangelical freedom subject it to the most unsparing criticism. We long ago drove back reward and punishment as dangerous educational measures, though we do not deny the fact that in the moral commandment there also lies a hygienic principle which provides information about the dangers threatening individual and social health, and which thus points to a system of law that decides on happiness and suffering and is definitive in the organization of life. For us, the moral world order is not a current state of affairs, but a norm in the sense noted above, a structure and regularity whose tendency we can recognize through observation of the reality of life; we attempt to express this tendency in moral precepts which we ethically formulate, specifically as an expression of the highest cosmic evolutionary striving, and which, in consequence of a relation to the Creator's will, we recognize as willed by God and sacred. Thus, morality is by no means based on a heteronomous authority, but on the autonomy of the individual and of society—yet not on their casual whim, but on their mode of being, which, in turn, refers back to the last conceivable, absolute legal authority.

Can we advise against this expansion of religion? Will the advance of the exact sciences make it superfluous? The contemporary march to the right, in the direction of orthodoxies, should not be decisive for our judgment. But, from the essence of humanity and from the narrow limits of the intellect, to Freud's prophecy of the future of an illusion I must oppose the no longer prophetic, but psychologically justified assertion of the illusion of such a future.

It is highly gratifying to me that Freud basically strives toward the same goal I do—he with his inspired researcher's gaze, I with my modest means. He is driven forward by his god Logos, whom he understands as the intellect—"presumably" [p. 139] toward the goal of human love and a decrease in suffering (p. 139). I am driven forward by my god Logos, whom I understand—admittedly based on the first chapter of the Gospel according to John—as divine wisdom and love, toward the same goals, beside which I would like to place the creation of positive interior and exterior values, more forcefully than Freud's statement reminiscent of Schopenhauer. It is not the declaration of religious faith that is the true criterion of a Christian. In John 13: 35 another criterion is given: "By this shall all men know that ye are my disciples, if ye have love one to another." At the risk of being ridiculed by loose tongues, I dare again to assert that Freud, in light of these words, with his view of life and his life's work, surpasses many a card-carrying church-Christian who considers him a heathen, as he also considers himself.

And thus *The Future of an Illusion* and "The Illusion of a Future" unite in a strong belief whose credo is:

"The truth shall make you free!" [John 8: 32].

Appendix B: Other Works by Freud and Pfister on Religion

[*The Future of an Illusion* was not Freud's first foray into the vexed subject of religion. In *The Psychopathology of Everyday Life* (1904), Freud argued that religion is an outward projection of inner processes, of psychology. But it was only in "Obsessive Actions and Religious Practices" (1907) that he engaged in sustained argument about the subject. In this work, abridged in what follows, Freud more explicitly connects religious belief with psychopathology—in particular "obsessional neurosis"—and telegraphs views immortalized in the *Future*. In particular Freud argues that neuroses are like "private religions," namely, actions defined by their ceremonies and rituals. "Obsessional neurosis presents a distorted image," as Freud puts it, "half comic and half tragic, as a private religion." According to Freud, psychoanalysis can penetrate to the hidden meanings of religion just as readily as it penetrates to the hidden meanings of neuroses. In both cases his goal is the "universal" significance that lies behind appearances.

Freud's next major statement on religion appeared in *Totem and Taboo* (1913), a work written under the influence of Carl Jung's defection from the psychoanalytic cause. In it Freud, an intrepid Sherlock Holmes, reveals the fantastical cause of civilization in our repressed history: the guilt that developed in the wake of the murder of the "primal father" by his sons. "The son-religion," Freud argues, "replaces the father-religion." This story of parricide and inherited conscience influenced the *Future* and, years later, *Moses and Monotheism* (1939). *Totem and Taboo* also lays out three grand phases of historical development—from animism to religion and then science—that capture Freud's faith in the ascendance of science.

Later in 1913 Freud wrote "Scientific Interest in Psychoanalysis" for the Italian periodical *Scientia*. The article contains a comprehensive account of psychoanalysis up to that point. From it I have selected his discussion on culture, which becomes increasingly important in the *Future* of 1927 and in *Civilization and Its Discontents* in 1930. In "Scientific Interest" Freud repeats his claims about the three phases of human history mentioned in *Totem* and extends the discussion in a direction that is of critical importance for understanding the "late works": his interest in "reality" and the "external world." His contention is that civilization is "therapeutic" insofar as it works to "relieve people of the tensions produced in them by [psychological] needs." In this respect religion, like philosophy, is useful as a compensatory belief system that will eventually be supplanted by the scientific understanding of the real world and its relation to human psychology.

Civilization and Its Discontents is well known for its argument that individual happiness is negotiated, and therefore compromised, by its proximity to *Kultur*—that is, by its proximity to society, to the masses, to other people. Or, once again, psychology must contend with the group when it is driven by biological self-interests that are given at birth. Freud's dark pessimism about the possibility of happiness culminates with his view, based on *Beyond the Pleasure Principle* of 1920, that progress, love, and pleasure are radically undercut by an essential death-drive, i.e., by a drive for non-existence. In the section included here, Freud clarifies his views from the *Future* and returns to some of the main themes of the late period: the pleasure and reality principles, the development of a sense of reality, the role of the external world, the limits of happiness, and the role of culture for psychology. Toward the end he admits (more explicitly than he does in "Scientific Interest") that religion has its uses: "by drawing them into a mass-delusion, religion succeeds in sparing many people an individual neurosis."

Moses and Monotheism is one of Freud's last works, demonstrating both that he was still committed to thinking psychoanalytically about religion at the end of his life and that this thinking was still determined by his belief in phylogenesis: the belief that the present is the accumulation and recapitulation of history at the level of individual and collective human biology. Clearly Freud's penchant for unchecked speculation, as in *Totem and Taboo*, shows no sign of abating in his late years. Just the opposite: Freud felt free to speculate about the deep (and frankly unknowable) prehistory of humankind and to couch those views in the "scientific" jargon of psychoanalysis. A generous selection from *Moses* is included here, not only to help readers understand these trends in psychoanalysis, but also because the work has sparked renewed interest from scholars since the early 1990s. Freud's fundamental idea is lifted from *Totem*: the historical Moses was actually an Egyptian leader killed by his followers who, tamed (or civilized) by a growing sense of guilt, founded a new monotheistic religion. That religion of Moses is Judaism, and its defining characteristics are derived from this original scene of parricide and guilt.

The significance of *The Future of an Illusion*, one of Freud's most well-read works, can be measured against these far-reaching and sometimes far-fetched speculations that form an important part of the corpus of Freud's late "cultural" period. Readers are encouraged to consult the full versions of these selections, most especially *Beyond the Pleasure Principle* and *Civilization and Its Discontents*. But they are also urged to read Oskar Pfister's critical response to the *Future*, included here as Appendix A. English readers have little access to Pfister's work, so I have also included (in consultation with Gregory C. Richter) a very short excerpt from Pfister's *On the Psychology of Philosophical Thought* (1923). In it Pfister foreshadows his rejection of any philosophy of "pure experience," which in "The Illusion of a Future" includes Freud's invocation of experience, the external world, and reality as presented in the *Future*.

All selections included in Appendix B have been translated from the German by Gregory C. Richter.]

1. Sigmund Freud, "Obsessive Actions and Religious Practices" (1907)[1]

I am certainly not the first to have noticed the similarity between the so-called obsessive actions observed in nervous disorders and the performances through which believers demonstrate their piety. The term *ceremonial*, with which some of these obsessive actions have been designated, gives me support in this. But this similarity strikes me as more than superficial: based on insight into the origin of the neurotic ceremonial one may presume to draw analogous conclusions about the mental processes of religious life.

People who carry out obsessive actions or ceremonials, as well as those who suffer from obsessive thinking, obsessive ideas, obsessive impulses, etc., belong to a particular clinical group suffering from a disorder commonly referred to as "obsessional neurosis" (Löwenfeld). But one should not seek to infer the characteristic features of this illness from its name, for strictly speaking, other types of pathological mental phenomena have equal claim to a so-called "obsessional nature." In place of a definition, we are currently seeking only detailed knowledge of these conditions, for we have not yet succeeded in identifying the criterion of the obsessional neuroses, which probably lies very deep, but whose presence seems to be felt everywhere in the expressions of those neuroses.

The neurotic ceremonial consists of small performances, additions, restrictions, or arrangements which, in certain actions of daily life, are always carried out in the same way, or vary according to a regular pattern. These activities give one the impression of mere "formalities"; they strike us as completely meaningless. Nor do they appear otherwise to those suffering from this illness, and yet such persons are inca-

---

1 "Zwangshandlungen und Religionsübungen," *Zeitschrift für Religionspsychologie* 1.1 (1907): 4–12.

pable of refraining from these practices, for any deviation from the ceremonial is punished by intolerable anxiety which immediately requires the completion of whatever has been omitted. Just as trivial as the ceremonial actions themselves are the occasions and activities that are elaborated, complicated, and in any case slowed down by the ceremonial—for instance, dressing and undressing, going to bed, or satisfying bodily needs. One can describe the practice of a ceremonial by replacing it, as it were, with a series of unwritten laws. In the bed-ceremonial, for instance, the chair must stand in a certain position before the bed, and the clothes must lie on the chair folded in a certain order; the blanket must be tucked in at the foot of the bed, and the sheet must be smoothed flat; the pillows must be arranged to lie in such and such a manner, and the body itself must lie in a precisely determined position. Only then may one fall asleep. Thus, in minor cases, the ceremonial merely resembles the exaggeration of a customary and justified orderliness. But the special conscientiousness in carrying out the details and the anxiety associated with an omission characterize the ceremonial as a "sacred act." Usually disturbances of such an act are poorly tolerated, and the presence of other persons during its execution is almost ruled out.

Any activities at all can become obsessive actions in a broader sense if they are elaborated by small additions or made rhythmic by pauses and repetitions. A sharp distinction between "ceremonials" and "obsessive actions" would not be expected. Usually obsessive actions have derived from ceremonials. Beyond these two, prohibitions and hindrances (abulias) form the content of the illness; actually, of course, they only continue the work of the obsessive actions, given that some things are not permitted at all to those suffering from the illness, while other things are permitted only if a prescribed ceremonial is observed.

It is remarkable that compulsion and prohibitions (being required to do something, and not being permitted to do something else) initially apply only to individuals' solitary activities and leave their social behavior unimpaired for a long period. For many years, then, those suffering from this illness can treat it as a private affair and conceal it. Indeed, many more people suffer from such forms of obsessional neurosis than are known to physicians. Furthermore, for many such individuals, concealment is made easier by the fact that they are completely capable of fulfilling their social duties for part of the day—after devoting several hours to their secret doings, secluded à la Mélusine.[1]

---

1 A legendary water-nymph.

It is easy to see where the similarity between the neurotic ceremonial and the sacred acts of religious ritual is to be found: in the guilty conscience associated with omission, in the complete isolation from all other activities (prohibition of disturbance), and in the conscientiousness of execution in every detail. But the differences are equally evident, and some so glaring that they render the comparison sacrilegious: the greater individual variability of the [neurotic] ceremonial acts versus the stereotypical nature of ritual (prayer, prostration, etc.), the private character of these acts versus the public and communal nature of religious practice, and especially the single fact that the minute details of the religious ceremonial are meaningful and conceived as symbolic, while those of the neurotic seem foolish and meaningless. Here, obsessional neurosis presents a distorted image, half comic and half tragic, as a private religion. But precisely this most trenchant difference between the neurotic and the religious ceremonial is eliminated when, with the help of the psychoanalytic investigative technique, one penetrates to an understanding of obsessive actions (Freud 1906).[1] In such an investigation the appearance that obsessive actions are foolish and meaningless is completely eliminated and the reason for such an appearance is revealed. It is found that the obsessive actions are fully meaningful in every detail, that they serve important interests of the personality, and that they give expression to still current experiences and to thoughts charged with affect. They do this in two ways—either as direct or as symbolic representations—and should thus be interpreted either historically or symbolically.

Here, I must present a few examples intended to clarify this point. Those familiar with the results of psychoanalytic investigation into the psychoneuroses will not be surprised to hear that what is represented in obsessive actions or in the ceremonial derives from the most intimate, usually sexual, experience of those affected.

(a) A young woman I observed was under the compulsion to rinse her wash basin several times after washing. The meaning of this ceremonial action lay in the proverbial saying: "One must not throw out dirty water before one has clean." This action was intended to admonish her beloved sister and to restrain her from divorcing her disappointing husband until she had established a relationship with a better man.

(b) A woman living apart from her husband was subject to a compulsion, whenever she ate, to leave the best untouched, e.g., to eat only the edges of a roast. This renunciation was clarified by the date of its

---

1 I.e., *Early Psychoanalytic Publications*.

origin. It appeared on the day after she had refused her husband further marital relations, i.e., had renounced the best.

(c) The same patient could actually sit only on one particular chair and could rise from it only with difficulty. For her, in connection with certain details of her married life, the chair symbolized her husband, to whom she remained faithful. To explain her compulsion, she declared: "It is so hard to part from anything (husband, chair) after getting settled."

(d) During a certain period of time she would repeat an especially noticeable and senseless obsessive action. She would go quickly from her room into another, in the middle of which was a table; she would straighten out the tablecloth in a certain way and ring for the maid, who would have to come up to the table, but whom she would then dismiss on some minor errand. In her efforts to explain this compulsion, it occurred to her that on one part of the tablecloth under discussion there was a discolored stain, and that she always laid out the cloth in such a way that the stain would be very noticeable to the maid. Indeed, all of this was a reproduction of an experience during her married life which had subsequently given her thoughts a problem to solve. On the wedding night her husband had experienced a not uncommon misfortune: he found himself impotent, and "came quickly many times in the course of the night from his room" into hers to repeat his efforts to succeed. In the morning he said he would be ashamed in the presence of the hotel maid who was to make the beds, and he therefore took a bottle of red ink and poured the contents over the sheet—but so clumsily that the red stain was produced in a place very unsuitable for his purpose. Thus, with her obsessive action, she was enacting the wedding night. "Bed and board" together make up marriage.

(e) She also acquired the compulsion to record the serial number of every banknote before spending it, and this too required a historical explanation. During the period when she still intended to leave her husband if she could find another more trustworthy man, she permitted herself the polite attentions of a man at a health resort, yet remained in doubt about the seriousness of his intentions. One day, lacking small change, she asked him to change a five Krone coin for her. He did so, placed the large coin in his pocket, and declared gallantly his intention never to part with it since it had passed through her hands. At subsequent meetings she was often tempted to ask him to show her the five Krone coin, as if to discover whether she could believe in his attentions. But she refrained—with the reasonable justification that coins of equal value cannot be distinguished one from another. Thus her doubt remained unresolved, but left her with the compulsion to record the serial number of every banknote, by which each note is distinguished from all others of equal value.

These few examples, selected from my wide experience, are intended merely to clarify the claim that everything in obsessive actions is meaningful and interpretable. The same holds for the actual ceremonial, except that the proof would require a more extensive discussion. In no way do I fail to recognize how far our explanations of obsessive actions seem to take us from the religious sphere of thought.

It is one of the conditions of the illness that the person obeying the compulsion must carry it out without knowing its meaning—or at least without knowing its main meaning. It is only through the efforts of psychoanalytic therapy that such persons become conscious of the meaning of the obsessive action and of the motives driving them to it. We shall express this significant fact by saying that the obsessive action serves for the expression of *unconscious* motives and ideas. Here, another distinction from religious practice seems to arise; but one must recall that the pious individual, too, normally performs the religious ceremonial without asking its meaning, though priests and researchers may be familiar with the mostly symbolic meaning of the ritual. Yet the motives impelling believers to religious practice are unknown to any of them, and are represented in their consciousness by motives advanced in place of the actual ones.

The analysis of obsessive actions has already enabled us to gain some insight into their causes and into the chain of motives decisive for them. One may say that those who suffer from compulsions and prohibitions behave as if they were dominated by a *sense of guilt*, of which they nevertheless know nothing—thus by an unconscious sense of guilt [*unbewussten Schuldbewusstsein*], as it must be expressed, disregarding the contradiction in terms. This sense of guilt has its source in certain early mental processes, but is constantly rekindled by the *temptation* renewed with each current provocation. It furthermore produces a constantly lurking *expectant anxiety*, an expectation of disaster—a feeling connected, by the concept of punishment, to the inner perception of the temptation. In the early stages of the formation of the ceremonial, those suffering from the disorder are still conscious that they must do this or that lest misfortune ensue, and their consciousness is still informed of the nature of the misfortune to be expected. The always demonstrable connection between the occasion provoking the expectant anxiety, and the content it threatens, is already hidden from them. Thus the ceremonial begins as an *act of defense* or *insurance*—as a *protective measure*.

To the sense of guilt of obsessional neurotics correspond the avowals of the pious that they know that in their hearts they are miserable sinners; the pious practices (prayers, invocations, etc.) with which they commence every daily activity and especially every unusual undertaking seem to have the value of defensive and protective measures.

One gains a deeper insight into the mechanism of obsessional neurosis if one considers the primary fact underlying it: this is in all cases the *repression of a drive impulse* (a component of the sex drive) that was contained in the person's constitution and was allowed to express itself for a time in childhood, but was later repressed. A special *conscientiousness* opposed to the aims of the drive is created when that drive is repressed, but this mental reaction formation feels insecure and constantly threatened by the drive lurking in the unconscious. The influence of the repressed drive is felt as temptation, and it is during the process of repression itself that the anxiety arises which, as expectant anxiety, gains control of the future. The process of repression leading to obsessional neurosis must be characterized as one that achieves only incomplete success, and threatens more and more often to fail. This process may therefore be compared to an unending conflict; new mental efforts are always required to balance the constant forward surge of the drive. Thus the ceremonial and obsessive actions arise partly as a defense against the temptation, partly as a protection against the expected misfortune. Against the temptation the protective measures soon seem insufficient; the prohibitions then arise, whose task is to keep at a distance the situation associated with the temptation. Prohibitions replace obsessive actions, as will be seen, just as a phobia has the task of averting a hysterical attack. On the other hand, a ceremonial represents the sum of the conditions under which other things not yet absolutely forbidden are permitted, just as the marriage ceremonial of the Church signifies for pious individuals permission for sexual enjoyment, otherwise a sin. It is also characteristic of obsessional neurosis and of all similar disorders that their expressions (symptoms, including obsessive actions) fulfill the condition of compromise between the mental forces in conflict. Thus, in addition, they always provide something of the pleasure it is their task to prevent; they serve the repressed drive no less than they serve the agencies repressing it. Indeed, as the illness progresses, actions originally more concerned with providing defense increasingly resemble the proscribed actions through which the drive was permitted to express itself in childhood.

Some aspects of this situation are also found in the realm of religious life. The repression and renunciation of certain drive impulses also seems to underlie the formation of religions. Yet these are not, as in the case of neurosis, exclusively sexual components; these are selfish, socially harmful instincts—in which a sexual contribution is usually not ruled out. A sense of guilt following ceaseless temptation, and expectant anxiety appearing as fear of divine punishment, have of course been familiar to us in the territory of religion longer than in that of neurosis. Perhaps because of the admixture of sexual components, or perhaps as a consequence of general characteristics of the drives, the repression of drives proves to be inadequate and interminable in religious life as well. Indeed, completely falling back into sin is more common among the pious than among neurotics, and leads to a new form of religious activity—acts of penance, for which one will find counterparts in obsessional neurosis.

We have regarded as a peculiar and degrading characteristic of obsessional neurosis the fact that the ceremonial is attached to small actions of daily life and expresses itself in foolish regulations and restrictions of those actions. One cannot understand this obvious feature in the symptoms of the illness until one realizes that the mechanism of mental *displacement*, which I first demonstrated in the formation of dreams (Freud 1900,[1] Chapter 6: Section B), dominates the mental processes of obsessional neurosis. From the few examples of obsessive actions discussed, it can already be seen that the symbolism and detail of execution arise through a displacement from the actual, significant thing to a minor object that replaces it—e.g., displacement from husband to chair. It is this tendency to displacement that progressively changes the picture of the symptoms, finally going so far as to turn the apparently most trivial detail into the most important and urgent thing. One cannot fail to recognize that in the religious realm there is a similar tendency to a displacement of mental values—and in the same way, such that gradually the petty ceremonial of religious practice becomes the essential thing, which has pushed aside the thought content of religious practice. Therefore religions are subject to retroactive reforms aiming to re-establish the original relation of values.

The compromising character of obsessive actions as neurotic symptoms is the one least clearly seen in the corresponding religious acts. Yet one is reminded of this trait of neurosis when one remembers how often all the acts religion rejects—expressions of the drives it represses—are carried out precisely in the name of religion, and supposedly for its sake.

Given these correspondences and analogies one might reasonably consider obsessional neurosis a pathological counterpart of the for-

---

1   I.e., *The Interpretation of Dreams.*

mation of religion; one might characterize neurosis as an individual religiosity, and religion as a universal obsessional neurosis. The most essential correspondence would be found in the underlying renunciation of the activation of drives constitutionally present; the most decisive difference would be found in the nature of these drives, which in neurosis are of purely sexual origin, and which in religion have an egoistic source.

A progressive renunciation of constitutional drives whose activation could give the ego primary pleasure appears to be one of the foundations of the development of human culture. A portion of this drive repression is achieved by religions in that they require individuals to sacrifice to the deity their pleasure connected with drives: "Vengeance is mine ... saith the Lord" [Romans 12: 19]. In the development of the ancient religions one seems to recognize that many things humankind had renounced as "iniquity" were given up to the deity and still permitted in his name, so that transferring such things to the deity was the way human beings freed themselves from domination by bad and socially harmful drives. It is therefore surely no coincidence that all human attributes, with the misdeeds ensuing from them, were without restriction ascribed to the ancient gods—and it is no contradiction that it was nevertheless forbidden to justify one's own iniquity through divine example.

2. From Sigmund Freud, *Totem and Taboo* (1913)[1]

III: Animism, Magic, and the Omnipotence of Thoughts (Section 3)

[...]
If we may regard the demonstration of the omnipotence of thoughts among primitives as evidence for narcissism, we may then presume to attempt a comparison between the stages in the development of mankind's view of the universe and the stages in the libidinal development of the individual. The animistic phase then corresponds both chronologically and in its content to narcissism; the religious phase corresponds to the stage of object-choice characterized by attachment to the parents; and the scientific phase has its complete counterpart in the stage of maturity in which individuals have renounced the pleasure principle, and, adjusting themselves to reality, seek their object in the external world.

---

1 *Totem und Tabu: einige Übereinstimmungen im Seelenleben der Wilden und der Neurotiker* (Leipzig and Vienna: Heller, 1913).

[...]

IV: The Return of Totemism in Childhood (Section 6)

[...]

In his great work, *The Golden Bough* [1890], Frazer[1] (1911, v. 2: Chapter 18) expressed the supposition that the earliest kings of the Latin tribes were foreigners who played the part of a god and in this role were solemnly executed at a particular festival. The annual sacrifice (variant: self-sacrifice) of a god seems to have been an essential trait of the Semitic religions. The ceremonial of human sacrifice in the most varied parts of the inhabited globe leaves little doubt that these persons met their end as representatives of the deity; and with the replacement of the living person by a lifeless effigy (puppet), this sacrificial rite can be traced into later times. The theanthropic sacrifice of a god, which unfortunately I cannot discuss here in as much depth as animal sacrifice, casts back a brilliant light upon the meaning of the older forms of sacrifice. With a frankness hardly to be outdone, it concedes that the object of the act of sacrifice has always been the same—precisely what is now worshipped as God: the father. The question as to the relation between animal and human sacrifice now finds a simple solution. The original animal sacrifice was already a substitute for a human sacrifice—the ceremonial killing of the father—and when the father-surrogate once again received its human form, the animal sacrifice could be transformed once again into a human sacrifice.

The memory of that first great sacrificial act had thus proved indestructible, despite all efforts to forget it; precisely when one wanted to distance oneself as far as possible from its motive forces, its undistorted repetition had to appear in the form of the sacrifice of a god. Here, I need not examine the developments of religious thought which, as rationalizations, made this recurrence possible. W. Robertson Smith,[2] of course unfamiliar with our derivation of the sacrifice from that great event in human prehistory, states that the ceremonies at the festivals in which the ancient Semites celebrated the death of a deity were interpreted as the "commemoration of a mythical tragedy" [Smith 413] and that in that context mourning did not have the character of spontaneous sympathy, but rather that of something obliga-

---

1   Scottish social anthropologist, James George Frazer (1854–1941), best known for studies of comparative religion.
2   Scottish orientalist and biblical scholar William Robertson Smith (1846–94).

tory and enforced by fear of divine anger.[1] We believe that this interpretation was correct, and that the feelings of the celebrants found a good explanation in the underlying situation.

Let us now take it as a fact that in the further development of religions as well, the two driving factors, the son's sense of guilt and the son's rebelliousness, never die out. Every attempt at solving the religious problem, every form of reconciliation between the two opposing mental forces, gradually breaks down—probably under the combined influence of historical events, cultural changes, and inner mental transformations.

The son's striving to put himself in the place of the father-god emerges more and more clearly. With the introduction of agriculture, the significance of the son within the patriarchal family increases. He permits himself new expressions of his incestuous libido, which find symbolic gratification in the cultivation of Mother Earth. Divine figures such as Attis, Adonis, and Tammuz emerge—spirits of vegetation and at the same time youthful divinities who enjoy the sexual favors of maternal goddesses and commit maternal incest in defiance of the father. But the sense of guilt, not allayed by these creations, is expressed in the myths that assign these youthful lovers of the mothergoddesses a short life, and require their punishment by emasculation or by the wrath of the father in animal form. Adonis is killed by the wild boar, the sacred animal of Aphrodite; Attis, the beloved of Cybele, dies by emasculation.[2] The mourning for these gods and the

---

1 "The mourning is not a spontaneous expression of sympathy with the divine tragedy but obligatory and enforced by fear of supernatural anger. And a chief object of the mourners is to *disclaim responsibility for the god's death*—a point which has already come before us in connection with theanthropic sacrifices, such as the 'ox-murder at Athens'" (Smith 412–13). [Freud's note]

2 In our youthful neurotics, fear of castration plays an extremely large role in the disruption of relations with their father. In Ferenczi's illuminating report we perceive how a boy sees his totem in the animal pecking at his little penis (Ferenczi). When our [Jewish] children learn of ritual circumcision, they equate it with castration. The socio-psychological parallel to this reaction by children has not yet been carried out to my knowledge. Circumcision, so frequent in primeval times and among primitives, occurs at the time of initiation into manhood, where its significance is to be found, and was only secondarily shifted back to earlier years of life. It is extremely interesting to find that among primitives circumcision is combined with cutting the hair and knocking out teeth, or is replaced by them, and that our children, who surely have no knowledge of this fact, actually treat these two operations—as evinced by their reactions of anxiety—as equivalents of castration. [Freud's note]

rejoicing over their resurrection passed over into the ritual of another son-deity, who was destined to achieve lasting success.

When Christianity first began its advance into the ancient world it met with competition from the religion of Mithras, and for a time it was doubtful which of the two deities would gain victory.

Yet the image, surrounded by light, of the youthful Persian god has remained dark to our understanding. From the depictions of Mithras slaying a bull one may perhaps conclude that he represented a son who carried out the sacrifice of the father alone, thus redeeming his brothers from the complicit guilt oppressing them. There was another path to allaying this sense of guilt, and this was first trodden by Christ. He went forth and sacrificed his own life, thereby redeeming the company of brothers from original sin.

The doctrine of original sin is of Orphic origin. It was retained in the [Eleusinian] mysteries, and spread from there to the philosophical schools of ancient Greece (Reinach 75ff.). Human beings were [seen as] descendants of the Titans, who had killed and dismembered the young Dionysos-Zagreus; the burden of this crime oppressed humankind.[1] A fragment of Anaximander states that the unity of the world was destroyed by a primeval crime,[2] and that all things that have proceeded from it must continue to bear the punishment. Through the traits of mobbing, killing, and dismemberment, the Titans' deed reminds one clearly enough of the totemic sacrifice described by St. Nilus[3] [Reinach 93]—as do many other myths of antiquity, e.g., the death of Orpheus—yet here we are disturbed by the deviation seen in the fact that it is a youthful god who is murdered.

In the Christian myth the original sin of humanity was doubtless a sin against God the Father. Yet if Christ redeems humanity from the burden of original sin by sacrificing his own life, he forces us to the conclusion that the sin was an act of murder. According to the law of

---

1 In Greek mythology, Zagreus was born of Zeus and Persephone and associated with Dionysus. In one story, a jealous Hera persuaded the Titans to attack and kill the young Zagreus. In his attempt to escape, Zagreus turned into various animals, the last of which was a bull. Having killed the bull, the Titans ate it. Zeus, in his turn, used lightning to turn the Titans to ash, while Persephone recovered their son's heart. These ashes and the heart they turned into a potion, and fed it to Semele, who conceived the reincarnation of Zagreus. In the meantime, the ashes of the Titans, infused with the flesh of Zagreus, became humankind.

2 "Une sorte de péché proethnique" [a sort of pre-ethnic sin] (Reinach 76). [Freud's note]

3 Nilus of Sinai, or Nilus the Ascetic (d. 430), a leading ascetic writer in the fifth century.

talion,[1] deeply rooted in human emotion, a murder can only be expiated by the sacrifice of another life; self-sacrifice points back to a case of blood-guilt.[2] And if this sacrifice of one's own life brings reconciliation with God the Father, the crime to be expiated must have been none other than the murder of the father.

Thus, in Christian doctrine human beings acknowledge in the most undisguised manner the guilty deed of primeval times, for now, in the sacrificial death of this one son, they have found the fullest atonement for that deed. The reconciliation with the father is all the more solid because, simultaneous with the sacrifice, there occurs the total renunciation of the woman on whose account the son had risen up against the father. But now the psychological ill fate of ambivalence comes into play. With the very deed that offers the father the greatest possible atonement, the son also achieves the goal of his wishes against the father. He himself becomes God—beside, indeed in place of, the father. The son-religion replaces the father-religion. As a sign of this substitution the old totem meal is revived as communion, in which the company of brothers now consumes the flesh and blood of the son— no longer that of the father; the brothers are sanctified in that act, and identify with the son. Through the ages we see the identity of the totem meal with animal sacrifice, with theanthropic human sacrifice, and with the Christian eucharist; in all these rituals we recognize the effect of the crime that so sorely oppressed all humans, but of which they must have felt so proud. The Christian communion, though, is essentially a renewed elimination of the father, a repetition of the deed to be atoned. We note the strong justifications for Frazer's pronouncement that "the Christian communion has absorbed within itself a sacrament which is doubtless far older than Christianity" (Frazer 1912, v.2: 51).[3]

---

1 Greek, meaning "same/equivalent," as in "an eye for an eye, a tooth for a tooth."
2 The suicidal impulses of our neurotics regularly prove to be self-punishments for death-wishes directed toward others. [Freud's note]
3 No one familiar with the literature on the subject will imagine that the derivation of Christian communion from the totem meal is an idea originating from the author of the present work. [Freud's note]

3. From Sigmund Freud, "Scientific Interest in Psychoanalysis" (1913)[1]

II. (E) The Interest of Psychoanalysis from the Point of View of the History of Culture

The comparison between the childhood of individuals and the early history of peoples has already proved fruitful in several directions, though it has only very recently been possible to undertake that work. Here, the psychoanalytic mode of thought functions as a new instrument of research. The application of its hypotheses to social psychology makes it possible to raise new problems, to see in a new light problems already worked on, and to contribute to their solution.

In the first place, it seems entirely possible to transfer the psychoanalytic view derived from work on dreams to products of ethnic fantasy such as myths and folktales (cf. works by Abraham,[2] Rank,[3] and Jung). The need for an interpretation of such constructions has long been clear; one senses a "secret meaning" within them, and is prepared to see changes and transformations that conceal that meaning. From its work on dreams and neurosis, psychoanalysis has gained enough experience to guess the technical means of these distortions. But in several cases it can reveal the hidden motives that have produced these modifications of myth from its original meaning. As the first impulse for the construction of myths, psychoanalysis sees no evidence of a theoretical need to explain natural phenomena or to account for cult observances and practices which had become incomprehensible, but rather seeks that impulse in the same mental "complexes," in the same emotional impulses it has demonstrated as the basis of dreams and symptoms.

Through a similar application of its points of view, hypotheses, and discoveries, psychoanalysis can cast light on the origins of our great cultural institutions—religion, morality, justice, and philosophy (cf. Jung 1912[4] and Freud 1913[5] for preliminary discussions). By exam-

---

1 "Das Interesse an der Psychoanalyse," *Scientia* 14.31–32 (1913): 240–50; 369–84.

2 Berlin psychoanalyst Karl Abraham (1877–1925) was one of Freud's closest followers, probably best known for his views on character formation and for his leadership role within psychoanalysis.

3 Otto Rank (1884–1939), a lay analyst, was a central figure in Freud's inner circle of adherents (ca. 1905–25). For years, Rank was Freud's favorite colleague, and they worked very closely—intellectually and institutionally—until Rank's own work drifted from Freud's.

4 I.e., *Psychology of the Unconscious*.

5 I.e., *Totem and Taboo*.

ining the primitive psychological situations from which the motivations for such creations were able to arise, it is in a position to reject various attempts at explanation that were based on provisional psychological assumptions and to replace them with deeper insights.

Psychoanalysis establishes an intimate connection between all these mental achievements as produced by individuals and as produced by societies in that it postulates the same dynamic source for both. It begins with the basic idea that the main function of the mental mechanism is to relieve people of the tensions produced in them by needs. One part of this task can be accomplished through gratification gained from the external world; for this purpose control over the real world becomes imperative. Gratification for another portion of these needs—mainly comprised of certain affective impulses—is regularly denied by reality. From this derives a second part of the task: that of providing another means of dealing with the ungratified impulses. In its entirety, the history of culture merely shows the methods humans adopt to bind their ungratified wishes under the shifting conditions (altered, furthermore, by technological progress) of favor and denial by reality.

An investigation of primitive peoples shows human beings caught, initially, in a childish belief in their own omnipotence (cf. Ferenczi; cf. Freud 1913: Chapter 3 ["Animism, Magic, and the Omnipotence of Thoughts"]), and allows a great number of mental constructions to be understood as efforts to deny disturbances of this omnipotence, and thereby to keep reality from affecting emotional life until it is possible to control reality better and exploit it for gratification. The principle of avoiding unpleasure dominates human activity until it is replaced by the better principle of adapting to the external world. Parallel with humans' increasing domination over the world goes a development of their world view, which increasingly turns away from the original belief in omnipotence, and rises from the animistic phase, through the religious, to the scientific one. Myth, religion, and morality fit into this interconnected pattern as attempts to seek compensation for the gratification of wishes that is lacking.

Knowledge of the neurotic illnesses of individuals has been of great use in our understanding of the great social institutions, for the neuroses themselves have proved to be attempts to solve, for the individual, the problems of compensation for wishes, while it is the purpose of the institutions to solve them socially. The diminished importance of the social factor and the predominance of the sexual one turns these neurotic solutions of the psychological task into distorted images serving no purpose except to cast light on these significant problems.

4. From Sigmund Freud, *Civilization and Its Discontents* (1930)[1]

II

In my essay *The Future of an Illusion*, the discussion was concerned much less with the deepest sources of religious feeling than with what the common man understands as his religion—the system of doctrines and promises that on the one hand clears up for him the riddles of this world with enviable completeness, and on the other hand assures him that a careful Providence will watch over his life and will, in an existence beyond this world, compensate him for whatever has been denied him. The common man cannot imagine this Providence other than in the person of an immensely exalted father. Only such a father can know the needs of human beings and be softened by their entreaties and placated by the signs of their remorse. All of this is so obviously infantile, so far from reality, that it is painful to anyone with convictions friendly toward humanity to think that the great majority of mortals will never be able to rise above this view of life. It is even more humiliating to discover how large a portion of those living today, who must surely see that this religion is untenable, nevertheless seek to defend piece after piece of it in a series of pathetic rearguard battles. One would like to mix in with the ranks of the believers so as to face the philosophers who believe they can rescue the God of religion by replacing him with an impersonal, shadowy, abstract principle, and so as to reproach them with the admonition: "Thou shalt not take the name of the Lord thy God in vain!" If some of the great minds of past times did the same, we cannot appeal to their example here: we know why they were obliged to do so.

We now return to the common man and his religion, the only one that should bear that name. The first thing we come across is the well-known comment of one of our great poets and thinkers that expresses the relation of religion to art and science:

> Wer Wissenschaft und Kunst besitzt, hat auch Religion;
> Wer jene beide nicht besitzt, der habe Religion![2]

---

1 *Das Unbehagen in der Kultur* (Vienna: Internationaler Psychoanalytischer Verlag, 1930).
2 "Whoever possesses science and art has religion too; / Whoever possesses neither one, let him have religion!" (Goethe, *Zahme Xenien* IX).

This saying on the one hand places religion in contrast with the two highest achievements of man, and on the other hand asserts that in creating value in life, religion can represent or replace science and art, and vice versa. Even if we wish to dispute the common man's religion, we clearly do not have the authority of the poet on our side. We will try out a particular path so as to come closer to an appreciation of his words. Life, as it is imposed on us, is too hard for us; it brings us too much pain, too many disappointments and unachievable tasks. To bear it, we cannot do without palliative measures. ("It's impossible without helpful measures," Theodor Fontane tells us [*Effi Briest,* 1895].) Of such measures there are perhaps three types: powerful deflections, which cause us to make light of our misery; substitute gratifications, which reduce it; and intoxicating substances, which make us insensitive to it. Something along these lines is indispensable.[1] Voltaire is thinking of deflections when, in the final words of *Candide* [1759], he advises that one should cultivate one's garden; scientific activity is another deflection of this kind. The substitute gratifications, as offered by art, are illusions contrasting with reality, but no less effective in the mind thanks to the role that fantasy has taken on in mental life. Intoxicating substances influence our body and alter its chemistry. It is not easy to identify the place of religion in this series. We shall have to look further.

The question as to the purpose of human life has been posed countless times; it has never yet received a satisfactory answer and perhaps such an answer is impossible. Some of those who have posed the question have added the following: if it should turn out that life has no purpose, it would lose all value for them. But this threat alters nothing. Rather, it seems that one has the right to reject the question. It seems to be a result of that human presumption already familiar to us in many other of its expressions. One does not discuss the purpose of the life of animals further than the claim, for example, that their purpose is to serve humankind. But even that is untenable, for there are many animals with which man can do nothing—except describe, classify, and study them—and countless animal species have escaped this use too, in that they lived and died out before humans ever saw them. Once again, it is only religion that has an answer for the question as to the purpose of life. One will hardly err in concluding that the idea of a purpose of life stands and falls with the religious system.

We therefore turn to the less ambitious question of what humans themselves show by their behavior to be the purpose and intent of

---

1 On a lower plane, Wilhelm Busch says the same thing in *Die fromme Helene* [1872]: "Whoever has cares has liquor too." [Freud's note]

their life, what they demand of life, and what they wish to achieve in it. The answer can hardly be in doubt: they strive for happiness, they want to become happy and to remain so. This striving has two sides, a positive and a negative goal: it wants, on the one hand, the absence of pain and unpleasure, and on the other hand, the experience of strong feelings of pleasure. In a narrower sense the word *happiness* refers only to the latter. Corresponding to this dichotomy of the goals, human activity develops in two directions, depending on whether it seeks to realize—chiefly or even exclusively—the one goal or the other.

It is, as one will see, the program of the pleasure principle alone that declares the purpose of life. This principle dominates the function of the mental apparatus from the very start. There can be no doubt as to its effectiveness, and yet its program is in conflict with the whole world, with the macrocosm just as with the microcosm. It simply cannot be carried out; all the institutions of the universe resist it. One has the urge to say that the intention that humankind be "happy" is not contained in the plan of "Creation." What is called happiness in the strictest sense arises from the relatively sudden satisfaction of needs that are, to a high degree, dammed up; happiness is by its very nature possible only as an episodic phenomenon. Any prolongation of a situation craved by the pleasure principle produces only a lukewarm feeling of well-being. We are so made that we can intensely enjoy only a contrast, and a state only in a very limited way.[1] Thus our possibilities for happiness are already restricted by our constitution. Far fewer difficulties arise in experiencing unhappiness. Suffering threatens us from three sides: from our own body, which, doomed to decline and dissolution, cannot even do without pain and anxiety as warning signals; from the external world, which can rage against us with overwhelming and inexorable destructive forces; and finally from our relations to other people. The suffering that arises from that last source we perceive as more painful, perhaps, than any other. We are inclined to regard it as a rather superfluous addition, although it cannot be any less fatefully inevitable than suffering from other origins.

It is no wonder that, under the pressure of these possibilities of suffering, people ordinarily reduce their claim to happiness, just as the pleasure principle too, under the influence of the external world, reconstituted itself as the more modest reality principle; it is no wonder that people think they are happy merely in having escaped unhappiness and in having survived suffering; it is no wonder that the

---

1   Goethe even admonishes us that "Anything in the world can be endured— except a succession of beautiful days" [*Sprichwörtlich*, 1815]. Still, that may be an exaggeration. [Freud's note]

task of avoiding suffering generally pushes that of obtaining pleasure into the background. Consideration of the facts shows that one can attempt to accomplish this task along very different paths; all these paths have been recommended by the various schools of worldly wisdom and trodden by humankind. An unrestricted gratification of all needs strongly suggests itself as the most enticing way to conduct one's life, but that means putting enjoyment before caution, and is soon punished. The other methods, in which the avoidance of unpleasure is the main goal, differ according to which source of unpleasure is their main focus. Some practices are extreme, some moderate; some are one-sided and attack the problem at different places simultaneously. Intentional isolation—keeping oneself away from others—is the most obvious defense against the suffering that can stem from human relationships. People understand that the happiness that can be attained along this path is that of quietude. Against the feared external world one can defend oneself in no other manner than by turning away in some fashion—if one intends to accomplish the task on one's own. But there is certainly another and better path: as a member of the human community, and with the help of technology guided by science, one can go over to the attack on nature and subject it to human will. Then one is working with all for the happiness of all. The most interesting methods of preventing suffering are, however, those that seek to influence our own organism. In the end, all suffering is only sensation; suffering exists only in so far as we feel it, and we feel it only as the result of certain aspects of the constitution of our organism.

The crudest, but also most effective method of influencing our organism is the chemical one—intoxication. I do not believe anyone fully understands its mechanism, but it is a fact that there are substances, foreign to the body, whose presence in the blood or tissues provides us direct pleasurable sensations, but also alters the conditions of our perceptive processes such that we become incapable of receiving unpleasurable impulses. Not only do these two effects occur simultaneously, but they seem to be intimately related. But in our own chemical processes there must be substances that achieve similar effects, for we are familiar with at least one pathological state, mania, in which a condition similar to intoxication arises without the introduction of intoxicants. Furthermore, our normal mental life shows swings between an easier and a more difficult discharge of pleasure, with which a decreased or increased receptivity to unpleasure runs in parallel. It is highly regrettable that this toxic side of mental processes has thus far escaped scientific research. The effect of intoxicating substances in the struggle for happiness and in keeping misery at a distance is so highly valued as a benefit that individuals as well as entire peoples have given them a permanent place in the economy of their libido. Such substances not only provide an immediate gain in pleasure, but also a strongly desired degree of independence from the external world. Indeed, one knows that with the help of this "drowner of sorrows" one can withdraw at any time from the pressure of reality and find refuge in a world of one's own, with better conditions of sensation. As is well known, it is precisely this property of intoxicants that also renders them dangerous and harmful. Under certain circumstances, they are at fault when large amounts of energy that could have been used for the improvement of the human condition are uselessly lost.

Yet the complicated structure of our mental apparatus entails a whole series of other influences. Just as the gratification of drives means happiness, great suffering is caused if the external world fails to provide for us, if it refuses to satisfy our needs. By influencing the drive impulses, one can therefore hope to become free from a portion of suffering. This way of averting suffering no longer attacks the sensory apparatus, but seeks to master the inner sources of our needs. This occurs in an extreme manner by killing off the drives, as taught by the worldly wisdom of the Orient and effected by the practice of yoga. If this succeeds, then one has of course given up all other activities as well—one has sacrificed one's life—and, by another path, attained only the happiness of quietude. The same path is followed, with reduced aims, if one strives merely to master the drive processes. Then the controlling forces are the higher mental functions, which have subjected themselves to the reality principle. Here the aim of gratification is by no means given up, but a certain protection against suffering is achieved since the non-gratification of those drives held in a dependent state is not felt as painfully as that of the uninhibited ones. However, there is an undeniable decrease in the possibilities for enjoyment. The feeling of happiness in the gratification of a wild drive impulse untamed by the ego is incomparably more intense than that found in the satisfaction of a tamed one. Here, the irresistibility of perverse impulses, and perhaps the attraction of the forbidden in general, finds an economic explanation.

Another technique for averting suffering utilizes the displacements of libido our mental apparatus permits, and through which its function gains so much flexibility. The task to be accomplished is to shift the goals of the drives such that they cannot be reached by the failures of the external world. For this purpose, the sublimation of drives lends its help. One achieves the most if one can sufficiently heighten the gain in pleasure from the sources of mental and intellectual work. Then fate can little harm one. Gratifications of this kind, such as the artist's joy in creating—in giving form to the constructions of his fantasy—or a researcher's joy in solving problems or recognizing the truth, have a special quality which some day we shall certainly be able to characterize metapsychologically. At the present time we can only say figuratively that they seem "finer and higher," but their intensity, compared to that produced by the satisfaction of crude, primary drive impulses, is muted; such gratifications do not convulse our physical framework. The weakness of this method, though, is that it is not applicable in all cases, but is accessible only to a few people. It requires special talents and gifts, which, on a practical scale, are not exactly common. Even to these few persons it cannot provide a complete defense from suffering; it creates for them no armor impenetrable to the arrows of fortune, and it regularly fails when one's own body becomes the source of suffering.[1]

If in this method there is already the clear intention of making oneself independent of the external world by seeking one's gratifications in inner, mental processes, in the next method the same traits emerge even more strongly. Here, the connection with reality is loosened still further; gratification is gained from illusions that are recognized as such, without allowing their divergence from reality to disturb one in one's enjoyment. The realm from which these illusions derive is that of fantasy life; at one time, when the sense of reality was developing, this realm was expressly exempted from the demands of reality-

---

1 When no special predisposition commandingly dictates the direction of one's interests in life, the ordinary professional work open to all can take the place assigned it by Voltaire's wise advice [to cultivate one's garden]. Within the limits of a brief survey, it is not possible to provide an adequate discussion of the significance of work for the economy of the libido. No other technique for the conduct of life binds individuals so firmly to reality as an emphasis on work, which at least fits them securely into a portion of reality, into the human community. The possibility of displacing a large number of libidinal components—narcissistic, aggressive, or even erotic—onto professional work and onto the human relations connected with that work lends it a value no less important than its indispensability in asserting and justifying one's existence in society. Professional activity provides special satisfaction when it is freely chosen—that is, when such work makes it possible, through sublimation, to utilize existing inclinations, persistent drive impulses, or constitutionally reinforced ones. Yet as a path to happiness, people do not value work highly. One does not strive for it as one does for other possibilities of satisfaction. The great majority of people only work because they must, and from this natural human aversion to work derive extremely difficult social problems. [Freud's note]

testing and remained apart, tasked with fulfilling those wishes that were hard to carry out. Chief among these fantasy gratifications stands the enjoyment of works of art; through the mediation of the artist, such an enjoyment is made accessible even to persons who are not themselves creative (cf. Freud 1911[1] and Lecture 23 in Freud 1917[2]). Those who are receptive to the influence of art cannot praise it highly enough as a source of pleasure and consolation in life. Yet the mild narcosis into which art brings us can produce only a fleeting withdrawal from the cares of life, and is not strong enough to make us forget real misery.

Another procedure goes forward more energetically and more thoroughly, seeing reality as the sole enemy, as the source of all suffering, with which it is impossible to live, and with which one must accordingly break off all relations if one wants to be happy in some sense. The hermit turns his back on the world and wants to have nothing to do with it. But one can do more; one can desire to recreate it, to build up another world in its place, in which the most unbearable features are eliminated and replaced by others conforming with one's own wishes. Whoever, in desperate outrage, takes this path to happiness will as a rule accomplish nothing; reality is too strong for him. He becomes a madman, who, in carrying out his delusion, usually finds no helpers. Yet it is claimed that each of us, in some respect, behaves like a paranoiac, corrects some intolerable aspect of the world by means of a wish-construction, and carries this delusion into reality. Of special significance is the case in which a considerable number of people, through a delusional reorganization of reality, collectively try to gain for themselves an assurance of happiness and a protection against suffering. We must also characterize the religions of humankind as mass delusions of this kind. The delusion, of course, is never recognized as such by anyone who shares it.

I do not think this is a complete enumeration of the methods by which people strive to gain happiness and to keep suffering away, and I also know that a different ordering of the material would be possible. There is one procedure I have not yet mentioned—not because I have forgotten it, but because it will concern us later in another context. How could one possibly forget this particular technique in the art of living? It is distinguished by an amazing combination of characteristic traits. It, too, naturally aims for independence from Fate—that is the best word for it—and with that intent shifts gratification to inner mental processes, making use here of the previously mentioned dis-

---

1 I.e., "Formulations on the Two Principles of Mental Functioning."
2 I.e., "The Paths to the Formation of Symptoms."

placeable nature of the libido. Yet it does not turn away from the external world. Rather, it clings to the objects of this world and gains happiness through an emotional relation to them. Nor is it content with the tired, resigned goal, as it were, of avoiding unpleasure. Instead, it passes that goal by without heed and holds firmly to the original, passionate striving for a positive fulfillment of happiness. Perhaps it really comes closer to this goal than any other method. I mean, of course, the orientation in life that takes love as the center of all things, and seeks all gratification in loving and being loved. Such a mental attitude is natural enough to all of us; one of the manifestations of love—sexual love—has given us the strongest experience of an overwhelming sensation of pleasure and has thus provided us with a model in our striving for happiness. What is more natural than continuing to seek happiness along the path where we first encountered it? The weak side of this technique of living is obvious; otherwise it would never have occurred to anyone to leave this path to happiness for another. We are never as unprotected against suffering as when we love, never so helplessly unhappy as when we have lost the beloved object or its love for us. But that is not all there is to say about the technique of living based on the value of love in providing happiness; there is much more to be said about it.

Here one may add the interesting case in which happiness in life is sought mainly in the enjoyment of beauty, wherever it presents itself to our senses and our judgment—the beauty of human forms and gestures, of natural objects and landscapes, of artistic and even scientific creations. This aesthetic orientation to the goal of life offers little protection against sufferings that threaten, but it can compensate for much. The enjoyment of beauty has a special, mildly intoxicating character in terms of sensation. Beauty has no obvious use, and it is not clear why culture has any need for it, yet culture could not do without it. The science of aesthetics investigates the conditions under which the beautiful is perceived, but it has been unable to give any explanation of the nature and origin of beauty; as usual, lack of results is concealed in a barrage of resounding and empty words. Unfortunately, psychoanalysis too is hardly able to say anything about beauty. It seems certain, though, that it is derived from the realm of sexual feeling. This would be a perfect example of an aim-inhibited impulse. *Beauty* and *attractiveness* are originally features of the sexual object. One notes that the genitals themselves, the sight of which is always exciting, are in fact almost never deemed beautiful; the quality of beauty seems, rather, to be associated with certain secondary sexual characteristics.

Despite the incompleteness of this discussion, I shall venture some remarks to conclude our investigation. The program for becoming happy imposed on us by the pleasure principle cannot be fulfilled; yet one must not—indeed, cannot—give up one's efforts to somehow bring it closer to fulfillment. One may take very different paths toward that goal, and may emphasize either the positive content of the goal, that of gaining pleasure, or the negative content, that of avoiding unpleasure. On none of these paths can we attain all we desire. Happiness, in the reduced sense in which it is understood to be possible, is a problem of the libido economy of the individual. There is no advice appropriate for everyone; everyone must find his own unique path to blessed happiness. The most varied factors will come into play to give direction in making the choice. It depends on how much real gratification one can expect from the external world, how far one is inclined to become independent of it, and finally, how much strength one is willing to exert in altering it to suit one's own wishes. In this, beyond the external circumstances, the mental constitution of the individual will be decisive. Predominantly erotic persons will emphasize emotional relationships to other people; more self-sufficient, narcissistic persons will seek their major gratifications in their inner mental processes; those who emphasize action will not give up the external world, in which they can test their strength. For the second of these types, the nature of one's talents and the degree of drive sublimation available will determine where one should place one's interests. Any extreme decision will be punished in that it will expose the individual to the dangers brought by the inadequacy of the technique of living chosen to the exclusion of the others. Just as a careful businessman avoids putting all his capital in one place, worldly wisdom will perhaps advise us not to expect all gratifications from one pursuit alone. Success is never certain; it depends on the convergence of many factors, and perhaps on none more than on the ability of the mental constitution to adapt its function to the environment and to exploit that environment for gaining pleasure. A person who comes with an especially unfavorable constitution of drives, and has not properly gone through the reconstruction and rearrangement of libidinal components—as is essential for later achievements—will have difficulty gaining happiness from the external situation, especially when faced with relatively difficult tasks. As a last technique of living, which at least promises substitute gratifications, such a person is offered flight into neurotic illness; this is usually accomplished at a young age. Those who in later years see their strivings for happiness come to naught may still find comfort in the gain of pleasure found in chronic intoxication, or they may undertake a desperate attempt at rebellion in psychosis.[1]

Religion impairs this play of choice and adaptation in that it imposes its own path to gaining happiness and to protection against suffering on all in the same way. Its technique consists in diminishing the value of life and distorting the picture of the real world through a delusion—which presupposes the intimidation of the intelligence. At this price, by forcibly fixing people in a state of mental infantilism and by drawing them into a mass-delusion, religion succeeds in sparing many people an individual neurosis. But that is the extent of it. As we have said, there are many paths which can lead to that happiness human beings can attain, but there is no path certain to lead there. Even religion cannot keep its promise. If, in the end, the believer finds himself obliged to speak of God's "inscrutable decrees," he is admitting that as a final possibility of comfort and source of pleasure in his suffering only unconditional submission is left to him. And if he is prepared for such submission, he could probably have spared himself the detour.

5. From Sigmund Freud, *Moses and Monotheism: Three Essays* (1939)[2]

II: If Moses was an Egyptian ...

(5)

[...]
[I]n 1922, Ernst Sellin[3] made a discovery that affects our problem decisively [Sellin]. In the Prophet Hosea (second half of the eighth century BCE) he found the unmistakable signs of a tradition based on the idea that the founder of the religion, Moses, met with a violent end in an uprising of his rebellious and stubborn people. Simultaneously,

---

1 I feel impelled to point out at least one of the gaps remaining in the presentation above. An examination of the possibilities for human happiness should not fail to consider the relation between narcissism and object libido. We desire to know what being essentially self-sufficient means for the economy of the libido. [Freud's note, 1931]

2 *Der Mann Moses und die monotheistische Religion: Drei Abhandlungen* (Amsterdam: Allert de Lange, 1939).

3 German theologian Ernst Sellin (1867–1946). Sellin incorporated archaeological findings into biblical studies.

the religion introduced by him was rejected. This tradition, though, is not restricted to Hosea: it returns in most of the later Prophets. Indeed, according to Sellin, it became the basis of all the later Messianic expectations. At the end of the Babylonian exile the hope developed among the Jewish people that the man who had been so shamefully murdered would return from the dead and lead his repentant people, and perhaps not them alone, into the kingdom of eternal bliss. The obvious connections with the destiny of a later founder of religion are not relevant here.

Again, I am certainly not in a position to determine whether Sellin has correctly interpreted the passages from the Prophets. But if he is correct we may attribute historical credibility to the tradition he discerned, for such things are difficult to invent. A tangible motive for doing so is lacking; if they really occurred, it is easy to understand that there would be a desire to forget them. We need not accept all the details of the tradition. Sellin is of the opinion that Shittim, in the land east of the Jordan, is to be identified as the place of the attack on Moses. We shall soon recognize that such a locale is unacceptable for our considerations.

We adopt from Sellin the hypothesis that the Egyptian Moses was killed by the Jews and that the religion introduced by him was abandoned. This hypothesis allows us to spin our threads further without contradicting credible results of historical research. But we shall otherwise presume to remain independent of those authors and to "venture along our own path." The exodus from Egypt remains our starting point. There must have been a considerable number of people who left the country with Moses; to this ambitious man aiming for great things, a small group would not have been worth the effort. The immigrants had probably been living in Egypt long enough to develop a population of considerable size. But we shall certainly not be in error if, with the majority of the authors, we assume that only a fraction of the subsequent Jewish people had experienced the turns of fate in Egypt. In other words, in the region between Egypt and Canaan, the tribe that returned from Egypt joined, subsequently, with other related tribes that had long been settled there. An expression of this union, from which the people of Israel arose, is seen in the adoption of a new religion common to all the tribes—that of Yahweh; according to Eduard Meyer[1] [Meyer 60ff.] this event occurred under Midianite influence at Qadesh. Thereupon, the people felt strong enough to undertake their invasion of the land of Canaan. It would be incompatible with this course of events to claim that the catastrophe to

---

1 German historian Eduard Meyer (1855–1930).

Moses and his religion took place in the territory east of the Jordan; it must have occurred long before the union of the tribes.

It is clear that highly diverse elements joined together in the formation of the Jewish people; but the greatest difference among these tribes must have been whether they had or had not experienced the sojourn in Egypt and what followed it. Regarding this point, one can say that the nation arose from the union of two components, and it accords with this that after a short period of political unity it split into two pieces—the kingdom of Israel and the kingdom of Judah. History is fond of such reinstatements, in which later fusions are canceled and earlier separations reappear. The most impressive example of this type is of course provided by the Reformation: after an interval of over a thousand years, it re-established the border between the Germany which had once been Roman and the Germany which had remained independent. In the case of the Jewish people it would not be possible to demonstrate such a faithful reproduction of the old situation; our knowledge of those times is too uncertain to justify the claim that the previously settled tribes joined together again in the Northern Kingdom, while those that had returned from Egypt did so in the Southern Kingdom; but here too the later division cannot have occurred without a relation to the earlier melding. Those who had once been Egyptians probably numbered fewer than the others, but they proved culturally the stronger; they had a more powerful influence on the further development of the people because they brought along a tradition the others lacked.

Perhaps they brought along something else more concrete than a tradition. One of the greatest mysteries of Jewish prehistory is the origin of the Levites. They are claimed to derive from one of the twelve tribes of Israel, the tribe of Levi, but no tradition has presumed to declare where that tribe was originally settled or what part of the conquered land of Canaan was allotted to it. They occupied the most important priestly positions but are distinguished from the priests: a Levite is not necessarily a priest. Nor is the term the name of a caste. Our supposition about the figure of Moses suggests an explanation. It is not believable that a great lord like Moses the Egyptian would have joined this alien people unaccompanied. He surely brought his retinue along—his closest followers, his scribes, his servants. That is who the Levites originally were. The traditional claim that Moses was a Levite seems to be a transparent distortion of the actual situation: the Levites were the people who accompanied Moses. This solution is supported by the fact, already mentioned in my earlier essay, that only among the Levites do Egyptian names still appear later.[1] It can be assumed that many of those who followed Moses escaped the catastrophe that struck him and the religion he founded. They multiplied in the subsequent generations and melded with the people among whom they lived, but they remained loyal to their master, preserved a memory of him, and practiced the tradition of his doctrine. At the time of the union with those who believed in Yahweh they were an influential minority, culturally superior to the others.

III: Moses, His People, and Monotheism—Part II

[...]

F. The Return of the Repressed

There are a number of similar processes among those with which we have become acquainted through the analytic investigation of mental life. A portion of them are designated as pathological; others are included within the great diversity of the normal. But that is of little import, for the boundaries between the two groups of processes are not sharply drawn, the mechanisms are largely the same, and it is far more important whether the relevant modifications play out in the ego itself, or approach it as alien entities—in which case they are called symptoms. From the abundant material, I shall first emphasize cases relating to character development. A girl has brought herself into a position of extremely decided contrast with her mother, has cultivated all the characteristics she finds lacking in her mother, and has avoided everything that reminds her of her mother. We may extend this by saying that in earlier years, like every female child, she had identified with her mother, and that she is now energetically rebelling against that identification. But when this girl marries and becomes a wife and mother herself, we should not be surprised to find that she starts to grow more and more like the mother toward whom she had felt such enmity, until, in the end, the surmounted mother-identification has been unmistakably restored. The same occurs with boys too; and even the great Goethe, who in the period of his genius certainly looked down upon his inflexible and pedantic father, developed traits in old

---

1 This hypothesis accords well with the information provided by Yahuda concerning the Egyptian influence on early Jewish literature (cf. Yahuda). [Freud's note]

age that had been found in the makeup of his father's character. The outcome is even more striking in those areas where the contrast between the two persons is sharper. A young man whose fate it was to grow up with a worthless father developed at first, in defiance of him, into a competent, reliable, and honorable person. In the prime of life his character reversed itself, and from then on he behaved as if he had taken this same father as his model. So as not to lose the connection with our theme, one must bear in mind that at the start of such a course of events, in early childhood, there is always an identification with the father. This is then rejected, even overcompensated, but in the end reasserts itself.

It has long been well known that the experiences of the first five years of life have a decisive effect on one's subsequent life—an effect that nothing later can oppose. Many things worth knowing, but not relevant here, might be said about the way these early impressions resist all influences occurring at subsequent ages. Yet it is probably less well known that the strongest compulsive influence derives from those impressions affecting the child at a time when the mental apparatus must be regarded as not yet completely receptive. There can be no doubt about the fact itself, yet we are so much taken aback by it that we can make it easier to understand by comparing it to a photographic negative that can be developed after any amount of delay and transformed into a picture. Still, it is nice to point out that it was an imaginative writer, who, with the boldness permitted to poets, anticipated this uncomfortable discovery of ours. E.T.A. Hoffmann[1] used to attribute the wealth of figures that put themselves at his disposal for his writings to the alternating images and impressions during a journey of several weeks in a postal chaise—a journey he had experienced while still an infant at his mother's breast. What children at the age of two have experienced but not understood they need never remember except in dreams. This material can only be introduced to them through a psychoanalytic treatment, but at some later time it will break into their life with obsessional impulses, direct their actions, and impose on them sympathies and antipathies; quite often it will determine their choice in love, a choice that so often cannot be rationally justified. There can be no doubt about the two points where these facts touch upon our problem. The first is the remoteness of the

---

1 Ernst Theodor Wilhelm (Amadeus) Hoffmann (1776–1822), a German romantic author and composer best known by his *nom de plume* of E.T.A. Hoffmann. Freud was greatly influenced by nineteenth-century Romanticism, of which Hoffmann was a major figure.

time[1]—a point recognized here as the actually determining factor, e.g., in the special state of memory which in the case of these childhood experiences we classify as "unconscious." There, we expect to find an analogy with the state we would like to attribute to tradition in the mental life of the people. It was not easy, of course, to bring the concept of the unconscious into mass psychology.

Regular contributions to the phenomena we seek are also made by the mechanisms leading to the formation of neuroses. Here, too, the decisive events occur in early childhood, but here the stress falls not upon the time, but upon the process that deals with the event, the reaction to it. The following schematic representation can be proposed. Resulting from the experience, a drive impulse arises, demanding gratification. The ego refuses to gratify it, either because it is paralyzed by the magnitude of the demand or because it recognizes it as a danger. The first of these reasons is the more basic; both of them are equivalent to the avoidance of a dangerous situation. The ego fends off the danger through the process of repression. The drive impulse is somehow inhibited; the cause, along with the associated perceptions and ideas, is forgotten. Thereby, however, the process is not complete: the drive has either retained its energies, or collects them again, or it is reawakened by a new cause. It then renews its demand, and, since the path to normal gratification remains closed to it by what we may call the scar of repression, somewhere, at a weak spot, it opens another path for itself to a so-called substitute gratification, which now appears as a symptom, without the consent of the ego, but also without its understanding. All the phenomena of the formation of symptoms may justly be described as the "return of the repressed." But the distinguishing characteristic of these phenomena is the extensive distortion the returning material has undergone in comparison to the original material. One may feel that with this last group of facts we have strayed too far from the similarity to tradition. But we should not regret it if, with these facts, we have approached the problems of the renunciation of drives.

---

1 Here, too, a poet may speak some words. In order to explain his attachment, he imagines: "Ach, du warst in abgelebten Zeiten / meine Schwester oder meine Frau [Oh, you were, in times previously lived / my sister or my wife]." [Freud's note. From a poem Goethe addressed to Charlotte von Stein: "Warum gabst du uns die tiefen Blicke?" (Why did you give us those penetrating glances?)]

G. The Historical Truth

We have undertaken all these psychological detours in order to make it more credible to us that the religion of Moses only established its effect on the Jewish people as a tradition. We have probably not reached more than a certain degree of probability. But even if we had successfully achieved a complete proof, the impression would remain that we had adequately addressed only the qualitative factor of the demand, but not the quantitative one as well. There is something magnificent associated with everything to do with the origin of a religion, certainly including the Jewish one, that has not been covered by our explanations up to this point. Some other factor must be involved beside which there is little that is analogous and nothing of the same type—something unique and of the same order of magnitude as what has come out of it, something as great as religion itself.

Let us try to approach the topic from the opposite side. We understand the fact that primitives need a god as creator of the universe, as chief of the clan, as personal benefactor. This god is positioned behind the departed ancestors about whom tradition still has something to say. People of later times, of our time, behave in the same way. They, too, remain childish and require protection, even as adults; they believe they cannot do without a dependence on their god. That much is undisputed, but it is less easy to understand why there can be only a single god, and why it is precisely the advance from henotheism[1] to monotheism that gains the overwhelming significance. As we have explained, believers certainly have a share in the greatness of their god; and the greater the god the more reliable is the protection he can provide. But a god's power does not necessarily require that he be the only one. Many peoples saw it only as a glorification of their chief god if he ruled over other deities subordinate to him; they saw no diminution of his greatness if other gods existed besides him. It would certainly mean a sacrifice of intimacy, too, if this god became universal and concerned himself with all lands and peoples. One was sharing one's god with foreigners, as it were; one had to compensate for this in the proviso that one was preferred by him. It can also be claimed that the very idea of a single god signifies an advance in intellectuality, but it is impossible to assign great value to this point.

Pious believers, though, have an adequate way to stop up this obvious gap in motivation. They say that the idea of a single god had

---

1 Henotheists worship one god only but allow for the existence of other deities. This is sometimes considered a stage in the development toward monotheism proper.

such an overwhelming effect on humankind because it is a portion of the eternal *truth* which, long concealed, at last appeared and then, of necessity, carried everyone along with it. We must admit that a factor of this kind at last accords with the magnitude of the topic and of its effect.

We too would like to accept this solution. But a doubt stops us short. The pious argument is based on an optimistic and idealistic premise. It has otherwise not been possible to demonstrate that the human intellect has an especially fine ability to scent out the truth and that the mental life of humans shows any particular inclination to recognize the truth. We have instead found, on the contrary, that our intellect very easily goes astray without warning, and that nothing is more easily believed by us than what, regardless of the truth, corresponds to our wish-illusions. We must therefore add a reservation to our agreement. We too believe that the solution of the pious contains the truth: not the *material* truth, but the *historical* truth. And we claim the right to correct a certain distortion this truth has undergone upon its return. That is, we do not believe that there is a single great god today, but that in early times there was a single person who must have appeared supremely great at the time and who then returned in human memory raised to the status of a deity.

We had assumed that the religion of Moses was initially rejected and half forgotten, and then broke through as a tradition. Now, we assume that this process was then repeated for the second time. When Moses brought the people the idea of a single god, this was nothing new, but signified the revival of an experience from the primeval eras of the human family—an experience that had long ago vanished from the conscious memory of humankind. But it had been so important and had produced or initiated such deeply penetrating changes in human life that we cannot avoid believing it left some lasting traces, comparable to a tradition, in the human mind.

We have learned from the psychoanalyses of individuals that their earliest impressions, received at a time when the child is still nearly incapable of speech, eventually express effects of a compulsive character without themselves being consciously remembered. We consider ourselves justified in assuming the same about the earliest experiences of humanity in general. One of these effects would be the appearance of the idea of a single great god—an idea one must recognize as a distorted memory, to be sure, but a completely justified one. Such an idea has a compulsive character: it must be believed. To the extent that it is distorted, one may characterize it as a *delusion*; to the extent that it brings the return of the past, it must be called *truth*. Psychiatric delusion, too, contains a small measure of truth and the patient's conviction extends from this truth to its delusional wrappings.

What follows from here to the end is a slightly amended repetition of the discussion in Part I [of Essay III].

In 1912, in *Totem and Taboo*, I attempted to reconstruct the early situation from which such effects proceeded. In so doing, I made use of certain theoretical ideas of Charles Darwin, James Atkinson, and particularly W. Robertson Smith; I combined them with findings and suggestions from psychoanalysis. From Darwin I borrowed the hypothesis that humans originally lived in small hordes, each horde under the despotic rule of an older male who appropriated all the females for himself and punished or eliminated the younger males, including his sons. In continuing this account, I took from Atkinson the idea that this patriarchal system met its end in a rebellion of the sons, who united against the father, overcame him, and devoured him collectively. In connection with Smith's totem theory, I assumed that subsequently the father-horde gave way to the totemic brother-clan. In order to be able to live in peace with one another, the victorious brothers renounced the women over whom they had, of course, killed the father: they instituted exogamy. Paternal power was broken and families were organized in a matriarchal structure. The ambivalent emotional orientation of the sons to the father remained in force during all subsequent developments. In place of the father, a particular animal was established as a totem. It was regarded as an ancestor and protective spirit, and no one was permitted to harm or kill it, but once a year the whole male community gathered for a ceremonial meal at which the totem animal, otherwise revered, was torn to pieces and collectively devoured. No one was permitted to miss this meal: it was the solemn repetition of the killing of the father, with which social order, moral laws, and religion had their beginnings. The correspondence between Smith's totem meal and Christian communion has been noticed by various authors before me.

Today I still hold firmly to this construct. I have repeatedly had to hear violent reproaches for not revising my opinions in later editions of the book, given that more recent ethnologists have unanimously rejected Smith's proposals and have in some cases brought forth other, completely divergent theories. I must respond that I am quite familiar with these supposed advances. But I have been convinced neither of the correctness of these innovations nor of Smith's errors. A contradiction is not a refutation; an innovation is not necessarily an advance.

Above all, though, I am not an ethnologist but a psychoanalyst. I had the right to select from ethnological literature what I found useful for work in analysis. The writings of the ingenious Robertson Smith have given me valuable contacts with the psychological material of analysis and connections for its utilization. My thoughts have never coincided with those of his opponents.

H. The Historical Development

Here, I cannot repeat the contents of *Totem and Taboo* in greater detail, but I must attend to filling in the long stretch between that hypothetical primeval era and the victory of monotheism in historical times. After the ensemble of brother-clan, matriarchy, exogamy, and totemism was established, there began a development best described as a slow "return of the repressed." Here I am using the term "the repressed" in an extended sense. We are dealing with something in the life of peoples that is in the past, has disappeared, has been surmounted—and which we shall presume to equate with the repressed material in the mental life of the individual. We cannot immediately say in what psychological form this past existed during the time when it was becoming obscure. It will not be easy for us to carry over the concepts of individual psychology into mass psychology, and I do not believe we will achieve anything if we introduce the concept of a "collective" unconscious. In any case, the content of the unconscious is certainly a collective, universal possession of humankind. Thus, for the time being, we will manage with the use of analogies. The processes we are studying here in the life of peoples are very similar to those familiar to us in psychopathology, yet not quite the same. We must finally resolve to accept the hypothesis that the mental precipitates of those primeval eras had become inherited property which in each new generation required only awakening, and not acquisition. This brings to mind the example of the surely "innate" symbolism that derives from the period of language acquisition, a symbolism familiar to all children without their receiving any instruction, and which can be stated in the same way for all peoples despite the differences in their languages. What we are perhaps still lacking in certainty we gain from other results of psychoanalytic research. We find that in a number of significant relations our children do not react in a way corresponding to their own experience, but instinctively, in a manner comparable to animals, which can only be explained as phylogenetic acquisition.

The return of the repressed occurs slowly and certainly not spontaneously, but under the influence of all the changes in the conditions of life that fill the history of human culture. Here, I can provide neither an overview of these dependent factors nor more than a fragmentary enumeration of the stages of this return. The father again becomes the head of the family, but is far less unchecked in his power than the father of the primeval horde had been. In a series of still very clear transitions, the totem animal yields its place to a god. Initially, the god in human form still has the head of the animal, and later he preferentially transforms himself into this particular animal; then this animal becomes sacred to him and is his favorite attendant, or he has killed the animal and bears the corresponding epithet himself. Between the totem animal and the god, the hero emerges, often as a preliminary step to deification. The idea of a supreme deity seems to appear early, at first only in a shadowy manner, without affecting the daily interests of human beings. With the joining together of tribes and peoples into greater unities, the gods too organize themselves into families and into hierarchies. One of them is often elevated to supreme lord over gods and men. Then, hesitantly, the further step is taken of revering only one god, and finally the decision is made to grant all power to a single god and to tolerate no other gods beside him. It was only in this way that the supremacy of the father of the primeval horde was restored and that the affects relating to him could be repeated.

The first effect of meeting him who had so long been missed and longed for was overwhelming, and was just as the tradition of the giving of the law from Mount Sinai describes it. Admiration, awe, and thankfulness that one had found grace in his eyes—the religion of Moses knows none but these positive feelings toward the father-god. The conviction of his irresistibility and the submission to his will could not have been more unconditional for the helpless, intimidated son of the father of the horde; indeed, they only become fully comprehensible by placing them in the primitive and infantile environment. The emotional impulses of children are intensely and inexhaustibly deep to a much greater degree than those of adults; only religious ecstasy can reproduce that. An ecstasy of devotion to God was thus the immediate reaction to the return of the great father.

The direction for this father-religion was thus established for all time, but this did not mean the conclusion of its development. In the essence of the relation to the father there is ambivalence: it was inevitable that in the course of time the hostility should also be aroused that had once driven the sons to kill their admired and feared father. Within the framework of the religion of Moses there was no room for the direct expression of the murderous hatred of the father. Only a powerful reaction against it could appear—the sense of guilt due to this hostility, a bad conscience for having sinned against God and for not ceasing to sin. This sense of guilt, which was continuously kept awake by the Prophets, and which soon formed an integral part of the religious system, had yet another superficial motivation that adroitly masked its real origin. Things were going badly for the people, the hopes placed on God's favor simply were not being fulfilled, and it was not easy to maintain the illusion, cherished above all else, of being God's chosen people. If one did not want to renounce this happiness, the sense of guilt due to one's own sinfulness offered a welcome exculpation of God. One deserved no better than to be punished by him, because one was not obeying his commandments; needing to gratify this sense of guilt, which was insatiable and came from a so much deeper source, one had to allow these commandments to grow ever stricter, more scrupulously precise, and indeed pettier and pettier. In a new ecstasy of moral asceticism, one continually imposed on oneself new renunciations of drives, thus achieving, at least in doctrine and law, ethical heights that had remained unattainable for other ancient peoples. In this higher development many Jews perceive the second main characteristic and the second great achievement of their religion. From our discussions it should be clear how this achievement is connected with the first one, the idea of a single god. Yet this ethical system cannot deny its origin in the sense of guilt arising from suppressed hostility toward God. In that it is incomplete and cannot be completed, it has the character of obsessional neurotic reaction formations; one further surmises that it also serves secret intentions of punishment.

The subsequent development goes beyond Judaism. The remaining material that returned from the tragedy of the primeval father could no longer be reconciled in any way with the religion of Moses. The sense of guilt felt at that time had long hence ceased to be restricted to the Jewish people; as a dull unease or as a premonition of calamity, whose source no one could point to, it had taken hold of all the Mediterranean peoples. Historical research of our day speaks of an aging of Classical civilization, but I suspect that such research has only grasped incidental causes and auxiliary factors in this depressed mood of the peoples. The elucidation of this depressed situation proceeded from the Jews. Irrespective of the various approximations and preparations all around, it was actually a Jewish man, Saul of Tarsus[1] (who, as a Roman citizen, called himself Paul), in whose spirit the realization first broke through: "It is because we have killed God the Father that we are so unhappy." And it is completely understandable that he could grasp this piece of truth in no other manner than in the delusional

---

1   The Apostle Paul, or Saint Paul (5–67 CE), was known as Saul of Tarsus before his conversion to the teachings of Jesus.

guise of the glad tidings: "we are redeemed from all guilt since one of us has sacrificed his life to atone for us." In this formulation the killing of God was of course not mentioned, but a crime that had to be atoned through the death of a sacrificial victim could only have been a murder. And the mediating step between the delusion and the historical truth was provided by the assurance that the sacrificial victim had been God's son. With the strength that flowed to it from the wellspring of historical truth, this new faith overthrew all obstacles; in place of the blissful sense of being chosen appeared liberating redemption. But in its return to human memory, the fact of the patricide had greater resistances to overcome than did the other fact that had comprised the content of monotheism; it also had to endure a more powerful distortion. The unnamable crime was replaced by the assumption of the actually shadowy notion of original sin.

Original sin, and redemption through the death of a sacrificial victim, became the foundational pillars of the new religion founded by Paul. For now, we shall not address the question as to whether, in the band of brothers who rebelled against the primeval father, there was really a leader and instigator to the murder, or whether this figure was later created by the fantasy of writers in the interest of turning themselves into heroes, and was thus introduced into the tradition. After the Christian doctrine had burst the bounds of Judaism, it took on components from many other sources, renounced several traits of pure monotheism, and supply adapted itself in various details to the ritual of the other Mediterranean peoples. It was as though Egypt was once again taking vengeance on the heirs of Akhenaton. It is worthy of note how the new religion dealt with the old ambivalence in the relation to the father. Its main content was, to be sure, reconciliation with God the Father and atonement for the crime committed against him, but the other side of the emotional relation showed itself in the fact that the son, who had taken the atonement on himself, became a god himself beside the father and, more precisely, in place of the father. Having emerged from a father-religion, Christianity became a son-religion. It has not escaped the fate of having to eliminate the father.

Only a portion of the Jewish people accepted the new doctrine. Those who refused to do so are still called Jews today. Due to this split, they are even more sharply divided from the others than before. From the new religious community (which, besides Jews, included Egyptians, Greeks, Syrians, Romans, and ultimately Germanic peoples as well), they were obliged to hear the reproach that they had murdered God. Unabridged, this reproach would be worded: "They will not accept the truth that they murdered God, whereas we confess it and have been cleansed of that guilt." One will then easily realize how much truth lies behind this reproach. As the topic of a special investigation, one could ask why it has been impossible for the Jews to participate in this forward step which was contained, despite all distortions, in the admission of having murdered God. In that way, they have in a sense taken upon themselves a tragic portion of guilt; they have been made to do a heavy penance for it.

Our investigation has perhaps cast some light on the question of how the Jewish people acquired the traits that characterize it. Less illumination has been cast on the problem of how the Jews have been able to maintain themselves as an individual group up to the present day. Yet, in fairness, exhaustive answers to such riddles can be neither demanded nor expected. A contribution, to be judged in view of the limitations mentioned at the beginning [of Essay III, Part II], is all that I can offer.

6. From Oskar Pfister, *On the Psychology of Philosophical Thought* (1923)[1]

IV: The Significance of Psychology for Understanding and the Normative Assessment of Philosophical Thought

[...]
It would be incorrect to attribute no significance whatsoever to logical argumentation. Yet one must not overestimate its power. For who would deny that the most astute philosophers calmly tolerate the most obvious contradictions in their philosophical thought, and fail to attribute the slightest significance to them?

Generally the rule applies: The more the manner of thought distances itself from the empirical, from elementary, a priori certainties, or from mathematical ones, the more strongly it becomes subject to the domination of affect.

A second rule follows: The more strongly a philosopher becomes introverted, i.e., pushed away from reality by affective influences, the more his philosophy loses its objectivity and bears the stamp of his subjectivity.

It is easy to see that both rules are related, but by no means express the same thing. The first rule, incidentally, in no way means that there can be empiricism free of subjective elements. There is no such thing as pure experience. In the hypotheses and theories of many natural

---

1 *Zur Psychologie des philosophischen Denkens* (Bern: Bircher, 1923).

scientists one can already clearly see their affect shining through. Just as little can there be an introversion in which all bridges to reality are completely severed and in which correction by reality of the postulates of affect is totally absent.

[...] Indeed, behind the supposedly purely objective determinations of many philosophical doctrines a hidden meaning can be shown. The solipsist, who declares that there is no exterior world, creates for himself in this statement a theoretical expression of the wish: "May it not exist!" The metaphysical philosopher, who in his system paints a portrait of his soul, wishes to portray an objective reality, but behind this lies the wish: "If only I were the creator of the world, capable of creating things according to the desires of my heart!" To the indicative mood of the philosophical doctrine corresponds an unconscious optative. Beside its open, theoretical content, philosophical doctrine possesses a secret and to an extent esoteric, symbolic sense, hidden even from consciousness. [...] The mental processes that play out beneath the threshold of consciousness and allow a philosophical persuasion, seemingly secured by theory, to arise in consciousness—often as an inspiration or enlightenment—can be very precisely identified in living persons. The analogy of poetic, artistic, and religious revelations, which often also present a philosophical manner of thinking, provides further insights, but the nature of the abstract inspiration or discovery, as well as its subsequent scientific elaboration, must be taken into consideration.

Efforts to provide a theoretical foundation for inspirations of the unconscious are called rationalizations. Here, if it were possible to provide a developed psychology of philosophical thought, it would also be necessary to discuss the psychology of rationalization, for it is beyond all doubt that a great portion of philosophical thinking consists only of rationalization. Similarly, theological dogma, which would like to grasp and justify religious experiences scientifically, is to be regarded in the same way.

[...] Let it now be stated that the completely conscious development of thoughts must become the ideal of all science. The unconscious makes the wish the father of thought, while conscious philosophical thought lends that role to reality itself. Between these two approaches there is a struggle in which, given the individual characteristics of the thinker, either wishful thinking arising from the unconscious or thinking based on reality is victorious. Often, the prevalence of one of these tendencies is so strong that the struggle goes completely undetected. For many thinkers in the higher and deeper regions, logical argumentation has almost no motivational power, while for others it possesses a great deal of power, thus producing an impression of pure objectivity.

[...]

References

1. Primary Works by Freud and Pfister

Abbreviations

GW: *Gesammelte Werke* (London: Imago). The publication date appears in brackets following the volume number.
SE: *The Standard Edition of the Complete Psychological Works of Sigmund Freud*, trans. James Strachey (London: Hogarth). The publication date appears in brackets following the volume number.

a. Sigmund Freud, The Future of an Illusion

Die Zukunft einer Illusion. Vienna: Internationaler Psychoanalytischer Verlag, 1927.
Die Zunkunft einer Illusion. GW 14 [1948]: 325–80.
The Future of an Illusion. Trans. William Robson-Scott. London: Hogarth, 1928.
The Future of an Illusion. *Standard Edition* 21 [1961]: 3–56.
The Future of an Illusion. In *"Mass Psychology" and Other Writings*. Trans. J.A. Underwood and Shaun Whiteside. London: Penguin, 2004. [Also *The Future of an Illusion*. London: Penguin, 2008.]

b. Other Works by Freud

Note: works by Freud are listed in chronological order, by their English titles, publication date, and *Standard Edition* reference. The German title and original publication information is then provided, followed by other translated English editions, where applicable.

Project for a Scientific Psychology. 1895. SE 1: 281–397.
The Interpretation of Dreams. 1900. SE 4 [1953]: vols. 4 and 5. [Orig. pub.: *Die Traumdeutung*. Leipzig and Vienna: Deuticke, 1900; GW 2 (1942)]
Early Psychoanalytic Publications. 1906. SE 3 [1962]. [Orig. pub.: *Sammlung kleiner Schriften zur Neurosenlehre*. Leipzig and Vienna: Deuticke, 1906; Gesammelte Schriften 3. London: Imago, 1952.]
"Obsessive Actions and Religious Practices." 1907. SE 9 [1959]: 116–27. [Orig. pub.: "Zwangshandlungen und Religionsübun-

gen." *Zeitschrift für Religionspsychologie* 1.1 (1907): 4–12; GW 7
(1941): 210–20.] [Trans.: "Obsessive Acts and Religious Practices." *Collected Papers* 2: 25–35. Trans. R.C. McWatters. London:
International Psychoanalytical Press, 1924.]

"The Future Prospects of Psycho-Analytic Therapy." 1910. SE 11
[1957]: 139–51. [Orig. pub.: *"Die zukünftigen Chancen der psychol-
ogischen Therapie."* *Gesammelte Schriften* 6: 25–36. Leipzig: Internationaler Psychoanalytischer Verlag, 1925 (1910).]

"Formulations on the two Principles of Mental Functioning." 1911.
SE 12 [1958]: 215–26. [Orig. pub.: "Formulierungen über die
zwei Prinzipien des psychischen Geschehens." *Jahrbuch für psychoanalytische und psychopathologische Forschung* 3.1 (1911): 1–8; GW
8 (1943): 130–38.]

"The Claims of Psycho-Analysis to Scientific Interest." 1913. SE 13
[1955]: 165–90. [Orig. pub.: "Das Interesse an der Psychoanalyse." *Scientia* 14.31–32 (1913): 240–50, 369–84; GW 8
(1943): 390–420.]

"Introduction to Pfister's *The Psychoanalytic Method.*" 1913. SE 12:
329–31. [Orig. pub.: "Geleitwort zu 'Die psychoanalytische
Methode' von Dr. Oskar Pfister, Zurich." Vienna: Internationaler
Psychoanalytischer Verlag, 1913; GW 10 (1913).]

*Totem and Taboo: Some Points of Agreement Between the Mental Lives of
Savages and Neurotics.* 1913. SE 13 [1955]: 1–161. [Orig. pub.:
*Totem und Tabu: einige Übereinstimmungen im Seelenleben der Wilden
und der Neurotiker.* Leipzig and Vienna: Heller, 1913; GW 9
(1940): 1–205.]

"The Paths to the Formation of Symptoms." *Introductory Lectures on
Psychoanalysis.* 1917. SE 16 [1963]: 358–77. "Die Wege der
Symptombildung." *Vorlesungen zur Einführung in die Psychoanalyse*,
Lecture 23. Leipzig and Vienna: Heller, 1917; GW 11 (1940):
372–91.

"From the History of an Infantile Neurosis." 1918. SE 17: 1–133.
[Orig. pub.: "Aus der Geschichte einer infantilen Neurose."
Vienna: Internationaler Psychoanalytischer Verlag, 1918; GW 12
(1940): 27–157.]

Beyond the Pleasure Principle. 1920. SE 18 [1955]: 3–64. [Orig. pub.:
Jenseits des Lustprinzips. Vienna: Internationaler Psychoanalytischer
Verlag, 1920; GW 13 (1940): 3–69.] [Trans.: *Beyond the Pleasure
Principle.* Ed. Todd Dufresne. Trans. Gregory C. Richter. Peterbor-
ough: Broadview, 2011.]

Group Psychology and the Analysis of the Ego. 1921. SE 18: 65–143.
[Orig. pub.: *Massenpsychologie und Ich-Analyse.* Vienna: Internationaler Psychoanalytischer Verlag, 1921; GW 13 (1940): 73–161.]

The Ego and The Id. 1923. SE 19: 1–66. [Orig. pub.: *Das Ich und das Es.* Vienna: Internationaler Psychoanalytischer Verlag, 1923; GW 13 (1940): 237–89.]

The Question of Lay Analysis. 1926. SE 20: 179–250. [Orig. pub.: *Die Frage der Laienanalyse.* Vienna: Internationaler Psychoanalytischer Verlag, 1926; GW 14 (1948): 209–86.]

"Postscript" to *The Question of Lay Analysis.* 1927. SE 20: 251–58. [Orig. pub.: "Nachtwort zur 'Frage der Laienanalyse.'" Vienna: Internationaler Psychoanalytischer Verlag, 1927; GW 14 (1948): 287–96.]

Civilization and Its Discontents. 1930. SE 21 (1961): 59–145. [Orig. pub.: *Das Unbehagen in der Kultur.* Vienna: Internationaler Psychoanalytischer Verlag, 1930. 2nd ed. 1931.] [Trans.: *Civilization and Its Discontents.* Trans. Joan Riviere. London: Hogarth, 1930; *Civilization and Its Discontents.* Trans. David McLintock. London: Penguin, 2002.]

New Introductory Lectures on Psychoanalysis. 1933. SE 22: 1–182. [Orig. pub.: *Neue Folge der Vorlesungen zur Einführung in die Psychoanalyse.* Vienna: Internationaler Psychoanalytischer Verlag, 1933; GW 15 (1940): 2–207.]

"Postscript" (to "An Autobiographical Study"). 1935. SE 20: 71–74. [Orig. pub.: "Nachschrift 1935." Vienna: Internationaler Psychoanalytischer Verlag, 1935; GW 14 (1948): 33–96.]

"Analysis Terminable and Interminable." 1937. SE 23: 209 53. [Orig. pub.: *Die endliche und die unendliche Analyse.* Vienna: Internationaler Psychoanalytischer Verlag, 1937; GW 16 (1950): 59–99.]

Moses and Monotheism: Three Essays. SE 23 (1964): 3–137. [Orig. pub.: *Der Mann Moses und die monotheistische Religion: Drei Abhandlungen.* Amsterdam: Allert de Lange, 1939; GW 16 (1950): 101–246.]

c. Works by Pfister

Note: works by Pfister are listed chronologically and by their English title.

The Psychoanalytic Method. [*Die psychanalytische Methode.*] Leipzig: Klinkhardt, 1913. [Trans. Charles Payne. New York: Moffat, Yard, 1917.]

Some Applications of Psycho-Analysis. [*Zum Kampf um die Psychoanalyse.*] Leipzig: Internationaler Psychoanalytischer Verlag, 1920. [Trans.: New York: Dodd, Mead, 1923.]

On the Psychology of Philosophical Thought. [*Zur Psychologie des philosophischen Denkens.*] Bern: Bircher, 1923.

Psychoanalytic Ministry: Introduction to Psychoanalysis for Pastors and Laymen. [*Analytische Seelsorge: Einführung in die praktische Psychoanalyse für Pfarrer und Laien.*] Göttingen: Vandenhoeck and Ruprecht, 1927.

"The Illusion of a Future: A Friendly Discussion with Professor Sigmund Freud." ["Die Illusion einer Zukunft: eine freundliche Auseinandersetzung mit Professor Doktor Sigmund Freud."] *Imago* 14 (1928): 149–84. [Trans.: *International Journal of Psychoanalysis* 74 (1993): 557–79. Ed. Paul Roazen. Trans. Susan Abrams and Tom Taylor.]

2. Other Primary Works

Dostoevski, Fyodor. *Notes from Underground.* 1864. New York: Vintage, 1918.

Falckenberg, Richard. *Geschichte der neueren Philosophie von Nikolaus von Kues bis zur Gegenwart* [*History of Newer Philosophy from Nikolaus von Kues to the Present*]. Leipzig: Veit, 1886.

Ferenczi, Sándor. "Ein kleiner Hahnemann." *Internationale Zeitschrift für Psychoanalyse* 1 (1913): 240 ff. [Trans.: "A Little Chanticleer." *First Contributions to Psychoanalysis*, Chapter 10. London: Hogarth, 1952.]

Feuerbach, Ludwig. *Das Wesen des Christentums.* Leipzig: Reclam, 1841. [Trans.: *The Essence of Christianity.* Trans. George Eliot. New York: Harper, 1957.]

Frazer, James. *The Magic Art.* [*The Golden Bough*, Part 1.] London: Macmillan, 1911.

———. *Spirits of the Corn and of the Wild.* [*The Golden Bough*, Part 5.] London: Macmillan, 1912.

Freud, Ernst, and Heinrich Meng, eds. *Sigmund Freud, Oskar Pfister: Briefe 1909–1939.* Frankfurt: Fischer, 1963. [Trans.: *Psychoanalysis and Faith: The Letters of Sigmund Freud and Oskar Pfister.* Trans. Eric Mosbacher. New York: Basic Books, 1963.]

Freud, Sigmund, and Lou Andreas-Salomé. *Sigmund Freud and Lou Andreas-Salomé: Letters.* Ed. E. Pfeiffer. Trans. William and Elaine Robson-Scott. London: Hogarth, 1966.

Freud, Sigmund, and Sándor Ferenczi. *The Correspondence of Sigmund Freud and Sándor Ferenczi.* Vol. 3. Ed. Ernst Falzeder and Eva Brabant. Trans. Peter Hoffer. Cambridge: Belknap, 2000.

Freud, Sigmund, and Oskar Pfister. *Psychoanalysis and Faith: The*

Letters of Sigmund Freud and Oskar Pfister. Ed. H. Meng. Trans. E. Mosbacher. London: Hogarth Press, 1963.

Freud, Sigmund, and Arnold Zweig. The Letters of Sigmund Freud and Arnold Zweig. Ed. E. Freud. Trans. William and Elaine Robson-Scott. London: Hogarth Press, 1970.

Jung, Carl. "Wandlungen und Symbole der Libido." Jahrbuch für psychoanalytische und psychopathologische Forschung 3–4 (1912): 120 ff. and 160 ff. [Trans.: Psychology of the Unconscious. London: Kegan, Paul, 1919.]

Kant, Immanuel. "An Answer to the Question: 'What Is Enlightenment?'" 1784. Kant's Political Writings. Ed. Hans Reiss. Trans. H.B. Nisbet. Cambridge: Cambridge UP, 1970: 54–60.

———. Critique of Pure Reason. 1781. Trans. Norman Kemp Smith. London: Macmillan, 1993.

Löwenfeld, Leopold. Die psychischen Zwangserscheinungen [Compulsive Mental Phenomena]. Bergmann: Wiesbaden, 1904.

Marx, Karl. A Contribution to the Critique of Hegel's Philosophy of Right. Vol. 3. 1843. Ed. Joseph O'Malley. Trans. Annette Jolin and J. O'Malley. Cambridge: Cambridge UP, 1982.

Meyer, Eduard. Die Israeliten und ihre Nachbarstämme [The Israelites and their Neighboring Tribes]. Halle: Niemeyer, 1906.

Nietzsche, Friedrich. Die Fröhliche Wissenschaft. Leipzig: Fritzsch, 1887. [Trans. The Joyful Wisdom. Trans. Thomas Common. New York: Ungar, 1973.]

———. "On Truth and Lie in an Extra-Moral Sense." In The Portable Nietzsche. Ed. and trans. Walter Kaufmann. 1873. New York: Viking, 1974: 42–47.

———. Twilight of the Idols. In The Portable Nietzsche. Ed. and trans. Walter Kaufmann. 1888. New York: Viking, 1974: 464–563.

Öttingen, Alexander. Die Moralistik in ihrer Bedeutung für eine christliche Socialethik [Morality in its Significance for a Christian Social Ethics]. Erlangen: Deichert, 1882.

Pfleiderer, Otto. Geschichte der Religionsphilosophie von Spinoza bis auf die Gegenwart [History of the Philosophy of Religion from Spinoza to the Present]. Berlin: Reimer, 1883.

Reinach, Salomon. Cultes, mythes, et religions. Vol. 2. Paris: Leroux, 1906.

Robitsek, Alfred. Symbolisches Denken in der chemischen Forschung [Symbolic Thinking in Chemical Research]. Imago 1 (1911): 83–90.

Schopenhauer, Arthur. Studies in Pessimism. 1851. New York: Cosimo, 2007.

Sellin, Ernst. Mose und seine Bedeutung für die israelitisch-jüdische Reli-

gionsgeschichte [*Moses and his Significance for Israelite-Jewish Religious History*]. Leipzig: Deichert, 1922.

Smith, W. Robertson. *Lectures on the Religion of the Semites*. London: Black, 1894.

Stevenson, Robert Louis. *The Strange Case of Dr. Jekyll and Mr. Hyde*. 1886. New York: Random House, 1945.

Vaihinger, Hans. *Die Philosophie des Als Ob*. [*The Philosophy of "As If"*] Leipzig: F. Mainer, 1922.

Yahuda, Abraham S. *Die Sprache des Pentateuch in ihren Beziehunge zum Ägyptischen*. Berlin: De Gruyter, 1929. [Rev. English ed. by author: *The Language of the Pentateuch in Its Relation to Egyptian*. London: Oxford UP, 1933.]

3. Secondary Sources

Brown, Norman O. "Instinctual Dialectics against Instinctual Dualism." 1959. In *Beyond the Pleasure Principle*, by Sigmund Freud. Ed. T. Dufresne. Trans. Gregory C. Richter. Peterborough: Broadview, 2011: 185–89.

Burston, Daniel. *The Legacy of Erich Fromm*. Cambridge, MA: Harvard UP, 1991.

Choisy, Maryse. *Sigmund Freud: A New Appraisal*. New York: Philosophical Library, 1963.

Crabtree, Adam. *From Freud to Mesmer: Magnetic Healing and the Roots of Psychological Health*. New Haven: Yale UP, 1993.

DiCenso, James J. *The Other Freud: Religion, Culture and Psychoanalysis*. London: Routledge, 1999.

Dufresne, Todd. "After *Beyond* Comes *The Future*: Freud's Absurdist Theatre of Reason." *English Studies in Canada* 32.1 (March 2006): 27–43.

———. "The Strange Case of 'Anna O.': An Overview of the 'Revisionist' Assessment." *Killing Freud: 20th Century Culture and the Death of Psychoanalysis*. London: Continuum, 2003: 4–25.

———. *Tales from the Freudian Crypt: The Death Drive in Text and Context*. Preface M. Borch-Jacobsen. Stanford, CA: Stanford UP, 2000.

Eliot, T.S. [Review of Freud's *The Future of an Illusion*]. *The Criterion* 8 (1928): 350–53.

Feigenbaum, Dorian. Review of *The Future of an Illusion*. *The Psychoanalytic Review* 16 (1929): 55–61. In Kiell, 581–87.

Fromm, Erich. "Freud's Model of Man and Its Social Determinants." *The Crisis of Psychoanalysis*. New York: Holt, Rinehart, Winston, 1970.

——. "A Humanist Response to the Death Instinct Theory." In *Beyond the Pleasure Principle*, by Sigmund Freud. Ed. Todd Dufresne. Trans. Gregory C. Richter. Peterborough: Broadview, 2011: 275–83.

——. *Psychoanalysis and Religion*. New Haven: Yale UP, 1950.

Gay, Peter. *Freud: A Life for Our Times*. New York: Norton, 1988.

Irwin, John E.G. "Oskar Pfister and the Taggert Report: The 'First Pastoral Counselor' and Today's Role Problems." *Journal of Pastoral Care* 27 (1973): 189–95.

——. "Pfister and Freud: The Rediscovery of a Dialogue." *Journal of Religion and Health* 12.4 (1973): 315–27.

Jones, Ernest. *The Life and Works of Sigmund Freud: The Last Phase, 1919–1939*. Vol. 3. New York: Basic Books, 1957.

Kiell, Norman. *Freud without Hindsight: Reviews of His Work (1893–1939)*. Madison, WI: International Universities Press, 1988.

Lehrer, Ronald. *Nietzsche's Presence in Freud's Life and Thought*. New York: SUNY Press, 1995.

Mahony, Patrick. *Cries of the Wolf Man*. New York: International Universities Press, 1984.

Marcuse, Herbert. "'A Decisive Correction': Non-Repressive Progress and Freud's Instinct Theory." 1970. In *Beyond the Pleasure Principle*, by Sigmund Freud. Ed. T. Dufresne. Trans. Gregory C. Richter. Peterborough: Broadview, 2011: 250–60.

——. *Eros and Civilization: A Philosophical Inquiry into Freud*. 2nd ed. Boston: Beacon Books, 1966 [1955].

Meissner, William W. *Psychoanalysis and Religious Experience*. New Haven: Yale UP, 1984.

Ornston, Darius. "Obstacles to Improving Strachey's Freud." *Translating Freud*: 191–222. Ed. Darius Ornston. New Haven: Yale UP, 1992.

Reich, Ilse Ollendorff. *Wilhelm Reich: A Personal Biography*. New York: St. Martin's, 1969.

Reich, Wilhelm. *Reich Speaks of Freud*. New York: Farrar, Straus, and Giroux, 1952.

Reik, Theodor. *From Thirty Years with Freud*. London: Hogarth, 1942.

Rieff, Philip [Susan Sontag]. *Freud: The Mind of the Moralist*. New York: Doubleday, 1961.

Richter, Gregory C. "Translator's Note." *Beyond the Pleasure Principle*. Ed. Todd Dufresne. Peterborough: Broadview, 2011: 37–47.

Roazen, Paul. "Introduction to The Illusion of a Future: A Friendly Disagreement With Prof. Sigmund Freud." *International Journal of Psychoanalysis* 74 (1993): 557–58.

———. "Nietzsche, Freud, and the History of Psychoanalysis." In *Returns of the 'French Freud.'* Ed. T. Dufresne. New York: Routledge, 1997: 11–23.

Strachey, James. "General Preface." *The Standard Edition of the Complete Psychological Works of Sigmund Freud*, v. 1: xiii–xxii. London: Hogarth, 1966.

Sulloway, Frank. *Freud, Biologist of the Mind: Beyond the Psychoanalytic Legend*. New York: Basic Books, 1979.

Zilboorg, Gregory. *Freud and Religion*. Westminster, MD: Newman, 1958.

Index

Gauss, Karl, 134
Gebhardt, Eduard, 146
Geibel, Emanuel, 134
Gladstone, William, 134
God, 12, 15f, 28, 47, 65, 84, 86, 95-103 passim, 105f, 110, 117,
    121-28 passim, 133ff, 137, 140, 143, 147, 150f, 163, 165f, 169,
    178, 188ff, 191
"God is dead," 12 n. 3, 16
Goethe, Johann Wolfgang von, 43, 43 n. 3, 116 n. 2, 134, 146, 169
    n. 2, 171 n. 1, 181, 183 n. 1
Graf, Herbert, 31 n. 1
Guilt, 16, 69, 145, 149, 153f, 165, 190f
    sense of, 154, 159, 161, 164f, 188f

Häckel, Ernst, 135
Happiness, 25, 49, 68, 119, 137, 143, 143 n. 1, 148 n. 2, 154, 171-
    78, 189
Hartmann, Eduard von, 143, 143 n. 1
Heer, Oswald, 134
Hegel, G.W.F., 25, 134
Heine, Heinrich, 109 n. 1
Herbart, Johann Friedrich, 130, 130 n. 2
Hitler, Adolf, 57
Hobbes, Thomas, 22, 22 n. 1, 25 n. 1
Hodler, Ferdinand, 145, 145 n. 2
Hoffmann, E.T.A., 182, 182 n. 1
Holbein, Hans, 146
Homer, 66, 132
Horde, 18, 149, 186, 188
Hume, David, 45, 141, 141 n. 1

Id, 12, 15, 56
Ideal (or ideals), 65, 117, 146, 148
    absolute, 127
    achievement, 122
    artistic creation and, 79
    communal existence, 23
    culture and, 79f
    ego, 42
    Enlightenment, 22, 42
    ethical, 126
    God as, 15, 147
    highest, 126

from the publisher

A name never says it all, but the word "broadview" expresses a good deal of the philosophy behind our company. We are open to a broad range of academic approaches and political viewpoints. We pay attention to the broad impact book publishing and book printing has in the wider world; we began using recycled stock more than a decade ago, and for some years now we have used 100% recycled paper for most titles. As a Canadian-based company we naturally publish a number of titles with a Canadian emphasis, but our publishing program overall is internationally oriented and broad-ranging. Our individual titles often appeal to a broad readership too; many are of interest as much to general readers as to academics and students.

Founded in 1985, Broadview remains a fully independent company owned by its shareholders—not an imprint or subsidiary of a larger multinational.

If you would like to find out more about Broadview and about the books we publish, please visit us at **www.broadviewpress.com**. And if you'd like to place an order through the site, we'd like to show our appreciation by extending a special discount to you: by entering the code below you will receive a 20% discount on purchases made through the Broadview website.

Discount code: **broadview20%**

Thank you for choosing Broadview.

Please note: this offer applies only to sales of
bound books within the United States or Canada.

FSC®
www.fsc.org

MIX
Paper from
responsible sources
FSC® C013916